Debates in Mathematics Ed

CW00385189

Debates in Mathematics Education explores the major issues that mathematics teachers encounter in their daily lives. It engages with established and contemporary debates, promotes and supports critical reflection and aims to stimulate both novice and experienced teachers to reach informed judgements and argue their point of view with deeper theoretical knowledge and understanding.

Written by experts in the field of mathematics education, it investigates and offers fresh insight into topics of central importance, including:

- Gender, social inequality and mathematics
- Mathematics, politics and climate change
- The history and culture of mathematics
- Using popular culture in the mathematics classroom
- The concept of 'ability' and its impact on learning
- What we mean by 'teaching for understanding'
- Choosing and using examples in teaching
- The fitness of formal examinations.

Designed to stimulate discussion and support you in your own research, writing and practice, *Debates in Mathematics Education* is a valuable resource for any student or practising teacher engaged in initial teacher training, continuing professional development or masters level study. It also has much to offer to those leading initial teacher education programmes, and to beginning doctoral students looking for a survey of the field of mathematics education research.

Dawn Leslie is Senior Lecturer in Education at Brunel University, UK.

Heather Mendick is Reader in Education at Brunel University, UK.

Debates in Subject Teaching Series

Series edited by: Susan Capel, Jon Davison, James Arthur, John Moss

The **Debates in Subject Teaching Series** is a sequel to the popular **Issues in Subject Teaching Series**, originally published by Routledge between 1999 and 2003. Each title presents high-quality material, specially commissioned to stimulate teachers engaged in initial training, continuing professional development and masters level study to think more deeply about their practice, and link research and evidence to what they have observed in schools. By providing up-to-date, comprehensive coverage the titles in the **Debates in Subject Teaching Series** support teachers in reaching their own informed judgements, enabling them to discuss and argue their point of view with deeper theoretical knowledge and understanding.

Titles in the series:

Debates in History Teaching
Edited by Ian Davies

Debates in English Teaching
Edited by Jon Davison, Caroline Daly and John Moss

Debates in Religious Education
Edited by Philip Barnes

Debates in Citizenship Education
Edited by James Arthur and Hilary Cremin

Debates in Art and Design Education
Edited by Lesley Burgess and Nicholas Addison

Debates in Music Teaching
Edited by Chris Philpott and Gary Spruce

Debates in Physical Education
Edited by Susan Capel and Margaret Whitehead

Debates in Geography Education
Edited by David Lambert and Mark Jones

Debates in Mathematics Education
Edited by Dawn Leslie and Heather Mendick

Debates in Mathematics Education

Edited by Dawn Leslie and
Heather Mendick

Heather Men.

To Vicky,
Happy Reading!
Heather

Have a great NQT year
...keep smiling!
Andy N.

To Vicky
You star! Keep in
touch
W... x

I hope this
enriches your
teaching
Mark

Routledge
Taylor & Francis Group

LONDON AND NEW YORK

First published 2014
by Routledge
2 Park Square, Milton Park, Abingdon, Oxon OX14 4RN

Simultaneously published in the USA and Canada
by Routledge
711 Third Avenue, New York, NY 10017

Routledge is an imprint of the Taylor & Francis Group, an informa business

British Library Cataloguing in Publication Data
A catalogue record for this book is available from the British Library

Library of Congress Cataloging in Publication Data
Debates in mathematics education / edited by Dawn Leslie and
Heather Mendick.
    pages cm
Includes bibliographical references and index.
1. Mathematics—Study and teaching. I. Leslie, Dawn, editor of
compilation. II. Mendick, Heather, editor of compilation.
QA11.2.D445 2013
510.71—dc23
2013008629

ISBN: 978-0-415-62383-4 (hbk)
ISBN: 978-0-415-62385-8 (pbk)
ISBN: 978-0-203-76258-5 (ebk)

Typeset in Galliard
by Cenveo Publisher Services

Printed and bound in Great Britain by
TJ International Ltd, Padstow, Cornwall

Contents

PART II
Debates in the teaching and learning of mathematics 67

PART III
Debates in mathematics curriculum and assessment 145

Illustrations

Contributors

Sunita Babbar's teaching career spans 17 years in a variety of roles in the secondary school setting. The experience she gained from her years as a classroom practitioner led to her role as a mathematics consultant for a local authority, which involved focusing on school improvement and developing teaching and learning in mathematics. Another key aspect of her role as a consultant was the provision of professional development both at departmental and whole school level, specialising in bespoke Inservice Training sessions. She now works at Brunel University, where she coordinates the secondary PGCert mathematics course. Sunita has always been interested in mathematics education, in particular curriculum development, transition and the development of problem solving skills in mathematics.

Richard Barwell is Professor of Mathematics Education at the Faculty of Education, University of Ottawa, Canada. His research is largely about the role of language and discourse in mathematics education. He has also written about climate change and mathematics education, motivated by a long-standing interest in environmental issues and a growing concern about the future of our planet. He has worked in the UK, Pakistan and Canada.

Mark Boylan is a Reader in Teacher Education at Sheffield Hallam University, Sheffield, England. He was a secondary school mathematics teacher before becoming a mathematics teacher educator. He had taught undergraduate and postgraduate students on both secondary and primary mathematics initial teacher education courses as well as qualified teachers on professional development courses. He has researched and published about emotional aspects of mathematics education and issues of social justice and teacher identity.

Margaret Brown is an Emeritus Professor of Mathematics Education at King's College London. Since teaching in primary and secondary schools and training mathematics teachers, she has directed over 25 research projects in the learning, teaching and assessment of mathematics. These have ranged over different contexts, from early years to undergraduate and adult education. She has been a member of several government and other committees advising on curriculum and assessment. She is a former president of the British Educational Research Association, and a former chair of the Joint Mathematical Council of the UK, and of the Educational Panel of the 2008 Research Assessment Exercise.

Peter Gates currently works at the University of Nottingham where he focuses on questions of access to mathematical knowledge. He edited the precursor to this book in 2001,

Issues in mathematics teaching and continues to write and argue for a fairer educational system in which working-class kids have greater opportunities. Peter has taught mathematics in London, Milton Keynes and Mozambique and taught mathematics teachers at The Open University, Bath University and now Nottingham. In his time he has been Chair of the British Society for Research into Learning Mathematics (BSRLM) and President of the International Group for the Psychology of Mathematics Education (PME). Peter is also an Adjunct Associate Professor at Griffith University in Brisbane. He has two daughters and two dogs; no guessing which two rush to the door to greet him when he arrives home.

Patricia George currently works as a researcher within the Ministry of Education, Antigua and Barbuda. She also works as an overseas research fellow for the Centre for Commonwealth Education, Faculty of Education, University of Cambridge, UK. These roles have enabled her to conduct educational research in Antigua and Barbuda as well as across some others of the smaller Caribbean countries. This research has to date focused on issues to do with access and equity in education, and on teachers authoring their own professional development via communities of practice. Patricia's research interests include students' and teachers' mathematical identities and more generally poverty and education and the education of at-risk and other vulnerable student groups.

Gwen Ineson started her career in teaching in primary schools in North London. She now works at Brunel University where she coordinates the primary PGCE course and the mathematics programme for primary trainee teachers. Her main research area involves the exploration of the relationships between the incidence of connected mathematical thinking in children and trainee teachers of primary mathematics and their mental mathematics competence, confidence and strategy choices in the context of primary mathematics. Her recently completed doctoral work used design-based research to design a one year intervention programme to develop the mental mathematics of trainee teachers for teaching.

Ian Jones is a Senior Research Fellow at the Mathematics Education Centre, Loughborough University and sits on the Royal Society's Vision Committee for Science and Mathematics Education 5–19. Ian was awarded a PhD in Mathematics Education from the University of Warwick and has worked as a Research Fellow on many mathematics education projects at several universities. Prior to his research work Ian was a school teacher in primary and secondary schools around the UK and overseas. His main research interests are in the assessment of mathematical knowledge and skills, and the role of equivalence relations in learning mathematics.

Dawn Leslie is a Senior Lecturer at Brunel University and is currently Subject Leader for Education (Initial Teacher Training). Her first five years at Brunel were spent working in Mathematics Initial Teacher Training, whilst the last two have seen her also working closely with Science trainees and overseeing the development of the Physics with Mathematics PGCert. Dawn's research background is in Physics and she currently works on experiments at the Large Hadron Collider, CERN, Switzerland as well as on a project concerning the development of an ionising radiation detector based on Quantum Dots. Her involvement in a range of outreach projects allows her to combine her two main fields of interest by working to promote STEM Education.

Anna Llewellyn works at the School of Education, Durham University. Previously she taught mathematics in secondary schools in Nottingham. Since joining Durham she has led the mathematics strand of the PGCE Secondary course as well as working on several masters and undergraduate programmes. Anna also leads on equality and diversity in the department; she runs workshops and support groups for LGBT+ inclusion in schools. Her research interests are in the areas of: discourses, normalisation, mathematics, identity, gender, sexuality and policy. She has a philosophical take on sociology and is primarily interested in poststructural forms of analysis. Anna is currently completing her doctoral studies which are based around unpacking taken for granted 'truths' of the mathematics classroom.

Rachel Marks works as a researcher in mathematics education at King's College London. Specialising in primary mathematics, she taught in primary schools across the UK for five years before entering academia. She has recently completed her Economic and Social Research Council (ESRC) funded doctoral study investigating the use of ability language and practices in primary mathematics education. Her research interests include ability, equity, assessment and the social context of mathematics teaching and learning. She has been involved in a range of research projects including an international comparative study of upper-secondary mathematics and an investigation into the numeracy needs of nursing students.

Mark McCormack is a Lecturer in Sociology at Durham University. His research examines the changing attitudes and behaviours of young people in cultures of decreasing homophobia. He has published widely in international journals including *Sociology*, *Sociology of Education* and *British Educational Research Journal*, and his book *The declining significance of homophobia: how teenage boys are redefining masculinity and heterosexuality* is published with Oxford University Press. He has also co-edited *Contemporary debates in the sociology of education* with Professor Rachel Brooks and Dr Kalwant Bhopal.

Heather Mendick works as Reader in Education at Brunel University. She worked as a mathematics teacher in secondary and post-16 education before becoming an academic. Her research is within the sociology and cultural studies of education and is focused on looking at issues of equity and identity within formal and informal learning. Within her funded research she has explored the gendering of the choice to study mathematics, the influence of popular culture on maths learners, the role of TV drama in young people's career choices, the identities of student teachers, online representations of women scientists and the relationship between ethnicity and physics. She is currently leading a study of the role of celebrity in young people's aspirations (www.celebyouth.org).

Marie-Pierre Moreau is Senior Research Fellow at the University of Bedfordshire, UK. Her research is at the nexus of education, work and equality issues, especially gender. She has published many articles in this area. Her recent book (*Les enseignants et le genre: les inégalités hommes–femmes dans l'enseignement du second degré en France et en Angleterre*) is an exploration of gender inequalities in the teaching profession. It was published in 2011 by the Presses Universitaires de France, Paris.

Andy Noyes is Deputy Head of the School of Education at the University of Nottingham. He joined the University in 2001, having taught in a local secondary school for a number of years. He has been programme leader for the Professional Doctorate in Education, PGCE course and the MA in Learning and Teaching. Andy has a wide variety of research interests within mathematics education and education more generally. He has recently directed large research projects on 14–19 mathematics education and is interested in multi-scale methods and the use of national datasets. Andy is a member of the Advisory Committee on Mathematics Education.

Alice J. Onion is a Visiting Senior Researcher at King's College London and strategic adviser to Bowland Maths. Her work on Bowland assessment tasks dovetailed well with her leadership of Nuffield AMP (Applying Mathematical Processes). Alice has worked with schools on assessment for learning across the curriculum. Her background is in teaching, advisory work and research and development including for Graded Assessment in Mathematics (GAIM). She has worked for four local authorities, leaving Croydon as a Senior Education Inspector in 2002 to join the Qualifications and Curriculum Authority (QCA), where her responsibilities included quality assurance of key stage mathematics tests. She left her post as head of the Mathematics, Science and Technology at QCA in 2007 to pursue an independent career.

Hilary Povey is Professor of Mathematics Education at Sheffield Hallam University where she is engaged in research, teaching and curriculum development. She has a long-standing commitment to working on social justice issues in education especially in the context of the teaching and learning of mathematics. She is an advocate for collaborative, dialogic pedagogies and against setting and tracking learners and the associated discourse of ability. The context for much of her research is in the teaching of undergraduate mathematics to students on secondary initial teacher education courses.

Leo Rogers is a founder member of the British Society for the History of Mathematics and founder of the International Study Group on the History and Pedagogy of Mathematics (HPM). He has taught in Primary and Secondary schools in England, and as a trainer of teachers, worked with pupils and teachers in a number of European Community school curriculum and university research projects. His principal interests are the Historical, Philosophical and Cultural aspects of Mathematics as they relate to the development of curricula, mathematical pedagogies, and individual learning. When not involved with mathematics education, he dances the Argentine Tango.

Tim Rowland is an Honorary Professor at the University of East Anglia, UK, Emeritus Reader in Mathematics Education at the University of Cambridge, Vice President of the International Group for the Psychology of Mathematics Education (PME), and Chair of the Joint Mathematical Council of the United Kingdom. Tim took an interest in mathematics from an early age, compulsively computing squares in his head whilst playing in defence for his primary school football team. He taught mathematics in two secondary schools before moving to teacher education and research in mathematics education. His current research focuses on mathematics teacher knowledge. He has a completed PhD in mathematics education and an uncompleted one (which took even longer) in mathematical logic.

Kenneth Ruthven joined the Faculty of Education at the University of Cambridge, where he is now Professor of Education and Director of Research, after teaching in schools in Scotland and England. His research focuses on curriculum, pedagogy and assessment, especially in school mathematics, and particularly in respect of the complex and contested process of adaptation to technological innovation. Ken(neth) is former Editor-in-Chief (and current Advisory Editor) of the international research journal, *Educational Studies in Mathematics*, recent Chair of the British Society for Research into Learning

Mathematics (and Advisory Editor of its journal, *Research in Mathematics Education*) and Chair of Trustees of the School Mathematics Project (SMP).

Cathy Smith is a Lecturer in Mathematics Education at the Institute of Education, London University. Her background is in secondary and undergraduate mathematics teaching and teacher education and she now leads the MA Mathematics Education. Cathy is interested in: choice and participation in mathematics at all ages; issues of teaching and learning mathematical thinking and content; supporting teachers in developing A-level pedagogy; and relationships between classroom practices and discourses of society and identity, particularly those that construct gender, ethnicity and social class. Her recent research has focused on participation in further mathematics A-level as an articulation of adolescence, neoliberal self-entrepreneurism and independence.

Hamsa Venkat holds the position of SA Numeracy Chair at the University of the Witwatersrand and is currently working on linked research and development work in primary mathematics. This project, entitled the Wits Maths Connect – Primary project, is working with ten partner schools in Johannesburg. Hamsa taught mathematics in London secondary schools for eight years before moving into mathematics teacher education and research. She completed a PhD at King's College London focused on the mathematics strand of the Key Stage 3 Strategy before moving to South Africa in 2005. Her early work in South Africa was on Mathematical Literacy and Hamsa continues to be interested in broadening access to mathematics, and understanding how the implementation of educational policies in classrooms works to support this broadening.

Introduction to the series

This book, *Debates in Mathematics Education*, is one of a series of books entitled *Debates in Subject Teaching*. The series has been designed to engage with a wide range of debates related to subject teaching. Unquestionably, debates vary among the subjects, but may include, for example, issues that:

- impact on Initial Teacher Education in the subject;
- are addressed in the classroom through the teaching of the subject;
- are related to the content of the subject and its definition;
- are related to subject pedagogy;
- are connected with the relationship between the subject and broader educational aims and objectives in society, and the philosophy and sociology of education;
- are related to the development of the subject and its future in the twenty-first century.

Consequently, each book presents key debates that subject teachers should understand, reflect on and engage in as part of their professional development. Chapters have been designed to highlight major questions, and to consider the evidence from research and practice in order to find possible answers. Some subject books or chapters offer at least one solution or a view of the ways forward, whereas others provide alternative views and leave readers to identify their own solution or view of the ways forward. The editors expect readers will want to pursue the issues raised, and so chapters include questions for further debate and suggestions for further reading. Debates covered in the series will provide the basis for discussion in university subject seminars or as topics for assignments or classroom research. The books have been written for all those with a professional interest in their subject, and, in particular: student teachers learning to teach the subject in secondary or primary school; newly qualified teachers; teachers undertaking study at masters level; teachers with a subject coordination or leadership role, and those preparing for such responsibility; as well as mentors, university tutors, CPD organisers and advisers of the aforementioned groups.

Books in the series have a cross-phase dimension, because the editors believe that it is important for teachers in the primary, secondary and post-16 phases to look at subject teaching holistically, particularly in order to provide for continuity and progression, but also to increase their understanding of how children and young people learn. The balance of chapters that have a cross-phase relevance varies according to the issues relevant to different subjects. However, no matter where the emphasis is, the authors have drawn out the relevance of their topic to the whole of each book's intended audience.

Because of the range of the series, both in terms of the issues covered and its cross-phase concern, each book is an edited collection. Editors have commissioned new writing from experts on particular issues, who, collectively, represent many different perspectives on subject teaching. Readers should not expect a book in this series to cover the entire range of debates relevant to the subject, or to offer a completely unified view of subject teaching, or that every debate will be dealt with discretely, or that all aspects of a debate will be covered. Part of what each book in this series offers to readers is the opportunity to explore the inter-relationships between positions in debates and, indeed, among the debates themselves, by identifying the overlapping concerns and competing arguments that are woven through the text.

The editors are aware that many initiatives in subject teaching continue to originate from the centre, and that teachers have decreasing control of subject content, pedagogy and assessment strategies. The editors strongly believe that for teaching to remain properly a vocation and a profession, teachers must be invited to be part of a creative and critical dialogue about subject teaching, and should be encouraged to reflect, criticise, problem-solve and innovate. This series is intended to provide teachers with a stimulus for democratic involvement in the development of the discourse of subject teaching.

Susan Capel, Jon Davison, James Arthur and John Moss

December 2010

Preface

Welcome to *Debates in Mathematics Education*

Our starting point is that teaching is a complex and multi-faceted activity that requires an awareness of issues that can be drawn on reflectively within practice. Lee Shulman (1987) classified knowledge for teaching into three types: content knowledge, pedagogical knowledge and pedagogical content knowledge. Effie MacLellan and Rebecca Soden (2003) explore this in their article 'Expertise, expert teaching and experienced teachers knowledge of learning theory' and, in characterising teachers as experts in the promotion of learning, argue that they should be knowledgeable about learning theory, requiring more than teaching skills, subject knowledge and classroom experience. This is particularly pertinent now in England, as we are being moved towards a more school-centred model of teacher education, urging us to consider how we marry the preparation of prospective teachers for the realities of the classroom with their acquisition of more than just practical skills and 'tips for teachers', but rather a broader view on education and a proper grounding of its history, philosophy, psychology and sociology (Korthagen and Kessels, 1999). By opening up debates and research in a way that is linked to practice, we hope that this book provides possibilities for going beyond commonsense understandings of how to teach mathematics and indeed how to teach more generally.

We view this book as a sequel of sorts to Peter Gates' *Issues in mathematics teaching*. Since that was published in 2001 there have been significant changes in educational policy and practice. As such, this book has been written to highlight some new issues and debates which we feel need to be addressed, including the move to Assessment for Learning and Personalisation. Also, where the same issues remain, such as differences in attainment and participation by social class and gender, they need to be reconsidered in light of recent developments and research evidence.

Following the example set by Peter Gates in the 2001 publication, we proceed here by considering who this book is for and how to read it. The purpose of the book is to highlight debates which are important in mathematics education and which teachers will have to address throughout their professional lives. It is designed therefore with beginning teachers in mind, aiming to enable them to consider and reflect on questions and issues, in order to reach their own informed judgements. Thus, whilst it is envisaged that this book will be of particular interest to those currently training and those in the first few years of their career in mathematics teaching, we also anticipate that the content will be of interest to many other people – notably to teachers working as mentors for student teachers and newly qualified teachers and to higher education tutors on secondary mathematics education courses, in England and beyond. Moreover, the chapters in this book have been written by active practitioners and researchers who are experts on the topics they are discussing so will provide valuable insights for those embarking on masters and doctoral programmes with a focus on the teaching and learning of mathematics.

We have divided the content into three areas: Debates in the social and political context of mathematics, debates in the teaching and learning of mathematics, and debates in mathematics curriculum and assessment. In the first section in particular but also elsewhere, we have included a focus on the social which makes this book distinctive from many others exploring practice. Whilst most chapters are rooted in the secondary phase of education we have included two chapters on primary maths and hope that all will offer something to a range of readers working in a range of contexts. Similarly, while most of the chapters are written from England, we have included chapters set in the Caribbean and in South Africa and those, for example, on climate change that take a global perspective.

In editing this book we have tried to create a collection of up-to-date, in-depth materials that can inform and help shape our readers' research, writing and practice. In bringing such content into one place, written accessibly, we aim to provide busy students and teachers with a much-needed, rich resource. Each of the chapters includes *key questions* – for you to consider, reflect upon and hopefully discuss with colleagues – and closes with suggestions for *further reading* as well as a full list of references. The style of writing is quite a relaxed one, which we hope will make reading the book enjoyable and engaging (and not too daunting!), while remaining rigorous and carefully argued. We have learned a great deal from this book, reading and rereading each chapter and engaging with the ideas therein, and we hope you find them similarly thought-provoking, challenging and inspiring.

References

Shulman, L. (1987) 'Knowledge and teaching: foundations of the new reform', *Harvard Educational Review*, 57, 1, 1–23.

MacLellan, E. and Sodon, R. (2003) 'Expertise, expert teaching and experienced teachers' knowledge of learning theory', *Scottish Educational Review*, 35, 2, 110–120.

Korthagen, F. A. J. and Kessels, J. P. A. M. (1999) 'Linking theory and practice: changing the pedagogy of teacher education', *Educational Researcher*, 28, 4, 4–17.

Acknowledgements

Even single-authored books are massive collective endeavours, but this applies even more to an edited collection like this one. We'd like to start by thanking all the amazing authors whose work features in the following pages for producing such wonderful chapters – the insights they contain and the connections between them are greater than we could have imagined when we wrote the book proposal. We appreciate that they responded constructively to our editorial ideas about their work (including sometimes telling us that we were wrong!) and generously reviewed other chapters in the book (as did our Brunel colleague Paul Ernest). Furthermore, the contributors to this book have agreed to donate all the royalties to Book Aid International. We'd also like to thank Routledge for welcoming and publishing this collection.

This editorial partnership came about through Heather's move to Brunel University where Dawn also works. We are both immensely grateful for the support we have received from our colleagues while carrying out the editorial work on this book. Heather would particularly like to thank the various people she's shared the corner of an office with during this time – Anne Chappell, Harriet Dismore, Laura Harvey, Sarmin Hossain and Sunita Babbar. Dawn would like to thank Sunita Babbar and Gwen Ineson for their support during the editing of this book and for the fantastic work they do in ensuring the high quality of Mathematics Initial Teacher Training at Brunel. Dawn would also particularly like to thank Susan Capel, for presenting her with the opportunity to edit this book and indeed Heather, for joining her in the endeavour – without your help Heather, this wouldn't have happened!

Our edited volume comes out of various mathematics education communities. This book and Heather's work generally owes much to the ideas she has encountered and the people she has met at the conferences of the British Society for Research into Learning Mathematics and Mathematics Education and Society, and at the meetings of the Critical Mathematics Education Group. In recent years, working with Anna Llewellyn and Cathy Smith has been productive and enjoyable and has kept her thinking about mathematics education even when her own research was taking her in other directions.

Finally, we'd like to acknowledge the work of Peter Gates, in his editing of *Issues in Mathematics Education*. We both love this book and have drawn inspiration from it.

Part I

Debates in the social and political context of mathematics education

Introduction to *Debates in the social and political context of mathematics education*

If you have picked up and started reading this book then the chances are you feel more positive towards mathematics than most people. Although few of us have a problem-free relationship with maths, you probably associate the subject more with pleasure than pain. This is in striking contrast to most of the population of the UK and many other countries, and it can make it difficult to be critical of mathematics education. In particular it can make the first section of this book a challenging and uncomfortable read as we ask you to engage with the ways in which mathematics is implicated in social inequality and in wider political issues. The chapters in this section cover issues that you won't always find in university courses of mathematics teacher education or on the agenda of mathematics departments in schools, colleges and universities. They deal with: the harm done by ideas that some people are naturally talented at mathematics (implying, of course, that some people aren't); how practices exclude some young people from access to the powerful knowledge that is mathematics; how mathematics reinforces inequalities of social class and gender; and how we cannot divorce what we do in maths from these processes or from the way maths is involved in everything from pop to politics.

The reasons these things are so rarely talked about, compared, for example, with how to deal with students' misconceptions about fractions or how to teach for deep understanding, is not just about how mathematics educators feel about maths. It is also because there is a dominant image of maths as *fixed* out there in the world and *fixed* inside people. Throughout this book we dispute this. Mathematics is *not* fixed out there in the universe waiting for people to discover it: people make mathematics. Mathematics is *not* an ability fixed inside people: what we are capable of mathematically is a product of our experiences and it changes in different contexts.

Thus, the chapter that opens this section, by Mark Boylan and Hilary Povey, takes apart what they call 'ability thinking': 'Mathematical ability, in this view, is an entity that helps to determine how much mathematics an individual can learn and how fast they can learn it. It is seen as determining and so predicting future attainment'. They show that, far from *describing* what people do, ability thinking *produces* some people who can do maths and some who can't. The views teachers take of mathematics and of mathematical ability are not peripheral matters to be dealt with – or not – once they have mastered how to teach long division and how to structure a set of examples on quadratics; they are at the heart of being a mathematics educator. They concern what we want for our society and what we think teaching (mathematics) is about. Mark and Hilary's list of possible aims for teaching maths is worth reproducing here because it shows how a subject that appears to be value-free is actually deeply imbued with values:

- To enable students to have mathematical skills to be active citizens.
- To maximise the highest attainment possible for the highest attaining individuals.
- To maximise the number of passes in the school leaving assessment.
- To promote enjoyment of mathematics.
- To develop problem-solving skills.
- To ensure all students have skills needed for daily life.
- To maximise the highest possible attainment for the lowest attaining individuals.
- To promote the social cohesion of the classroom.

The next chapter, by Heather Mendick and Marie-Pierre Moreau, tracks one source of 'ability thinking': popular culture. This chapter – and the next one on mathematics and politics – ask readers to look for mathematics in perhaps unexpected places, within TV drama and climate change debates, for example. The stories that Heather and Marie-Pierre recount of geniuses and nerds, of obscure and everyday mathematics, are familiar ones. The challenge is to see them differently – to understand their familiarity as deriving from their constant repetition rather than from their intrinsic truth – and to think about how they exclude some and include others in mathematics. Something that all the authors featured in this book share is a desire to interrupt the repetition of the stories and practices of mathematics-as-normal and to find ways of doing otherwise in mathematics education.

Looking for mathematics within TV and film dramas, within puzzles and quiz shows, Heather and Marie-Pierre suggest a way to open up questions about what counts as mathematics and what skills are mathematical (empathy, creativity, communication, etc.). This is a theme picked up in the next chapter by Richard Barwell who advocates teaching mathematics to promote young people's critical engagement. The examples he offers from the mathematics of climate change disrupt our ideas of what constitutes 'hard mathematics'. For here, what makes a mathematical problem complex is not what most of us call mathematics. Instead it is thinking about what version of the world is constructed within any particular model and about what effects these models have. Mathematics becomes about posing problems at least as much as it is about solving them (Brown and Walter, 2005). For teachers, this requires letting go of covering the maths content – something which, even if teachers are willing, they are rarely able to do, because of the systems of accountability in which they are embedded.

In showing us that politics is mathematical and mathematics is political, Richard once again asks us to rethink some old stories of mathematics. Many people when asked for an everyday example of maths will mention shopping. In saying this, they are usually referring to adding up the bill and working out the change. These are things that, we suspect, few people actually do. Yet, beyond this commonsense but artificial story, Richard reminds us that mathematics has changed the relationship between shop workers and customers and, more generally, de-skilled these workers. He asks us to look at the – sometimes sordid – underside of mathematics and the way that mathematics moves decisions 'out of sight'.

Following this chapter, we encounter two further ways that maths is political, through its role in reproducing social class and gender inequalities. There are interesting contrasts and connections between these two dimensions. As Peter Gates and Andy Noyes state, differences in attainment by social class, at least in the UK, remain vast and entrenched, yet they garner very little coverage in the media. This contrasts with gender differences which, as Mark McCormack points out in his chapter, are the subject of strident headlines every August despite being small and changing. However, this coverage of gender is not a sign of media engagement with the continuing gender inequalities in schooling, but instead unhelpfully reduces gender issues to a matter of boys vs. girls. Mark's chapter on gender asks us to think about inequalities beyond a narrow idea of attainment to take account of the choices students make and how differences between them become naturalised. For example, he discusses 'stereotype threat' which 'refers to the phenomenon by which when people are reminded of a stereotype about themselves, they perform in such a way that conforms to that stereotype'. This does not mean that teachers should ignore gender and social class differences when they work with students but instead that they need to be aware that how they talk about them can be part of the problem.

Schools are very particular places, which, as Peter and Andy show, match the culture of some homes more than others. Increasingly the UK education system models itself on middle-class parenting practices and tries to reform parenting in its own image; a pattern that Sharon Gewirtz (2001) has referred to as 'cloning the Blairs' (after the family of the UK's former Prime Minister Tony Blair). The value of such practices are assumed within much policy despite evidence of children and young people's increasing unhappiness and growing rates of physical and mental health problems. As Andy and Peter say, to ask about the mathematics of *different* communities and homes is political. Doing this in anything beyond a superficial way forces us to see the dominant (school) mathematics as specific, not universal. The idea of alternative, indigenous mathematics is something which has been developed within work on ethnomathematics (d'Ambrosio, 2001) and on the mathematics involved in what we think of as 'women's work' (Harris, 1997).

Finally Patricia George's chapter brings us back to where we started as her 'made for maths' view parallels what Mark and Hilary called 'ability thinking'. Her focus is slightly different as she looks in detail at the role of teachers in perpetuating this view and challenges them/us to do otherwise. In this way we hope Patricia's work offers a bridge to the next section of the book on teaching and learning. Bookending this first section with chapters about 'ability' reflects how this idea runs through all the other chapters: it's in popular culture images of geniuses, it's a way that mathematics formats our world, and it is tied to class and gender, naturalising very social inequalities. Patricia's chapter marks a move to the Caribbean; although mostly set in England we hope this book has a global outlook and that chapters like this offer a comparative approach.

Patricia also raises the issue that we used to open this introduction: how our own relationships with mathematics constrain what we can do as teachers. 'Teachers' views of mathematics are not formed in isolation, but in a context of having themselves had long years of experience in classrooms as learners of mathematics where mathematics teaching and available ways of learning were modelled before them as well as societal beliefs about mathematics and expectations of what is possible in it and with whom these possibilities lie'. Teachers need spaces to reflect on their own relationships with mathematics, to be re-introduced to maths (to adopt a metaphor from one of the teachers who participated in Patricia's research). They need to 'open up avenues and environment[s] for students to really dance in the classroom, see connections, see worlds … to navigate, to meander, to dream, to dance'.

All the authors who have contributed to this section remind us what's at stake in mathematics education; maths has the power to give young people access to critically engaged citizenship and enhanced life chances. Mark and Hilary's vision of an entitlement to mathematics is one shared by all the authors in this book and is a great way to open the volume.

References

Brown, S. I. and Walter, M. I. (2005) *The art of problem posing (3rd edition)*. Mahwah, New Jersey: Lawrence Erlbaum Associates.

d'Ambrosio, U. (2001) 'What is ethnomathematics, and how can it help children in schools?', *Teaching Children Mathematics*, 7, 6, 308–310.

Gewirtz, S. (2001) 'Cloning the Blairs: New Labour's programme for the re-socialization of working-class parents', *Journal of Education Policy*, 16, 4, 365–378.

Harris, M. (1997) *Common threads: women, mathematics and work*. Stoke-on-Trent: Trentham Books.

Chapter 1

Ability thinking

Mark Boylan and Hilary Povey

Introduction

> *There are many words and phrases used in schools by teachers and students that refer to or describe mathematical 'ability'.*
>
> *Make a list of words that you have used or heard others use. If you are working or placed in a school you might keep a record of the different ways teachers and students use ability and other labels.*
>
> *Which of the words on your list are useful and helpful for teachers and learners and which do you think are unhelpful and damaging?*

This chapter is about an important aspect of the way people in the UK and in some other countries think about how mathematics is taught and learnt. We call this 'ability thinking'. The central belief in this mindset is that each person has a particular level of mathematical ability that is relatively stable. Mathematical ability, in this view, is an entity that helps to determine how much mathematics and how fast an individual can learn. It is seen as determining and so predicting future attainment. It is also claimed that learners with similar levels of attainment and so, it is assumed, ability, are best taught together. This idea is the basis for either setting or banding of learners in secondary schools in the UK. Primary schools either use within-class ability grouping or setting, with the latter becoming increasingly common. These grouping practices are outcomes of ability thinking and also help to produce it because they shape how we think about our own and others' capacity to learn mathematics.

Much of our discussion in this chapter is about setting and grouping as these are the clearest manifestations of ideas of ability and symbolise this way of thinking. However, the lens of ability influences everyday interactions between teachers and learners and the way learners relate to each other. It is the dominant way that teachers, children, parents and policy makers think about attainment in mathematics. It is so dominant that it is often taken for granted as obviously true. Because of this it is rarely debated. We think it should be. A recent international study by the Organisation for Economic Cooperation and Development concluded that setting students should be avoided at least until upper secondary education as it is unfair and has negative effects on overall attainment (OECD, 2012).

In this chapter we look at five areas. We begin by further discussing ability thinking and questioning the idea of mathematical ability as it is used in everyday talk in schools and classrooms. We go on to examine the impact of setting on attainment; this is followed by a discussion of the unfairness of setting practices and the effects setting has on teaching. Setting and ability thinking have significant impacts on learners' beliefs about mathematics and themselves. We discuss the short- and long-term consequences of these ability mindsets. We conclude by considering alternatives to ability thinking.

ABILITY THINKING

Consider this statement: your mathematical ability is something about you that you cannot change very much. How far do you agree?

If you broadly agree with the above statement it is likely that you have an entity or fixed view of mathematical ability. You are likely to think that whilst people can learn more mathematics each person has an underlying level of mathematical ability which is the main factor in determining, and so is predictive of, future attainment. It is not surprising if you believe this. It is probably shared by the majority of mathematics teachers in the UK. If educated here, your own experience of being taught in mathematical sets and being labelled by ability is likely to have shaped your beliefs. Further, evidence from schools appears to support this view. After all, some students do know more mathematics than peers of the same age and do seem to understand new mathematical ideas more quickly.

The fixed view of mathematics ability is linked to a more general view of 'inborn intelligence'. In the space we have here we can only summarise some key reasons why this innate view of ability is wrong. The statistical basis for this theory is fundamentally flawed (Gould, 1981). Success in tests that purport to measure innate mathematical ability is not independent of cultural knowledge or formal and informal education. With practice it is possible for people to increase their test scores which should not happen if the tests were measuring something fixed. Recent studies have also shown a link between intelligence test outcomes and motivation. If you believe that success in a test will lead to a reward you tend to do better (BBC, 2011).

Further, the capability to carry out even relatively simple calculations is situated by context. What people can do in informal situations in their daily lives is very different from the knowledge they display in formal school environments or in tests. Attainment on mathematics tests is not only determined by how much mathematics is known but also by a host of other factors including: physical wellbeing on the day; level of motivation; general test-taking skills; emotional issues such as test anxiety; and the amount of revision an individual might have done. These are only some of the reasons why tests are unreliable and different tests produce different results. Teachers are also used to the experience of finding that students with very similar test scores have quite different capacities to engage in classroom activities. Even those who believe that cognitive ability can be measured estimate that differences in scores on cognitive ability tests only explain 36% of the variance in attainment outcomes (Ireson and Hallam, 2001).

Ability thinking also supposes that mathematical ability is a single entity that is generally disconnected from other human capacities. However, mathematics is much more diverse than the content that is included within tests of mathematical ability. For example, research shows that young children's creativity and the depth of imaginative play they engage in give good indications of later mathematical attainment (Hanline, Milton, and Phelps, 2008). The current curriculum has tended to be shaped by what can be easily tested rather than reflecting the diverse ways that mathematics is used in society or important aspects of mathematical activity. Ability thinking entails and is supported by a narrow view of what mathematics is that can exclude these other aspects of thinking mathematically including problem solving, communicating about mathematics and collaborating with others.

Labels for mathematics learners such as high or low ability are used to predict future attainment outcomes. However, it has long been established that students will tend to fulfil the expectations that teachers and the education system place on them (Rosenthal and Jacobsen, 1968/2003). Ability labels tend to lead to a series of self-fulfilling prophecies, lowering expectations of teachers and students as to what is possible. They tend to narrow and restrict learning objectives. By questioning the idea of mathematical ability we are not suggesting that there are not differences in people's capacity to do mathematics, or to learn mathematics. Clearly, learners are not the same and it is important that teachers understand these differences to inform their teaching. However, we do not believe that these differences are fixed, unchanging and context-free. Further, ability thinking can get in the way of understanding and appreciating these differences as it can lead to 'seeing and teaching the label' rather than the student.

SETTING AND ATTAINMENT

Consider the following possible purposes a mathematics teacher might have:

- *To enable students to have mathematical skills to be an active citizen.*
- *To maximise the highest attainment possible for the highest attaining individuals.*
- *To maximise the number of passes in the school leaving assessment.*
- *To promote enjoyment of mathematics.*
- *To develop problem-solving skills.*
- *To ensure all students have skills needed for daily life.*
- *To maximise the highest possible attainment for the lowest attaining individuals.*
- *To promote the social cohesion of the classroom.*

Which of these purposes do you think are the most important and which the least important and why?

What tensions might exist between these different purposes?

How might setting in mathematics influence or impact on achieving these purposes?

The most visible outcome of ability thinking in secondary schools is teaching students in sets. Setting has been the dominant form of organisation for mathematics lessons in most secondary schools in the UK for a long time. In primary schools it is more common to place students in small groups that are seen as having the same ability for mathematics lessons.

In response to the pressure to 'raise standards' and official government encouragement for these approaches, since the start of the century these practices have become even more embedded and accepted in England (Ofsted, 2008). Indeed, in one recent extreme example students were required to wear different coloured ties to indicate their different perceived levels of attainment (David, 2011).

Although ability grouping and thinking is the norm in England there are other countries that do not organise mathematics learning in this way. Attainment in England is lower than in those countries that do not segregate learners. Over the last 20 years, comparing mathematics education internationally has become a 'hot topic' for politicians and journalists, as well as mathematics educators, and it is important to be cautious about drawing conclusions. Politicians' declarations that England has gone down the international league tables do not entirely stand up when these studies are critically examined. The actual differences in attainment in mathematics between all prosperous and relatively industrialised countries as measured by international comparison surveys TIMSS (Trends in International Mathematics and Science Study) and PISA (Programme for International Student Assessment) are relatively small (Askew, Hodgen, Hossain and Bretscher, 2010). Most learners in most of these countries have quite similar levels of attainment. The reasons for the differences that do exist between them are complex and multiple and so it is possible to find evidence from international comparisons to support a variety of views on setting. However, no high-performing country groups students by ability in mathematics in the rigid and fine ranked way we often do in England. The countries that are most successful, such as Finland, generally teach mathematics in all-attainment groups and this is generally true of the other highly ranked European countries. Thus it is ironic that the drive to increase setting, which has come in part from politicians' desire to compete with other countries in international comparisons, does not take into account the lessons we can potentially learn from such countries.

Teachers in these other countries are experienced in teaching all attainment groups. Further, they will generally have experienced this way of learning in their own education, and importantly their beliefs about learning mathematics are not constricted by ability thinking. In the UK attainment grouping in mathematics has often been put into practice in a hostile policy context, by teachers with little support from initial teacher education or continuing professional development, and where the assessment regime is based on and backs up ability thinking.

Given this, we might expect to find that setting in the UK leads to higher outcomes than all-attainment teaching. However, comparisons of different forms of grouping within the UK also show that grouping by perceived ability does not generally raise attainment when compared with alternatives. The evidence from various studies is somewhat contradictory due, perhaps, to the effects of other features associated with setting such as different curricula and teaching practices. Some studies have shown that no groups of students benefit from setting or tracking in terms of attainment (for example, Boaler, 1997). Other studies have shown that those who are of highest attainment on entry to secondary school may get some limited benefit in terms of attainment outcomes but that lowest attaining students suffer and do less well when segregated (Ireson and Hallam, 2001). Once placed in a lower set, students usually suffer from lower expectations and a restricted curriculum and may be given less qualified or experienced teachers. Students with very similar levels of attainment when placed in different sets have very different outcomes and in mathematics this can be as much as a GCSE grade (Wiliam and Bartholomew, 2004).

SETTING PRACTICES AND TEACHING

> *Investigate how individuals are allocated to particular sets or groups in mathematics and their educational experience in those sets.*
>
> *You might reflect on your own experience as well as talk to other people about theirs. If you always were in one type of set then it is valuable to talk to people who were in different types of grouping.*
>
> *If you are currently working or placed in a school enquire into the process by which students are placed in sets. What influences those decisions?*

Setting practices are deeply inequitable. Some gain at the expense of others and often the ones who appear to do well out of setting tend to be students who are already advantaged. Teacher beliefs about students rather than attainment evidence can be significant in deciding on sets. Such perceptions can be influenced by cultural stereotypes. This may explain why, for example, a lower proportion of African-Caribbean students are entered for the higher mathematics tier than would be expected on the basis of their prior attainment (Strand, 2011). Because movement between sets is rare (Hart *et al.*, 2004) once allocated to a particular set educational opportunities may be curtailed for the rest of the student's schooling. Students from groups who experience social and economic disadvantage are more likely to be found in the lower sets (Wiliam and Bartholomew, 2004) as are girls (Brown, Brown, and Bibby, 2008). Our view, and one we hope you would share, is that mathematics teachers have a responsibility to support all students to achieve mathematically and to develop a positive relationship with the subject.

When students are taught in sets few students receive an appropriate level of challenge. It is all too easy to teach a class in which the range of attainment is narrowed as if the attainment, motivation, and disposition of all students in the class is the same. In top sets the usual assumption is that learners benefit from or need a fast pace and instrumental proficiency even though evidence suggests that many learners, and in particular girls, are alienated in this environment (Boaler, Wiliam and Brown, 2000). Further, such practices appear to put learners off studying mathematics once the subject becomes optional (Brown *et al.*, 2008). Offering those with the highest previous attainment or with a particular interest or disposition for mathematics a diet of mathematics in pre-digested bite-sized pieces 'delivered' at pace may also leave them unchallenged.

Those in lower sets in secondary schools will often only be offered material that they have previously encountered and so meet a narrow and restricted curriculum (Watson and De Geest, 2005). Through adherence by teachers and schools to a simplistic theory of learning styles, they may be labelled kinaesthetic and so be required to use practical equipment even when it does not support mathematical learning (Marks, 2011). At the same time students in high sets may not be offered the opportunity to develop their thinking through engaging with manipulatives, physical models or embodied learning that can stretch understanding and provoke debate about the meaning of mathematical concepts. As discussed in the chapter by Peter Gates and Andy Noyes, there appears to be a link to the type of curriculum and learning experiences that are offered and the patterns of social class background found in different types of set. Groups in which working-class students are more likely to be found are offered a more 'manual' curriculum.

ABILITY MINDSETS

Setting and the ability thinking that supports it is unjust and damaging in other ways. It not only creates barriers to attainment – it also can have profound impacts on learners' beliefs about themselves and their relationship to mathematics. There is now extensive evidence of the ways in which children, including from young ages, are highly aware of their relative position in the class or year group (for example, Hodgen and Marks, 2009). The process of measuring and being measured affects how children see themselves and others. For some, including those who appear to gain by being labelled clever or 'top set', it can lead to profound anxiety (Boaler, Wiliam and Brown, 2000). Mathematics comes to be seen as an elitist activity that only some can do (Nardi and Steward, 2003). One understandable response by teachers of previously low attaining students is to try to further simplify or reduce the challenge in mathematics – to try to make mathematics easy. Unfortunately, this is counterproductive: it makes learners over-reliant on teachers doing the mathematical thinking on their behalf; it robs the mathematics studied of meaning and purpose thus making it harder to learn; and it makes students unwilling to tackle questions or topics that appear difficult when first encountered, to engage in problem-solving or to apply mathematics in unfamiliar contexts.

The effect on identities lasts beyond compulsory mathematics education. Mathematical anxiety and shame experienced at school can still be felt in adulthood (Bibby, 2002). Jo Boaler (1997) carried out a celebrated study in the 1990s of the experience of school mathematics in two schools that were similar in terms of attainment and socioeconomic profiles but which had different approaches to teaching mathematics. In one, mathematics teaching focused on a problem-solving curriculum and students worked in all-attainment groupings. Hilary discusses this approach in more detail in a later chapter. In the other school students learnt through a more traditional approach and learning took place in sets. When Jo Boaler later interviewed participants from her original study as adults, she found that those who had learnt mathematics in all-attainment classrooms were more likely to be working in higher-paid and more highly skilled occupations. She concludes that setting can limit the aspirations of those who are placed in lower sets. One of her interviewees who had experienced setting reflected on the effects on his peers:

> You're putting this psychological prison around them [...] It kind of just breaks all their ambition [...] It's quite sad that there's kids there that could potentially be very, very smart and benefit us in so many ways, but it's just kind of broken down from a young age. So that's why I dislike the set system so much – because I think it almost formally labels kids as stupid.
>
> (Boaler, 2005, p.142)

We believe it is not only those who find themselves in lower sets who may experience psychological prisons. There is evidence that not just setting but ability thinking itself damages all learners.

Carol Dweck (1999; 2006) and colleagues have done extensive research into the way people's self theories or 'mindsets' about ability influence their achievements. She identifies two contrasting theories or beliefs. One is to see intelligence as 'malleable' or changeable. Learners with this incremental view tend to stick at challenges. They see effort as the key to success. The other theory is at the heart of what we call ability thinking. Here intelligence or ability is seen as an entity and is fixed. The consequence of this mindset when met with challenge or difficulty is often to give up due to a belief that ability equates to being able to do a task straightaway. If the task is challenging then this, it is supposed, means that the task is beyond their ability. Success for the entity theorists should be effortless and there is little point trying. Carol Dweck has found that learners with the same level of initial attainment given the same learning opportunities but with different mindsets have different outcomes. Those with a fixed view of ability tend to do worse.

Dweck's research is able to explain why, for example, even those who go on to achieve highly in mathematics may still feel insecure about their competence or mathematical identity (Black *et al.*, 2009). We have a culture in school mathematics where if someone is placed in the top set through their effort they are not seen as being as 'bright' as others; achievement in mathematics is supposed to be effortless, thus reinforcing entity theories. Most teachers, of course, encourage their students to try hard and not to give up when meeting challenges. However, this encouragement cannot, on its own, develop or sustain an incremental view if the language of the classroom, the emphasis on measurement, the pedagogy, curriculum and the experience of setting all assert a fixed view of ability. Whatever the form of classroom organisation, often the most significant lesson learnt by students is that in mathematics what counts and is valued is speed, competition and the amount 'covered'.

> *How far does Carol Dweck's research reflect your own experience or that of people you know?*
>
> *What are the implications of Dweck's research for how mathematics should be taught and organised in schools?*

ALTERNATIVE MINDSETS

In this chapter we have discussed the negative effects of the setting practices that flow from ability thinking. However, adopting all-attainment groupings will not by itself create inclusive classrooms where the attainment of all can be fostered. The negative consequences of ability thinking can and do happen in mixed-ability classes as well, if the ability mindset is the way teachers and learners are thinking about learning mathematics (and as Patricia George shows in her chapter, many of them do hold this mindset).

Fortunately, there are other ways to think about mathematical capacity and learning than ability thinking. We have discussed Carol Dweck's concept of malleability emphasising that human cognitive and social capacities are not fixed. Susan Hart and colleagues propose a similar concept of 'transformability' that focuses on the potential for change (Hart *et al.*, 2004). There are many ways in which classroom mathematics can be taught based on the principle of transformability and Hilary discusses a number of these in a later chapter in this book: 'A pedagogy of attainment for all'.

However it may not be the teaching practices, classroom organisation or curriculum that are most important in supporting success for all learners, but rather the beliefs of teachers and so of learners themselves. We noted above that there are many countries which do not think about mathematical capacities and learning in terms of ability and who successfully support high attainment for the majority. These countries differ in their approaches to teaching mathematics but what they have in common are:

- High expectations of all students.
- Allowing all to access a challenging curriculum.
- Valuing current effort rather than previous attainment.
- Striving for the achievement of all rather than of a few.

These countries demonstrate what is possible on a national scale. Obviously individual teachers cannot reproduce their pedagogical approaches or the culture that supports them. However, we can, as teachers, change our own mindsets and strive to teach our students rather than teach to labels. When we do this, remarkable and surprising outcomes are possible. Brent Davis, Dennis Sumara and Rebecca Luce-Kapler (2008), for example, offer the story of Krista, who is labelled as having a learning disability in mathematics but goes on to achieve highly when her learning needs are addressed.

Anne Watson and Els De Geest (2005) point to what is possible for whole classes of, what they describe as, previously low-attaining students. They identify the principles that underlay the practice of teachers who were particularly successful with such students in spite of the restriction of rigid curricula or prescribed types of lessons. These principles include: access to a broad mathematics curriculum; supporting students to develop reasoning and thinking and to become mathematical learners; supporting students' self-esteem through mathematics; giving students freedom to exercise rights and responsibility; taking into account the power of external measures but not being driven by them; and providing extended thinking time and extended tasks. It is principles rather than practices, they argue, that are key. These principles also provide their own challenge to the restrictions generated by ability thinking. When low-attaining, demoralised students are given 'more choice, freedom, challenge, responsibility and time' (Watson and De Geest, 2005, p.230) they are enabled to succeed.

In the UK there is general agreement on the need to support more learners to be successful in mathematics and to address the disengagement of many from the subject. In recent times this has been addressed, in the main, by focusing on differences between learners. National curriculum levels, and more recently the fictitious idea of sub-levels, are used as tools to identify ever more narrow diets of mathematical content for specific groups of learners. The increased use of setting has tended to predetermine the range of possible outcomes for students. Resources and attention has tended to flow to whichever groups of students are designated as being of most concern by whatever measure is used, at any particular point in time, to judge school success. The alternative we propose is one which:

> emphasises *universal entitlement* rather than differences: *everybody* counts, *everybody's* learning is equally important, *everybody* contributes to the learning environment. And so it follows that teachers work constantly to create – and if necessary invent – approaches that allow everybody without exception, to engage in the activities provided, to have the experience of being excited by learning, to gain something worthwhile, and to feel a sense of safety and belonging.
>
> (Dixon *et al.*, 2002, p.9, original emphasis)

Challenging our own and others' ability thinking offers the possibility of honouring this entitlement.

Further reading

Dweck, C. (1999) *Self-theories: Their Role in Motivation, Personality, and Development*. Philadelphia: Psychology Press. This is an engaging digest of a body of research that demonstrates that ability thinking is damaging for learners. Dweck also challenges 'commonsense' ideas about praise and feedback, emphasising the importance of valuing effort, challenge and the development of strategies rather than ability.

Hart, S., Dixon, A. Drummond, M. J. and McIntyre, D. (2004) *Learning without limits*. Maidenhead: Open University Press. This book is based on a research project which studies the practices of a group of teachers who teach all-attainment or widely attaining classes. They propose the concept of transformability as an alternative to ability. Chapter 2 – 'What's wrong with ability labelling' – is particularly relevant to the ideas we have presented in this chapter.

Wiliam, D. and Bartholomew, H. (2004) 'It's not which school but which set you're in that matters: The influence of ability grouping practices on students progress in mathematics', *British Educational Research Journal*, 30, 3, 279–293. This article provides a summary of key research on setting in mathematics as well as evidence from a study that tracked the progress of 950 students. The study showed how setting can affect attainment and teaching practices.

Watson, A. and De Geest, E. (2005) 'Principled teaching for deep progress: improving mathematical learning beyond methods and materials', *Educational Studies in Mathematics*, 58, 2, 209–234. This article reports on a two-year action research project with ten teachers to improve the achievement of previously low-attaining secondary students. A key finding was that effective practices were based on common principles. These principles represent, in our view, an alternative to ability thinking.

References

Askew, M., Hodgen, J., Hossain, S. and Bretscher, N. (2010) *Values and variables: Mathematics education in high performing countries*. Nuffield Foundation: London.

BBC. (2011) 'IQ tests measure motivation – not just intelligence'. Available at: http://www.bbc.co.uk/news/health-13156817 (accessed 15 January 2012).

Bibby, T. (2002) 'Shame: an emotional response to doing mathematics as an adult and a teacher', *British Educational Research Journal*, 28, 5, 705–722.

Black, L., Mendick, H., Rodd, M., Solomon, Y. and Brown, M. (2009) 'Pain, pleasure and power: selecting and assessing defended subjects', in L. Black, H. Mendick and Y. Solomon (eds) *Mathematical relationships: Identities and participation*. London: Routledge.

Brown, M., Brown, P. and Bibby, T. (2008) '"I would rather die": reasons given by 16 year olds for not continuing their study of mathematics', *Research in Mathematics Education*, 10, 1, 3–18.

Boaler, J. (1997) *Experiencing school mathematics: Teaching styles, sex and setting*. Buckingham: Open University Press.

Boaler, J. (2005) 'The "psychological prisons" from which they never escaped: The role of ability grouping in reproducing social class inequalities', *Forum* 47, 2 and 3, 125–134.

Boaler, J., Wiliam, D. and Brown, M. (2000) 'Students' experiences of ability grouping – disaffection, polarisation and the construction of failure', *British Educational Research Journal*, 26, 5, 631–648.

David, R. (2011) 'School colour codes students by ability', *The Guardian*. Available at: http://www.guardian.co.uk/education/2011/jul/25/secondary-school-streaming (accessed 28 July 2011).

Davis, B., Sumara, D. and Luce Kapler, R. (2008) *Engaging minds: Changing teaching in complex times*. New York: Routledge.

Dixon, A., Drummond, M., Hart, S. and McIntyre, D. (2002) 'Developing teaching free from ability labelling: back where we started?', *Forum*, 44, 1, 7–11.

Gould, S. (1981) *The mismeasure of man*. London: Penguin.

Dweck, C. (1999) *Self-theories: their role in motivation, personality, and development*. Philadelphia: Psychology Press.

Dweck, C. (2006) *Mindset*. New York: Random House.

Hanline, M., Milton, S. and Phelps, P. (2008) 'A longitudinal study exploring the relationship of representational levels of three aspects of preschool sociodramatic play and early academic skills', *Journal of Research in Childhood Education*, 23, 1, 19–28.

Hart, S., Dixon, A., Drummond, M. J. and McIntyre, D. (2004) *Learning without limits*. Maidenhead: Open University Press.

Hodgen, J. and Marks, R. (2009) 'Mathematical "ability" and identity: A sociocultural perspective on assessment and selection', in L. Black, H. Mendick, and Y. Solomon (eds), *Mathematical relationships: Identities and participation*. London: Routledge.

Ireson, J. and Hallam, S. (2001) *Ability grouping in education*. London: Paul Chapman Publishing.

Marks, R. (2011) '"Ability" in primary mathematics education: patterns and implications', *Proceedings of the British Society for Research into Learning Mathematics (BSRLM)*, 31, 1, 91–96.

Nardi, E., and Steward, S. (2003) 'Is mathematics T.I.R.E.D.? A profile of quiet disaffection in the secondary mathematics classroom', *British Education Research Journal*, 29, 3, 345–367.

Organisation for Economic Cooperation and Development (OECD) (2012) *Equity and Quality in Education: Supporting Disadvantaged Students and Schools*. Paris: OECD.

Office for Standards in Education (Ofsted) (2008) Mathematics: understanding the score. Available at: http://www.ofsted.gov.uk/resources/mathematics-understanding-score (accessed 6 February 2012).

Rosenthal, R. and Jacobsen, L. (1968/2003) *Pygmalion in the classroom: teacher expectation and pupil's intellectual development*. Carmarthen: Crown House.

Strand, S. (2011) 'The White British-Black Caribbean achievement gap: tests, tiers and teacher expectations', *British Education Research Journal*, 38, 1, 75–102.

Watson, A. and De Geest, E. (2005) 'Principled teaching for deep progress: improving mathematical learning beyond methods and materials', *Educational Studies in Mathematics*, 58, 2, 209–234.

Wiliam, D. and Bartholomew, H. (2004) 'It's not which school but which set you're in that matters: The influence of ability grouping practices on students progress in mathematics', *British Educational Research Journal*, 30, 3, 279–293.

Chapter 2

From *Good Will Hunting* to *Deal or No Deal*

Using popular culture in the mathematics classroom

Heather Mendick and Marie-Pierre Moreau

This chapter is about mathematics and popular culture. So, before you start reading, can you remember any times you've seen mathematics and/or mathematicians in popular culture? Try to think of at least one example for each of these categories: film, television, advertising, newspapers, magazines, computer games, clothing, the internet, music, comedy, books. Now try to describe a couple of them and how you feel about them.

Mathematics is both ubiquitous and invisible in popular culture; it is everywhere and nowhere. This chapter draws on our research into how representations of mathematics and mathematicians in popular culture impact on learners. We interviewed over 130 people during this research in 2007 but, first, in 2006, we surveyed 556 14–15-year-old school students and 100 university students and asked them, as we've just asked you, to recall two examples of popular culture images of mathematics or mathematicians. Twenty-four percent left the first example blank and 50 percent left the second blank. We don't think this signals an absence of mathematical images, but their invisibility. Only ten of the examples came up more than five times but a huge number, 71, came up fewer, with 47 being noted just once. Some we had anticipated but expected to come up more often, including: *Rainman* (film), sport and *The Da Vinci Code* (book). Others took us by surprise, including: *Mission Impossible* (film), *Friends* (TV), Mambo Number 5 (music) and Wolfram (website).

In the years since 2006, the presence of mathematics has increased. Alan Sugar, the entrepreneur at the centre of the UK *Apprentice*, regularly berates contestants for their computational incompetence. Global phenomenon *High School Musical* features a cake bearing the symbol pi and, when we first meet its star Gabriella Montez, she is correcting a mathematical formula. YouTube has recently launched Numberphile, a channel where people enthuse about their favourite numbers. We hope to show that, rather than ignoring this proliferation of popular mathematics and carrying on with 'mathematics-as-usual', teachers and learners should engage with these images in their classrooms.

In this chapter, we see learning mathematics as about more than acquiring a range of skills in arithmetic, algebra, geometry, statistics and problem solving. Learning mathematics involves forming a relationship with the subject – of love, hate, pain and/or pleasure. Central to this are the stories people tell about mathematics and about themselves in relation to it. By 'stories', we mean ways of seeing and making sense of the world.

What stories do you tell about your own and other people's relationships to mathematics? Where do these stories come from?

The stories we tell about mathematics come from various places: school mathematics, other people (not just maths teachers, but parents, siblings, friends, other teachers) and popular culture. They include stories in which those doing mathematics are 'geniuses' and stories in which they're 'nerds', stories of mathematics as abstract and of mathematics as everyday. These stories of mathematics and mathematicians circulate in popular culture texts (e.g. films, television programmes, websites). Children, like all of us, do not see things on TV, for example, and then copy them, but the things they see are part of the resources that they use to make sense of who they are and what happens to them. Because popular culture plays a key role in shaping relationships with mathematics, our view is that, as teachers, we should care about that rather than ignore it.

The next section focuses on the image of the mathematical genius. There are lots of these in popular culture, for example, in Good Will Hunting *and* Numb3rs. *In these stories, where does mathematical ability come from? Does it matter whether learners think that mathematicians are born or made?*

BORN THAT WAY: THE STORY OF NATURAL MATHEMATICAL ABILITY

We have organised this chapter around stories about mathematics giving examples of how they circulate in popular culture and how these are taken up by students we spoke to within our research. We begin with one of the most widespread and influential stories about mathematics: that being good (or bad) at it is in your genes. The film *Good Will Hunting* is a classic example of this idea that mathematicians are born not made. The central character Will Hunting (played by Matt Damon) has more than 'natural ability'; he's a 'genius'. A self-taught, working-class janitor at MIT, overnight he solves problems which took a Fields Medallist, MIT Professor years.

Stories of *natural* mathematical abilities are usually supported by being associated with other characteristics that are seen as natural: mental health issues, autism, obsession. In *Good Will Hunting*, Will loses control and uses physical violence early in the film landing him a lengthy course of therapy. Similarly, in the book *The Curious Incident of the Dog in the Night-time* and the film *Rainman*, the main characters combine mathematical abilities with autistic spectrum disorders. While in the film *A Beautiful Mind*, based on the life of mathematician John Nash, exceptional mathematical ability is closely related to schizophrenia, paranoia and social anxiety. This pattern repeats in the films *Pi* and *Enigma* whose genius mathematicians both have breakdowns. In *Pi* this breakdown results in the loss of all mathematical abilities but increased mental calm, happiness and connection with other people. This parallels the ending of *Good Will Hunting*, when Will abandons a high-powered career in mathematics in pursuit of love and connection with girlfriend Skylar.

In popular culture, mathematical ability is double-edged. It carries power (to control the stock market and access the divine in *Pi*, and to win the Second World War in *Enigma* and the cold war in *A Beautiful Mind*) yet is often linked to disabilities. The students we spoke to picked up on this, sometimes reproducing these stories and sometimes challenging them. School student Bob said about *The Curious Incident of the Dog in the Night-time*: 'most people that do have Asperger's syndrome are actually amazing at maths but they have like side effects like schizophrenia and things like that that stop them going out'. When we showed people a picture of *A Beautiful Mind*'s John Nash, this provoked talk about the boundaries between genius and madness: 'is he crazy or is he just clever?'. People who did not like mathematics tended to position these attributes negatively as something with which they didn't identify. However, those who'd chosen mathematics (or were planning to), were more likely to frame this positively as 'skill', 'commitment' or 'devotion'. Young women presented more negative perceptions than young men, constructing Nash as 'disturbed', 'nuts', 'weird', 'mental'.

For many people we talked to, this story of natural mathematical geniuses coexists with another story: that most people can do mathematics and get better at it through practice. The tension between these two stories is resolved by the problematic idea that there are two sorts of mathematics, esoteric and everyday, associated with two sorts of people, geniuses and normal people. School student Firefly distinguished between 'genius maths, which is working out these equations and winning big prizes' and 'the sort of maths that [you can] apply to engineering or … accountancy or anything'. He continued, genius maths 'is more a thing that you see as someone who just sits at home with a desk, staying up till two o'clock working out this equation. Whereas applied maths you just think someone, just like a more normal person in a job, even though the maths might be similar'. In describing this as how 'you just think' things rather than how things really are, Firefly implicitly recognises there's a problem with his image. His final 'even though the maths might be similar' also shows awareness of contradictions in his account. However, not everyone expressed such reflexivity and, even when they did, they had no alternatives with which to replace this image of the crazy, isolated, obsessive mathematical genius.

This association between being a mathematician and the exceptional figure of the genius makes it difficult for individuals to identify *themselves* with mathematics. Even when they are good at it by school standards, the spectre of those who are natural-born geniuses renders their own achievements as second-class in comparison. In the case of women and of minority ethnic groups, this is complicated by the fact that in popular culture these exceptional individuals are usually white males and, with the notable exception of Will, come from middle-class backgrounds.

The next section focuses on images of geeks. What makes someone a geek? (How) is this different from being a nerd, boffin or dork? Do you see yourself as a geek? Do you think others see you in this way?

GEEK CHIC: THE STORY OF THE SOCIALLY-AWKWARD, BUT CUTE (MALE) MATHEMATICIAN

The story of 'geeky' mathematicians relates to the 'genius' story, extending how mathematical ability is seen as written on the body. Geekiness is an imprecise term but generally encompasses a range of behaviours including having no fashion sense, social incompetence and an inability to relate to the opposite sex. This is part of a wider story in which mathematicians' lives are seen as dominated by mathematics, so that it consumes their whole personality.

TV sitcom *The Big Bang Theory* centres on four male geeks and their unlikely friendship with the blonde, fashionable, chatty Penny. Although they are physicists and engineers, they are often shown doing mathematics. Three are white (one of whom is Jewish) and one is Indian. Within this show, we see a spectrum of geekiness. Leonard, the most conventional and the most sexually and romantically successful of the four, still suffers many health problems and nervous disorders including lactose intolerance, sleep apnoea, migraines, carsickness, nose bleeds and asthma. He regularly applies excessive hair gel and wears mismatched clothing. At the other extreme is Sheldon, who interprets everything literally, feels compelled to order his surroundings (even when this involves invading his neighbour's flat) and feels that massaging his own shoulders involves excessive physical contact. In between are Howard, who lives with his mother, and Raj, who can't talk to women unless he's drunk. Most of the female characters, like Penny, exist to contrast with the male geeks, and implicitly emphasise their heterosexuality. The two female geeks are peripheral characters introduced as potential love interests for the men. They stand out like the one female geek and one gay geek included in a total of 42 geeks featuring across five seasons of US Reality TV show *Beauty and the Geek*.

Geek stories in popular culture, like those of geniuses, are double-edged. Geeks are strange but also valued for their 'geek chic', being intelligent and unafraid of being different. Despite varying levels of social and emotional incompetence, they all attract the attention of beautiful women. In *The Big Bang Theory*, Penny clearly enjoys hanging out with the geek gang and she dates Leonard and has a one night stand with Raj.

We found that the more distant (in time and feelings) a person was from mathematics, the more likely they were to present geeks as weird, as in this extract from an interview with sociology undergraduate Ellie:

> My friend who was the maths geek, he came back this summer and he has got like the pi symbol and it's about an inch big tattooed on the underside of his wrist. Everyone was telling me he had 'pi' and I was thinking, 'why has he got a pie tattooed on his wrist? … What kind of pie would it be and why would you think "let's have a pie"?'. And then everyone was like, 'what are you on about? Pi, you know'. And I was like 'oh'. But he thinks it is like the best thing ever, so much so that he has had it now permanently tattooed on him. [laughter] You wouldn't go and get Marx, you know, 'I really like Marx let's have him tattooed'.

Ellie uses geek stories to distance herself from mathematicians, compounded here by multiple misunderstandings: that it is mathematical pi not edible pie; how anyone can relate to the symbol pi like that; and even more, how someone can relate to a subject like that.

The comparison with Marx renders this obsessive and excessive. It's also typical of how, whether they like and do mathematics or not, people expect mathematics to be (literally in this case) written on the body.

It was the mathematics undergraduates who were most likely to present geek as chic. For example, Dave referred to film *Jurassic Park*'s Ian Malcolm (played by Jeff Goldblum) as 'the first cool mathematician, ever ... When I was younger, I always wanted to be a writer, then I remember ... [Ian Malcolm] was described as New Age mathematician. He wasn't a regular mathematician. ... I remember saying I wanted to become a New Age mathematician, whatever the hell that was'. Nathan, a school student who aspired to study mathematics at university, mentioned a mathematician he saw in a cartoon: 'it sounds a bit stupid, but when I was little I watched this cartoon and there was a mathematician in it ... I suppose he was like, seen as really cool I suppose, and he went to work for NASA. So that sort of made me like maths, I think'.

However, there is a striking difference between Nathan and Dave. While Dave embraced the character of Ian Malcolm, Nathan is more hesitant in recognising the influence of the character he mentioned, as reflected by his wording (*'I suppose* he was like, *seen as* really cool *I suppose* ... So that *sort of* made me like maths *I think*'). Nathan is still in a school environment where claiming maths is cool may risk rejection and ridicule (Francis, 2009). In contrast, Dave is part of a university mathematics community so the risk is less and claiming 'mathematical coolness' is more acceptable within his peer group.

EUREKA: THE STORY OF MATHEMATICS AS AN ABSTRACT, INDIVIDUAL ACTIVITY

Mathematicians don't actually do much mathematics in popular culture. When they do, it is usually presented as mystifying, in a pace and manner which make it nearly impossible to understand. There are frenzied scenes in which Will Hunting and John Nash are seen scribbling on all available surfaces, including mirrors and windows. These texts present mathematics as an individual rather than collective endeavour, as the result of sudden revelation rather than ongoing effort, as something associated with youth, precocity and madness, and so as enacted by the kinds of mathematical geniuses discussed earlier. This contrasts with the complex and subtle accounts of real-life mathematicians by Leone Burton (2004) and Claudia Henrion (1997) which show professional mathematics to be a collaborative activity where 'inspiration' is dependent on ongoing work.

It's useful to look at how gender and class relate to this image of mathematical activity by focusing on the one scene from *A Beautiful Mind* where John Nash comes up with the original mathematics that won him the Nobel Prize.

> The scene is a bar with upbeat music playing. The camera focuses on a tall blonde (among a group of women) and then on a group of male mathematics graduate students staring at her. The exception is John Nash who is working, surrounded by papers and books, piled haphazardly and with a pint of beer. His fellow students draw his attention to 'the blonde'. They look at the group of young women, who then look back at them. Nash looks uncomfortable. One student, Martin, makes reference to Adam Smith's theory that 'in competition, individual ambition serves the common good'. 'The blonde' looks at Nash. His fellow students joke about Nash's lack of

success with women. There is a change in Nash's posture and a change from upbeat jazzy music to softer piano music. He smiles and says 'Adam Smith needs revision'. He explains that if they all go for 'the blonde' they will block each other and upset the other women; however, if they cooperate, and none of them go for 'the blonde', they can all be successful. During this exposition the images become surreal and blur slightly, as if the characters are puppets illustrating Nash's conjectures. We get an aerial view where, in a geometrical pattern, we see all the men going for 'the blonde', then going for the other women. The camera pans from a close-up of Nash to his mathematical 'visions'. This happens alongside changes in Nash's tone of voice from nervous to authoritative and the loss of his bodily twitches. This sequence ends with Nash saying 'That's the only way we win, that's the only way we all get laid', the music returns to jazzy. Hastily, Nash gathers his papers and leaves. He pauses by 'the blonde', says 'thank you' and rushes out. She looks puzzled.

Here, 'the blonde' acts as the silent muse for the creativity of the male genius. This positioning of women as handmaidens to inspire creativity, but not as creative agents in their own right, is common (see the chapter by Mark McCormack). This scene represents mathematics as esoteric, abstract, detached from the everyday. In many Western countries abstract academic knowledge is associated with middle-classness and concrete vocational knowledge with working-classness. Thus, these images make it more difficult for women and working-class young people to identify with mathematics.

This is the esoteric, genius mathematics discussed above and which Firefly contrasted with everyday mathematics. It takes mathematics and those who do it out of the normal run of things. Both people studying and enjoying mathematics and those who disliked and had chosen away from the subject used this story. For example, when we asked people to imagine a world where mathematicians appear on TV regularly, many found this impossible:

> I think like trying to make something that everyone will love out of maths is never going to happen. Because music, ... I mean you never really meet anyone who says "I don't like music". ... Whereas loads of people say "I don't like maths". But that's because ... it connects to your emotions, it's more ... primal, ... it's just more of an instinctive natural thing, and maths ... it's only like intellectual and if that's the way that your mind works then so be it, but a lot of people's mind isn't bent towards that. So I don't think that that would ever happen.

> Um, I can't really imagine it. I don't know really. ... From my point of view of what it's like being at uni[versity], it'd just be completely opposite. Like if I meet new people and everyone's like 'What course are you doing? What year are you in?' and you say 'maths', it's a bit of a standing joke that it just kills the conversation. ... Like we were even told at school ... 'when you get to uni, everyone will think you're weird for doing maths'. It's true, it's completely true. So I suppose it'd just be the opposite to that.

The first of these quotations comes from a sociology undergraduate and the second from a mathematics undergraduate. Their refusals draw on oppositions: the musical vs. the mathematical; the instinctive and emotional vs. the intellectual; our world where most people don't like maths and see it as weird vs. the world posited in the question where most people enjoy doing maths and watching other people doing it. In order, to allow more people to identify with mathematics we need to find ways to cut across these oppositions.

'WE ALL USE MATHS EVERYDAY': STORIES OF MATHEMATICS AS OPEN AND ACCESSIBLE

The voiceover in the opening credits to seasons one and two of mathematics-solves-crimes TV drama series *Numb3rs* assures us that 'We all use math every day; To forecast weather; To handle money'. These vague references (how many people use maths to forecast the weather?) are in stark contrasts to the images of genius Charlie doing mathematics in the show. He is usually either frenziedly covering one after another of the many blackboards he keeps in the attic of the house he shares with his father, or surreally mathematising the world in a similar sequence to the one from *A Beautiful Mind* described above. So popular culture representations of mathematics, like those of mathematicians, are full of tensions. While stories of mathematics as abstract, individual, and open only to a few natural geniuses dominate, popular culture also offers us alternative storylines in which mathematics is beautiful, empathic and accessible. Even the scene we described above from *A Beautiful Mind* is infused with a strong notion of mathematics as beautiful, linked to pattern, with carefully constructed sound- and vision-scapes used to present mathematics. This links the process of doing mathematics to artistic, musical and other forms of creativity, which, if explored with students, have the potential to challenge some of the oppositions identified in student talk in the last section.

The idea of mathematics as empathic turns up in teen comedy film *Mean Girls*. In the sudden-death round of a 'mathlete' scholastic competition, the lead character, Cady Heron (played by Lindsay Lohan), has a revelation when presented with a limit to evaluate. Her internal monologue during this runs: 'Calling somebody else fat won't make you any skinnier. Calling someone stupid doesn't make you any smarter. And ruining [former friend] Regina George's life definitely didn't make me any happier. All you can do in life is try to solve the problem in front of you'.

Games shows, as various as *Deal or No Deal* and *The Weakest Link*, present mathematics as part of 'general knowledge' and humanity, rather than being the province of the lucky (or unlucky) few. The success of sudoku also brings mathematics into people's lives as do computer games like *Tetris*, magazine quizzes and sport. This is not unproblematic. For example, many newspapers feel the need to reassure people that 'there's no maths involved' in sudoku. However, there is much potential for using these examples with students. Our research and that of others suggests that many students, particularly young women, are put off studying the subject by ideas that mathematics excludes emotion, creativity and fantasy, and present it as rigid, certain and absolute (Boaler 1997; Mendick 2006).

These alternative images featured occasionally in student talk. Several related mathematics to patterns and to modelling. For example, a mathematics undergraduate said: 'Most of it boils down to like theories or … patterns … and you can use them to explain things in the world'. A school student said of a picture of Romanescu cauliflower (a vegetable fractal):

> You know everything that it's about just by looking at it. … It's maths in the world we live in and … maths really, it's about perfection, … and with that it's like, it's just so right, it's just perfect, the symmetry and the way it fits together.

Finally, one mathematics undergraduate articulated a strong sense of mathematics as empathic:

> When you understand mathematics, the why and the how, then you can understand life. ... Your idea is right but I have to understand. I have to know why you are telling that, why you are doing this, why you are doing this. ... That is why people have told me that I am so quiet, that is right, because I am always thinking.

People drew on a range of resources to support these 'alternatives' including their experiences of doing mathematics investigations and proofs, of exploring mathematical ideas such as Fibonacci sequences in art and things that their teachers, parents and friends had told them. They also used popular culture, particularly sudoku, gambling and sport.

What is your experience of how young people engage with popular culture? How could you use this in a classroom setting?

BRINGING TOGETHER SCHOOL MATHEMATICS AND POPULAR MATHEMATICS

Our research has shown that stories about mathematicians constrain how learners think about the mathematically able. As the examples above show, they are not simply absorbing these stories, rather they are negotiating the meanings in them and making them their own. But we need to engage critically with clichéd images and to develop more inclusive images of mathematics and mathematicians, so that learners can draw on these to tell their own stories.

As we said earlier, there's an increasing range of popular cultural representations of mathematics and mathematicians. However, as shown by people's resistance to imagining a world where mathematicians appear regularly on TV, these examples are often not connected to school mathematics. In this section, we explore one method of how teachers can bring these examples together in order to open up ways of being a mathematician and doing mathematics.

Sarah Greenwald and Andrew Nestler (2004) describe using an episode of cartoon sitcom *The Simpsons* where one character, Homer, gets transported into a parallel universe that appears to be three-dimensional. Greenwald asks her students to write a letter from 3D Homer to his 2D wife Marge explaining his new spatial environment. They discuss whether the original world of *The Simpsons* really has two dimensions and extend the exercise to thinking about the difference between three- and four-dimensional spaces.

> The advantage of beginning with *The Simpsons* ... is that students relate to them and find them amusing. This helps students feel more comfortable with challenging material. ... After watching the movie clip, without even being prompted, students immediately argue about whether the Simpsons are 2D or 3D.
>
> Greenwald and Nestler (2004, p.35)

This approach makes creativity intrinsic to mathematical learning. Skills not normally valued in maths classrooms (communication, creativity, imagination, empathy) are central to the task. Mathematical knowledge is no longer a matter of rights and wrongs with the teacher's role being to correct students' errors. It is negotiable and the teacher's role is to attempt to understand the students. It is often tempting, as a pressed-for-time teacher, to try to extract the maths from a text and abandon the rest. However, this can reinforce the opposition between the mathematical and the everyday instead of disrupting it. In this example, maths is not extracted from *The Simpsons* and then worked on separately, but is embedded in the characters and their relationships. Similarly, the popular culture texts mentioned in the Further Reading and Further Viewing sections below could be used to extend the way students think about mathematics/mathematicians as can the examples of working with the mathematics of climate change and income inequality discussed in the chapters by Richard Barwell and Hamsa Venkat respectively.

Popular texts create spaces for learners' own views and so give people alternatives to the current limited range of ways of relating to maths. The patterns of emotional investment and identification with characters and stories make these potentially ways of doing maths differently and more inclusively. For example, interaction with sudoku provoked one school student to reflect on the nature of mathematics:

> Before I came to this meeting, I just thought that maths was a thing that has divide, times and plus and minus and all that stuff. … The question 'what is maths?', I don't think it will ever be answered because it just goes on and there are so many different things and I think you have to spend like at least I don't know, more than a lifetime thinking about what maths is.

This indicates that popular maths may open more spaces than school maths for people to shift their ideas about what maths is and to build positive relationships with the subject.

Further reading

Appelbaum, P. M. (1995) *Popular culture, educational discourse and mathematics*, Albany: State University of New York Press. Peter Appelbaum uses juxtapositions between popular and school mathematics to challenge how we think about knowledge and education. He also makes suggestions for incorporating his ideas into the classroom.

Evans, J., Tsatsaroni, A. and Staub, N. (2007) 'Images of Mathematics in Popular Culture/Adults' Lives: a Study of Advertisements in the UK Press', *Adults Learning Mathematics: an International Journal*, 2, 2, 33–53. This paper looks at patterns and meanings in newspaper advertising featuring mathematics.

Mendick, H., Moreau, M.-P. and Hollingworth, S. (2008) *Mathematical Images and Gender Identities: a report on the gendering of representations of mathematics and mathematicians in popular culture and their influences on learners*, Bradford: UKRC. This report explores the ideas in this chapter in detail focusing on gender issues. Available online: http://brunel.academia.edu/HeatherMendick/ Books/74972/Mathematical_Images_and_Gender_Identities. Further information can be found on the project website: http://sites.brunel.ac.uk/mathsimages.

MathFiction: http://kasmana.people.cofc.edu/MATHFICT. Compiled by Alex Kasman, this is a near comprehensive collection of instances of mathematics and mathematicians in short stories, plays, novels, films and comic books. There is a detailed description for each entry and ratings of their literary and mathematical quality based on user votes.

The Math and Science Performance Festival Website: http://www.edu.uwo.ca/mpc/mpf2011/index.html. Compiled by George Gadanidis, this website contains examples of children and young people mixing mathematics with storytelling, singing, dancing, etc.

simpsonsmath.com: http://mathsci2.appstate.edu/~sjg/simpsonsmath/, This website from Sarah J. Greenwald and Andrew Nestler tracks the mathematics in *The Simpsons* TV animated sitcom and provides ideas for incorporating this into mathematics classrooms. Sarah has written extensively on using popular culture and living mathematicians to teach mathematics to undergraduates, see her website: http://mathsci2.appstate.edu/~sjg/.

Acknowledgements

We are grateful to the Economic and Social Research Council and the UK Resource Centre for Women in Science Engineering and Technology for funding our research; to Debbie Epstein who worked with us on the project; and to the students and staff at the schools and universities where we carried out interviews.

Further viewing

These are our main film and television sources with references to the International Movie Database where you can find out more:

A Beautiful Mind: http://www.imdb.com/title/tt0268978/
Beauty and the Geek: http://www.imdb.com/title/tt0460625/
Enigma: http://www.imdb.com/title/tt0157583/
Good Will Hunting: http://www.imdb.com/title/tt0119217/
Jurassic Park: http://www.imdb.com/title/tt0107290/
Mean Girls: http://www.imdb.com/title/tt0377092/
Numb3rs: http://www.imdb.com/title/tt0433309/
Pi: http://www.imdb.com/title/tt0138704/
Rainman: http://www.imdb.com/title/tt0095953/
The Big Bang Theory: http://www.imdb.com/title/tt0898266/

References

Boaler, J. (1997) *Experiencing school mathematics: teaching styles, sex and setting*. Buckingham: Open University Press.

Burton, L. (2004) *Mathematicians as enquirers: learning about learning mathematics*. Dordrecht: Kluwer Academic Publishers.

Francis, B. (2009) 'The role of The Boffin as abject Other in gendered performances of school achievement', *Sociological Review*, 57, 4, 645–669.

Greenwald, S. J. and Nestler, A. (2004) 'r dr r: Engaging students with significant mathematical content from *The Simpsons*', *PRIMUS – Problems, Resources, and Issues in Mathematics Undergraduate Studies*, XIV, 1, 29–39.

Henrion, C. (1997) *Women in mathematics: the addition of difference*. Bloomington, Indiana: Indiana University Press.

Mendick, H. (2006) *Masculinities in mathematics*. Maidenhead: Open University Press.

Chapter 3

Mathematics and politics?

Climate change in the mathematics classroom

Richard Barwell

Wait. Are you thinking 'Teaching mathematics is not political – this chapter has nothing to do with me'? You are probably in a hurry to get to something that sounds more practical. I want to challenge the idea that teaching mathematics is not political. I don't mean Political (capital P) – I don't want to know who you vote for. By political, I mean that there are links between mathematics, the way society is organised and the way things get decided. Mathematics teaching can help students be aware of these links and participate in democratic debate and social action.

An example: climate change is, whatever you think about it, one of the top political issues of the 21st century. Its increasing significance is reflected by the recent creation of a new department of the UK government: the Department of Energy and Climate Change (DECC). The name of the department reflects the contested nature of climate change as a political issue, both at a societal level and at an individual level. The department's website includes a section on 'tackling climate change' and another on 'meeting energy demand' (DECC, 2012). The two are arguably in conflict. For example, meeting energy demand, according to the website, will mean using coal: 'Coal is an abundant and flexible energy source that remains an important part of the energy mix, both globally and in the UK' (DECC, nd). It also, of course, happens to be one of the most polluting forms of energy. Most of what we know about climate change and energy use is intimately related to mathematics. Mathematics is part of the debate. That is where you come in.

In this chapter, then, I use the political debates relating to climate change to illustrate how mathematics and politics are linked. How does mathematics shape what we know about the world? How does mathematics shape our lives? And how, as mathematics teachers, can we engage with how mathematics is used in our society and what it is used to do? To respond to these questions, I present two related ideas: *politics is mathematical* and *mathematics is political*. Each idea is explained in general terms, followed by some illustration based on the issue of climate change.

POLITICS IS MATHEMATICAL

Politics is mathematical in a fairly simple sense: there is hardly a single political debate that does not involve data, statistics, projections and other mathematical information. Debates about unemployment include jobless totals, unemployment rates expressed as a percentage of the working population, costs of unemployment benefits and so on. Debates about transport policy include trends in car, train or plane use, data on greenhouse gas emissions, and economic costs associated with road congestion. Debates on health include cancer cure rates, life expectancy data and figures demonstrating the benefits of exercise and a balanced diet. Debates about wars involve claims about costs and the calculation of the number of civilian deaths. And the world of politics is obsessed with opinion polls, voting intentions and demographics. The presence of mathematics in political debate is fairly simple to observe but has serious consequences. It means, in particular, that in a democratic society, citizens must be able to engage with mathematics in order to participate.

Our society is now so complex and so technological that participation in democratic processes is no simple matter, whether with national politics or at a very local level. This participation requires what is sometimes called *democratic competence*, which can be understood as what citizens need to know and understand in order for the 'ruling class' to be held to account (Skovsmose, 1994, p.34). If no one understands what the rulers are doing, they can act in their own interests and not in the interests of society at large. By 'ruling class' I am referring not just to politicians, but to scientists, civil servants, the judiciary and so on. Moreover, the same arguments apply at the local level, even within a school, for example, where the ruling class would be the headteacher and staff. For democracy to be democratic, then, it is not enough simply to have elections; citizens need to monitor what their elected governments are doing and challenge them when their actions are problematic. Given the ubiquitous presence of mathematics in political debate, as well as in technology and the instruments of government, it is clear that democratic competence must involve some level of mathematical understanding. Citizens need to be able to interpret the mathematical information used in political debates and need some sense of where this mathematical information comes from, of how it is produced.

The mathematical dimension of democratic competence has been compared to the role of literacy in empowering citizens to participate in political debate and action. By becoming literate, citizens do not simply gain access to information; they are able to question, to challenge and to make the case for alternative courses of action (Freire, 1972). This perspective is known as *critical literacy*, since it includes critique as a key aspect of literacy. Mathematics can play a similar role: Ole Skovsmose (1994) proposes the term *mathemacy*, to capture the sense that mathematics, too, can be empowering. Mathemacy can 'help people to reorganise their views about social institutions, traditions and possibilities in political actions' (p.26). This view of mathematics goes beyond 'the basics' and implies a mathematics education that is about more than providing numerate workers for the labour market. It suggests that mathematics education should empower students to participate in the democratic process through a critical understanding of the mathematical aspects of political debate.

Mathematics and climate change

The issue of climate change is replete with mathematics. In fact, it is difficult to say anything very specific about climate change, or even to be sure that climate change is occurring, without mathematics. So what kind of mathematics might be included in the democratic competence necessary to participate in debates about climate change? First, it is helpful to understand the role of mathematics in climate change research.

The mathematics of climate change can be divided into roughly three areas: *description*, *prediction* and *communication* (Barwell, 2013). The mathematics involved in describing climate change includes the measurement and recording of things like temperature, sea level, glacial mass, the onset of spring, greenhouse gas emissions and so on. It also includes the statistical treatment of this kind of data to describe the climate or emissions and to identify trends. This mathematics is not particularly advanced: key concepts include statistical mean, distribution and some basic statistical tests. The huge volume of data does, however, introduce considerable complexity.

For example, the calculation of global mean temperature involves compiling data from weather stations around the world. In fact, scientists do not simply average all this data, since such an average would be meaningless – it does not make much sense to average the temperature in the Arctic with the temperature in Basingstoke. Instead, scientists proceed in a number of steps – those shown below are about the annual mean temperature, but the same general method applies for monthly or daily means, or means for any other period.

- For each weather station, they work out a long-term annual mean over a selected 30-year period.
- For each station, for any given year, they work out the mean temperature.
- They then work out the difference between the mean temperature for the given year and the long-term mean. This difference is known as a temperature anomaly.
- The global temperature anomaly for any given year is the mean of the temperature anomalies for all the weather stations.

The global temperature anomaly is, in effect, the average difference in temperature from the long-term mean around the world. Some stations may have been colder, others warmer than the long-term average. If this figure is above zero, it means that, on average, the world is warmer than the long-term mean. This is a simplified account, but it gives a good idea of the mathematics involved (means) and the complex nature of the data.

The prediction or projection of climate change involves much more advanced mathematics, the most fundamental of which is the creation and use of mathematical models of the climate. These models use sets of equations to model different aspects of the climate – the seas, the atmosphere, land surfaces and so on. These equations are all linked together and tested by simulating past climates for which we have measurement data. If the model can simulate the past in a way that fits well with this data, then the assumption is made that it will simulate the near future with a similar degree of accuracy. Climate models are different from weather forecasts in at least one key respect: they are not precise. They offer 'projections' rather than predictions, giving a broad sense of likely trends over the coming decades. Other areas of mathematics that are involved in predicting climate change include differential equations, non-linear systems and advanced probability.

Finally, mathematics is used to communicate climate change, whether in a television news report or in a scientific article. The communication of climate change includes both the production of information about climate change and the consumption of that information. Both production and consumption require an understanding of graphs, tables and other forms of graphic presentation, as well as an understanding of the mathematical processes involved in describing and predicting climate change, though not necessarily at the level of an expert. For example, it is important for citizens to understand how the climate modelling process works, even if few will ever learn the advanced mathematics that this modelling entails.

Mathemacy and climate change

There are many political debates related to climate change. Many of them are about how to respond to climate change, when, for example, formulating energy policy or transport policy, or planning where to build new houses. At international level, debate is fierce on what agreements should be put in place to reduce as much as possible the future warming of the planet. The first such agreement, the Kyoto protocol, appears to have had a limited impact on global warming. There are, of course, also claims and counter-claims about whether human-induced climate change even exists. This last debate is a good example with which to illustrate how mathemacy is an important aspect of democratic competence.

In recent years, Nigel Lawson has emerged as a sceptical voice on climate change. In 2008, Lawson published a book setting out his thoughts, which he has also expressed in interviews and other public appearances. One of the claims he advanced was that 'global warming ... is not at the present time happening' (Interview in *The Guardian*, 3 May 2008). In his book, he states that 'there has, in fact, been no further global warming since the turn of the century' (p.7) and supports this claim with some data. Specifically, he lists the global mean temperature anomalies for the years 2001–2007. They are, in degrees centigrade, 0.40, 0.46, 0.46, 0.43, 0.48, 0.42 and 0.41. He also mentions that the anomaly for 1998 was 0.52C. He sums up the situation as follows:

> the 21st century standstill (to date), which has occurred at a time when CO_2 emissions have been rising faster than ever, is something that the conventional wisdom, and the computer models on which it relies, completely failed to predict.
>
> Lawson (2008, p.7)

These claims are related to all three aspects of the mathematics of climate change mentioned above. The reference to recent global temperature data is an example of the description of climate change. The comment in the quotation about computer models refers to the prediction of climate change. And the whole text, including the selection and presentation of some data, involves the communication of climate change.

The information presented by Lawson is, despite the simplicity of the arguments, mathematically non-trivial. A key mathematical idea that is rather implicit in these arguments is the notion of trend. Lawson argues that, although there was a clear warming trend from 1970 until 2000, since that time the warming has stopped. This position assumes that global warming should be a smooth process, with a clear, regular trend. For example, global temperature anomalies would increase by a steady amount from one year to the next. His position also assumes that seven data points are sufficient to establish a counter-trend. Figure 3.1 shows global mean temperature anomalies since 1850, based on the same data set cited by Lawson. It is clear from the graph that global temperature, even averaged over a planet for a whole year, is not smooth in its behaviour – there are peaks and troughs from year to year. Hence, for example, the 1950s were, relatively speaking, a little cooler than surrounding decades. But set against the long-term trend, this cooling is of limited duration. So the seven years referred to by Lawson appears to be part of the general fluctuation in global temperature that goes on all the time.

My point here is not that Lawson is wrong (although I believe he is), but that in order to critically engage with what he is saying, a degree of mathematical sophistication is required. Moreover, the mathematics that forms part of the democratic competence to participate in such a debate is not simply an understanding of average, of measurement and of ideas about trends. Such mathematics must also include the capacity to ask questions, to think about the author's agenda and the way mathematics is used in support of that agenda.

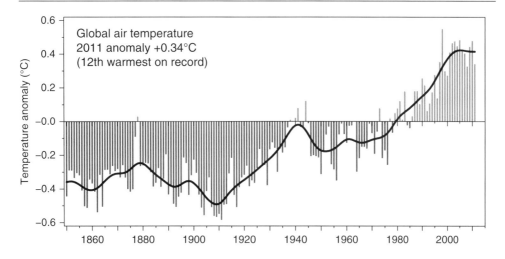

Figure 3.1 Global Temperature Record.
(Source: http://www.cru.uea.ac.uk/cru/info/warming/)

The example of climate change I have elaborated illustrates how mathematics is vital to understand and participate in political debate. Given that mathematics is so prevalent in political discourse, democratic competence must include an element of critical mathematics – the capacity not just to make sense of mathematical information, but to question, to challenge and interrogate how that information has been shaped by different agendas. Moreover, the nature of many of the most challenging problems facing our society are too complex to leave to experts, even when we have elected them or they are appointed in our names. Issues like swine flu, mad cow disease, nuclear power or, for that matter, climate change, are so complex that developing a response requires the participation of engaged citizens from the start of the process. Mathematics education, therefore, has a role to play in preparing students to participate actively and critically in these debates (Barwell, 2013). For me, this means that simply teaching mathematics well is necessary but not sufficient. Our students not only need to be able to do mathematics, but to think critically with mathematics.

> *Consider a couple of political issues that interest you. What mathematics do they involve? How could this mathematics be drawn on in teaching? Should it?*

MATHEMATICS IS POLITICAL

If politics is fairly clearly mathematical, in the sense that political debate makes widespread use of mathematical information, the converse is less obvious, but no less important. Mathematics is political because of its role in organising our society and our lives. Mathematics is used to take decisions that affect us. Indeed, mathematics can be seen to have a direct, though often invisible effect on our daily lives. This idea runs contrary to the view of mathematics as a neutral activity that has little to do with everyday life, beyond a bit of basic numeracy.

As a brief illustration, consider a weekly supermarket run. Supermarkets are organised around highly mathematical systems of distribution, stock control and checkout procedures embedded in IT systems, scanners and barcodes. These systems are mathematical because they are built around mathematical algorithms that model the production and consumption of hundreds of products, or that enable detailed tracking of products and customers. They have changed our lives in numerous ways. Shopping is more efficient than ever, we have access to a wider range of products and costs are kept low. On the other hand, much supermarket work is increasingly unskilled and involves ever less interaction with customers (think about self-service checkouts). Mathematisation of stock control is also mathematisation of workforce control. So there is a link between mathematics and such basic aspects of our lives as shopping.

Skovsmose (1994) highlights the role of mathematics in shaping our lives by giving it a name: he calls it the *formatting power* of mathematics. How does mathematics format our society and our lives? Partly through technology, such as the supermarkets' IT systems; but technology is in many respects simply the vehicle for human designs. These designs are expressed mathematically in the form of algorithms, models and computer code. In mathematical form, human designs are abstract in nature. Once they are embedded in technology, they start to become real. For example, commodities like wheat or oil are traded on international markets. When they are traded on futures markets, they appear as variables in sophisticated differential equations. When the prices fluctuate, however, they can affect the price of a loaf of bread and, in extreme situations, lead to hunger. So the abstractions of the traders' equations become the reality of some (other) people's hunger.

It is in this sense that mathematics is political. Many aspects of our lives are shaped by mathematics, generally embedded in IT systems. Think, for example, about the mathematics involved in mortgages, insurance, medicine, transportation, health care, banking, gambling, communications and so on. Or, closer to the classroom, think of how mathematics is used to process children's scores on national tests, in order to rank children, teachers and schools. On the whole, we pay little attention to this mathematics – after all, it makes our lives easier. The problem is that this mathematics *does not do itself*: someone is creating the algorithms, writing the software and selecting which variables to include and which to leave out. And these someones are largely invisible. Another aspect of democratic competence, then, must be the ability to hold to account the people who are making decisions that affect us. And this ability involves mathematics. Of course, society is not *only* organised using mathematics; my point is simply that mathematics is one important way in which society is organised. As a result, mathematics education needs to empower students to participate in the democratic process, not just through a critical understanding of the mathematical aspects of political debate, but also through a critical understanding of the role of mathematics in shaping our society and our lives.

Mathematical formatting and climate change

The political role of mathematics in the issue of climate change comes from its formatting power. This formatting power has two slightly different but interrelated effects. Both are fairly subtle. First, there is a chain of interconnection from mathematics, via technology, to a globalised consumer society. Much of the basis for this society lies in fossil fuels. Let's pay another visit to the Department of Energy and Climate Change:

> Energy Minister Charles Hendry said: "I am very pleased to launch the 27th offshore oil and gas licensing round. This is shaping up to be a very prosperous year for the North Sea as we expect a substantial increase in field approvals. With around 20 billion barrels of oil still to be extracted, the UK Continental Shelf has many years of productivity left."
>
> (DECC press release, 1 February 2012)

The press release does not make any reference to climate change. Twenty billion barrels of oil is difficult to imagine and yet in global economic terms, 20 billion barrels is a modest quantity.

There is, of course, a direct link between the use of fossil fuels, like North Sea oil, and climate change. Use of fossil fuels results in greenhouse gas emissions, increasing concentrations of these gases in the atmosphere and, thanks to the greenhouse effect, higher temperatures. Fossil fuels, however, are not, on the whole, simply burned to keep us warm. Between the extraction of fossil fuels and the emission of greenhouse gases lies our global consumer society. And, as I have argued already, this global consumer society relies on mathematics embedded in technology. This embedded mathematics is extremely powerful: it enables us, as a species, to do things like control and eliminate diseases, provide clean water and sanitation, and produce all the comforts of modern life. It also enables us to have a huge impact on our environment.

Mathematics helps to hide the human role in making decisions that shape this global consumer society and the environmental impact of these decisions. To return to the supermarket, the mathematics of stock control and of international communication means that we can eat fresh apples in February, imported from South America. The apples are marked with a barcode – just scan and eat! The barcode is the tip of a mathematical iceberg that links your apple to a producer in Argentina, via trucks, planes and automated distribution centres, all for an amazingly low price. The barcode hides the role of mathematics. But it also hides the decisions made to sell apples in February, to source them from South America, to set price levels and shipping times, and so on. You do not see all these decisions because they are embedded in the algorithms and models that run the technology. IT systems do not make decisions, they simply move them out of sight.

So when a minister in the Department of Energy and Climate Change talks about the prosperity that North Sea oil brings, he is talking about our global, consumer society, a society that depends on mathematics, embedded in technology, which hide its worst effects. I am not suggesting that oil is bad or that mathematics is bad. Rather, I am arguing that if citizens are to participate in finding a way to deal with climate change, they need to be aware of much that is hidden.

The second link between the formatting power of mathematics and climate change concerns our understanding of climate change itself. One of the challenges of climate change is that it is a global phenomenon. It is difficult for any individual to really experience climate change on a global scale. We can only develop a clear picture of climate change by collecting measurements around the world and analysing these data, as shown in the example about mean annual global temperature. This kind of work is important, but it does have a kind of side effect. Climate change is formatted in a particular way, as a quantified, mathematical phenomenon. For example, the communication of climate change includes graphs or charts, or references to averages or extremes, whether of temperature, sea level, storm frequencies or other indicators. This mathematisation of climate change does not easily capture the qualitative nature of climate change – the loss of habitat, the subtle changes to ecosystems, or the dislocation of climate refugees.

For example, one effect of climate change in the UK is the desynchronisation of ecosystems. In spring, birds and animals produce offspring to coincide with an abundance of suitable food. Climate change, however, interferes with the behaviours of different parts of this delicate system in different ways. Some creatures may produce offspring earlier, while food sources may move to cooler locations, or new predators may move in. Changes can interfere with the interrelated life-cycles of different species so that some struggle to find food. While all this can be documented statistically (e.g. Thackery *et al.*, 2010), mathematics does not capture suffering or the ethics of human-induced species loss, or the intrinsic value of an ecosystem.

In this respect, an awareness of the formatting power of mathematics includes an awareness of its limitations. Mathematics is a powerful way of manipulating our environment and of representing the world. But it leaves out some important things including ethics, beauty, relationships or values. Mathematics education, therefore, has a role to play in teaching students not only the power of mathematics and the effects of mathematics, but also the limitations of mathematics.

> *Consider two or three aspects of modern society that you particularly appreciate in some way (Your car? Central heating? ...). What mathematics is hidden in your choices? What does this mathematics enable? What issues does this raise? How might these issues be addressed by students?*

Conclusions

Mathematics plays a key role in our society, but this role is often overlooked. In this chapter, I have shown how *politics is mathematical* and how *mathematics is political*. Mathematics teachers have the possibility of preparing students to participate in political debate, to look at our society critically, and to be aware of the role of mathematics in shaping their lives. Teachers, therefore, must decide whether to respond to issues like climate change in their teaching. Indeed, for some, we have a *responsibility* to respond to such issues (d'Ambrosio, 2010). But what kind of response? To address the two themes described in this chapter, mathematics teaching needs to address both democratic competence and the formatting power of mathematics.

Moshe Renert (2011) describes a useful framework designed to link mathematics teaching with sustainability, which can be adapted to think about the political dimension of mathematics teaching more generally. The framework involves three levels or stages: accommodation, reformation and transformation. An *accommodation* approach aims simply to pass on knowledge. Mathematics teachers would address social and political issues within teaching largely through using them as examples or contexts with which to teach particular mathematical concepts. In the case of climate change, for example, students might learn about the planetary temperature changes discussed above, as part of work on data handling.

Climate change simply provides a convenient context to do some work on averages. This approach is informative, but does not have a strong critical dimension – it does little to promote democratic competence and nothing to highlight the formatting power of mathematics.

A *reformation* approach aims to promote a degree of critical thinking. Students are invited to consider values (ethics, beauty, etc.) as well as knowledge (averages, data handling, etc.) and to think about ways to make the world better – without necessarily questioning underlying assumptions. In particular, students are encouraged to use mathematics to think about how to reform the way things are, but only within existing parameters. For example, students might use carbon calculators to think about how to reduce their greenhouse gas footprints, without going so far as to question the consumerist nature of our economy. Or, to give a different example, they might use data and calculations relating to the Gini coefficient to debate the issue of national and global inequality, without considering why such inequality arises in the first place (see the chapter by Hamsa Venkat for discussion of this example). A reformation approach is different from an accommodation approach in its greater attention to social and political issues. In an accommodation approach, such issues are secondary to mathematics curriculum content – climate change is a convenient context through which to teach averages. In a reformation approach, the assumption is still that mathematics will be learned, but a parallel goal is to deepen understanding of social and political issues. A reformation approach, therefore, does address democratic competence, through a focus on social and political issues.

A *transformation* approach is perhaps more challenging to achieve, since it includes a recognition that education itself is part of the equation and may need to change. Not only, then, can we say that politics is mathematical, and that mathematics is political, we must also recognise that *mathematics education* is political. Teaching mathematics has a political dimension (even if we choose not to recognise it). A transformation approach to teaching mathematics will include aspects of an accommodation approach and a reformation approach. Students still need to learn mathematics and critically relate mathematics to particular contexts and issues. A transformation approach, however, goes beyond these goals. Renert (2011) argues that such an approach includes the awareness that 'teachers are not the only source of ingenuity in mathematics classrooms, and that deconstruction and critique ought to be followed by innovation and transformation' (p.23). He goes on to give an example of how the topic of 'large numbers' might be tackled from a transformational perspective. Rather than simply teaching the key ideas and, perhaps, using a topic like climate change to provide some context, students could be provided with the following prompt:

> Many adults are having a hard time comprehending large numbers and as a result find it difficult to relate to issues of the environment. How would you explain the meaning of some large numbers (for example, the number of kilograms of carbon emitted daily into the atmosphere) to adults in your life in order to move them to action?
>
> Renert (2011, p.23)

This kind of task requires students to think about the nature of large numbers and the way they are represented, but it also requires them to think about the political meaning of these numbers in the context of climate change, and in particular, the role of mathematics in communicating and formatting climate change.

Of course, a transformation approach is risky. We cannot know the kinds of responses students will generate and some responses may be provocative and challenging. In working on climate change, for example, students may challenge the way their class or school is managed. And for teachers, there is a fine balance to be struck between promoting critical thinking and promoting a particular agenda. In a world in which mathematics, politics and education are interrelated, we need our students to be critical thinkers and we must trust them to use the democratic competence we foster to transform their world.

> *What kind of approach to teaching mathematics will you adopt?*

Further reading

Coles, A., Barwell, R., Cotton, T., Winter, J. and Brown, L. (2013) *Teaching Secondary Mathematics as if the Planet Matters*. London: Routledge. This book, written for teachers, proposes ways to teach mathematics for global sustainability. It presents key concepts and many examples. One half of the book starts from sustainability, and includes chapters on climate change, biodiversity and economics. The other half starts from mathematics, and includes chapters that look at number, probability and algebra in relation to sustainability.

Gutstein, E. (2005) *Reading and Writing the World with Mathematics: Toward a Pedagogy for Social Justice*. New York: Taylor and Francis. Gutstein, a mathematics teacher and educator in Chicago is a leading advocate of the power of mathematics teaching to give students the tools to engage with the mathematics of political issues. Indeed, he sees mathematics teaching as a way to awaken an awareness of political issues that are directly relevant to students. This book provides both a framework for implementing this kind of approach and many useful examples of what it can look like in the classroom.

Renert, M. (2011) 'Mathematics for life: sustainable mathematics education', *For the Learning of Mathematics*, 31, 1, 20–26. This article proposes a framework for thinking about sustainability issues in mathematics education. Parts of the framework are referred to in this chapter but the article elaborates on these ideas and gives some examples of how it might be used to inform mathematics teaching.

Skovsmose, O. (1984) Mathematical education and democracy, *Educational Studies in Mathematics*, 21, 2, 109–128. One of the first articles to relate mathematics education with political issues and the origin of ideas like mathemacy and democratic competence in mathematics.

References

Barwell, R. (2013) 'The mathematical formatting of climate change: critical mathematics education and post-normal science', *Research in Mathematics Education*, 15, 1, 1–16.

d'Ambrosio, U. (2010) 'Mathematics education and survival with dignity', in H. Alrø, O. Ravn, and P. Valero (eds), *Critical mathematics education: past, present and future*. Rotterdam: Sense Publishers.

Department of Energy and Climate Change (DECC) (2012) Department of Energy and Climate Change Website. Available at: http://www.decc.gov.uk/ (accessed: 4 December 2012).

Department of Energy and Climate Change (DECC) (nd) Coal. Available at: http://www.decc.gov.uk/en/content/cms/meeting_energy/coal/coal.aspx (accessed: 4 December 2012).

Freire, P. (1972) *Pedagogy of the oppressed*. Harmondsworth: Penguin.

Jones, P. (2012) 'Information Sheet 1: Global Temperature Records'. Available at: http://www.cru.uea.ac.uk/cru/info/warming/ (accessed 29 February 2012).

Lawson, N. (2008) *An appeal to reason: a cool look at global warming.* London: Duckworth Overlook.

Renert, M. (2011) 'Mathematics for life: sustainable mathematics education', *For the Learning of Mathematics*, 31, 1, 20–26.

Skovsmose, O. (1984) 'Mathematical education and democracy', *Educational Studies in Mathematics*, 21, 2, 109–128.

Skovsmose, O. (1994) *Towards a philosophy of critical mathematics education.* Dordrecht: Kluwer.

Skovsmose, O. (2011) *An invitation to critical mathematics education.* Rotterdam: Sense Publishers.

Thackeray, S. J., Sparks, T. H., Frederiksen, M., Burthe, S., Bacon, P. J., Bell, J. R., Botham, M. S., Brereton, T. M., Bright, P. W., Carvalho, L., Clutton-Brock, T., Dawson, A., Edwards, M., Elliott, J. M., Harrington, R., Johns, D., Jones, I. D., Jones, J. T., Leech, D. I., Roy, D. B., Scott, W. A., Smith, M., Smithers, R. J., Winfield, I. J. and Wanless, S. (2010) 'Trophic level asynchrony in rates of phenological change for marine, freshwater and terrestrial environments', *Global Change Biology*, 16, 12, 3304–3313.

Chapter 4

School mathematics as social classification

Peter Gates and Andy Noyes

WE NEED TO TALK ABOUT... 'CLASS'

> *Imagine… you meet up with your teacher friends one evening and start discussing your most challenging group, and some of your most challenging students. How would you describe them?*

Probably in doing that you will have used some terms which compared students against others; you will have classified students according to some criteria. Classifying students is something that teachers and schools engage in all of the time; ranking, grouping, setting, allowing some onto courses, keeping others out and so on. Classification is not only a fundamental process of mathematical activity, but also is fundamental to mathematics education itself, at least as we know it in England. Yet there is a particular type of classification that is of interest to us in this chapter – sorting students by their social and economic backgrounds. So we begin this chapter by asking the following questions:

- How do young people become classified through mathematics education?
- How do our professional practices (our pedagogy, curriculum, assessment, etc.) contribute to this?
- How might we respond in light of this awareness of our collusion in such classificatory processes?

Why is this tendency toward classification such an issue for mathematics teachers that we need a chapter on it? Paul Connolly's (2006) study of GCSE performance highlights that student socioeconomic background (rather than gender or ethnicity) is the greatest predictor of learning outcomes. This is not to say that these three social characteristics should be seen as unconnected, or that they are unproblematic; all three can be difficult to pin down sometimes and we know that gendered and ethnic identities are complex and can, for some young people at least, be problematic.

Social class is a complex, shifting and contested notion and often goes unrecognised which makes its influence hard to see and to measure. In a recent study drawing on three large datasets in the UK, Alissa Goodman and Paul Gregg (2010) reported that 'only 21% of the poorest fifth (measured by parental socioeconomic status – SES) manage to gain five good GCSEs (grades A*–C, including English and mathematics), compared to 75% of the top Quintile' (p.7).

The term 'socioeconomic' oversimplifies things somewhat and we find the idea of '*capital*' helpful. Capital is usually thought of as financial resources or *economic capital*, but this was extended by Pierre Bourdieu, a French sociologist, into *cultural capital* (buying into particular, 'cultured' ways of living) and *social capital* (having connections and knowing people with relevant influence).

Think about a diverse collection of young people (think of your students if you're working in a school). What can you 'see' as the different forms and levels of economic, cultural and social capital they have?

IDENTIFYING 'CLASS'

It is quite difficult to provide a simplistic definition or measurement of someone's social class background and we generally use some form of '*proxy* indicator'. A first attempt could use '*occupational indicators*'. If we use the terms 'working class' or 'middle class', we could classify by the parental occupation and income if we knew them. These two measures will be closely related but not uniquely so. Some 50 years ago this terminology would not have been too problematic – yet as the economy has become more segmented, fragmented and dynamic, such occupational measures become more difficult to depend on.

We might alternatively use some '*economic indicators*' and use the terms 'poor', 'deprived' or 'disadvantaged' to indicate some sense of being denied some opportunities or economic resources. This too is difficult to measure, but one approximation to being poor is being eligible for free school meals so this is often used as a proxy. This is not foolproof as students can easily move in and out of such categories.

A third approach is to use '*aggregated geographical measures*' which are based upon postcodes and census output areas. An example of this is the UK government's *Income Deprivation Affecting Children Index* (IDACI). This measures the proportion of children under the age of 16 that live in low-income households in a particular area and is used when calculating school contextual value added scores (for more information on these measures in the UK go to http://www.education.gov.uk/cgi-bin/inyourarea/idaci.pl).

Finally you can use data on '*consumer spending habits*' or '*geodemographic segmentation*'. The system called MOSAIC has been developed by Experian in the UK and creates 155 person types aggregated into 67 household types. As with the IDACI this assumes we are like the people we live near; which to some extent we all are. At one stage we asked our pre-service teachers to drive or walk around the school neighbourhood to get a sense of the area. You might find this a useful exercise in your own context.

MAKING JUDGEMENTS

UK Governments use a number of these proxy measures in their analyses of student progress – and other countries will undoubtedly use similar measures. The weakness of these sorts of measures is that they rely heavily on economic capital and on spatial aggregation and ignore the equally import dimensions of cultural and social capital. So although there are certain allocation problems for some students (transgender, dual heritage, etc.), analysing educational outcomes by gender and ethnicity are relatively straightforward. However, statistical analyses and classifications made on the basis of socioeconomic status are fraught with problems. Research in the US shows that the mathematics achievement gap related to *socioeconomic status* (SES) is roughly *ten times* the size of the gender gap (Lubienski, 2002, p.105). However, although socioeconomic status is arguably the most important dimension of educational achievement, it is the one most often systematically overlooked. It is tricky to separate out the effect sizes of class, ethnicity and gender and to understand the intersection of these: being a white working-class boy makes you as complex as a Chinese middle-class girl.

Having argued that social class is a problematic and contested construct, it *is* the case that we all classify on the basis of some measure of socioeconomic status. Indeed, as we have said, everyone is engaged in classifying, at a more or less conscious level, all of the time. Our categories and strategies for doing this are themselves a product of our own social backgrounds and upbringing. Part of the way teachers classify their students is through the assessment of mathematical skills but another part is through implicit and often subconscious judgements of the students' cultural capital, even in the form of their names (Noyes, 2003). Do we picture a Kylie or a Dwayne in the same way as a Katherine or a David? There is never a truly fresh start at school!

> *Think of the time you met one of your classes for the first time, try and become aware of what you noticed about the students. What judgements were you forming and how? Write down some notes, reflect on them and prepare yourself to be surprised by a) your skills as an amateur sociologist and b) your prejudices. Then consider the implications of those initial judgements for your future interactions with these students.*

So, whether we like it or not, we are all involved in classificatory practices, and these are probably not fair; they tend to benefit people like ourselves, and teachers are more likely to be certain kinds of people. To talk about 'class' then is to organise the world around us, whether we do this organising and classifying in school or in society more generally. A key sociological idea since the 1960s is that schools are one of the key sites of social reproduction; hence the use of class as an organising principle in school and society is not at all accidental. Neither is the fact that it remains largely hidden, or at best misrepresented in various ways.

ATTAINMENT AND CLASS

In a recent study of GCSE mathematics attainment across the Midlands of England by Andy (Noyes, 2009, p.177) the relationship between the level of income deprivation and attainment became clear (see Table 4.1).

Students from the households in the lowest quintile of IDACI scores (i.e. the least deprived areas) were over twice as likely to achieve a grade C in GCSE than those in the most deprived fifth of households. This grade C is critical for accessing many education, employment and life opportunities. Students from the least deprived homes were over *five* times as likely to get A*/A grades than those in the most deprived households. These grades are the desired prerequisite in most schools/colleges for progression to Advanced-level mathematics (see the later chapter by Cathy Smith).

Table 4.1 GCSE Mathematics Grade and Income Deprivation (cumulative percentage)

GCSE Mathematics Grade	IDACI quintile				
	1 (least deprived)	*2*	*3*	*4*	*5 (most deprived)*
A*	5.7%	3.8	2.8	1.7	0.8
A or above	18.9	14.1	10.5	6.6	3.8
B or above	42.5	34.3	27.7	19.7	13.2
C or above	68.6	60.3	52.2	41.6	31.8
G or above	98.4	97.7	96.8	94.7	91.9

(Source: Noyes 2009; National Pupil Database)

When this attainment pattern is combined with the fact that low levels of numeracy have been shown to be the strongest predictor of unemployment (Bynner and Parsons, 1997), and that those who complete an A-level in mathematics are likely to earn more in the future (Wolf, 2002), there is a convincing argument that the rankings and classifications undertaken through school mathematics have a great influence on organising social classifications for the future – possibly more so than any other school subjects. Pierre Bourdieu puts it quite starkly:

> Often with a psychological brutality that nothing can attenuate, the school institution lays down its final judgements and its verdicts, from which there is no appeal, ranking all students in a unique hierarchy of all forms of excellence, nowadays dominated by a single discipline, mathematics.
>
> (Bourdieu, 1998, p.28)

In the light of all this, it is really important that teachers of mathematics think about their own roles and the role of the education system in social classification. So, who gets what in school mathematics in your school, and in your classes?

VIRTUAL SCHOOL BAGS

In a study of disadvantaged young people in Adelaide, Pat Thomson (2002) talked about the '*virtual school bag*' to explore how schooling interacts with the *stuff – the 'baggage'* that young people bring to school. Rarely do teachers of mathematics get to look into these school bags. If we ignore the different contents of these virtual bags and treat all students equally we give *de facto* support to those who arrive at school with the right kinds of *kit* that is necessary for success in schools. This kit does not just include a pencil, ruler and pen, it also includes ways of thinking, speaking and writing that are common in schools but not common in all kinds of homes.

If you are working in a school, identify two contrasting students in your classes and find out as much as you can about them. If you have access to their postcode use the Department for Education (DfE) site to identify their IDACI measure.

In a study of two very different children (Caitlin and Cory) attending the same school (Jorgensen *et al.*, submitted), differing learning trajectories in mathematics have resulted from the influences of family culture and linguistic capital as well as the ability group that they were taught in; Caitlin was in the top ability group, Cory in the lowest. Analysis and experience in schools suggests it is very unlikely that either of them will change ability group even at an early stage of their secondary education, as this grouping seems in many ways to be a product of much more than mathematical knowledge.

> *In your experience, how often do setting decisions get changed and students move between sets? What are the implications for students and teacher?*

Both students lived with their mothers. Caitlin lived in an affluent area; she used similar language and had similar values to her teachers. Her parents have endowed their daughter with much social, cultural and linguistic capital. In the educational field, she has distinct advantages; her capital earns her an enhanced reputation, a comfortable position in the highest ability set and high attainment.

Cory's progression was not so smooth and he did not achieve the same degree of academic success as Caitlin. Cory and the school system did not fit together as naturally as Caitlin and school seem to. Cory's view of education was narrower than Caitlin's; for him the purpose of school is purely functional and looks at individual skills and knowledge as opposed to the value of an all-round education. This agrees with Andy's findings that 'the economically and culturally more well-endowed make the most of moving school' (Noyes, 2006, p.43).

> *How are students' backgrounds and prior experience integrated into curricular and pedagogic decisions in classrooms where you have taught and learned maths?*

One of the ways in which 'class' works in schools is through language, and a number of researchers have explored how language helps in the classificatory and discriminatory practices of school mathematics. Robyn Zevenbergen (2001) highlights the fact that school language is middle-class and therefore presents an obstacle to working-class children who may not have the dispositions tacitly required by schools. This means that those children without the same language competence are disadvantaged in the classroom.

HOW WE ORGANISE LEARNERS

In our organisational and pedagogical decisions, how do we treat all learners? What are our expectations? Here is Pierre Bourdieu again:

> to penalize the underprivileged and favour the most privileged, the school has only to neglect, in its teaching methods and techniques and its criteria when making academic judgements, to take into account the cultural inequalities between the different social classes. In other words, by treating all pupils, however unequal they may be in reality,

as equal in rights and duties, the educational system is led to give its *de facto* sanction to initial cultural inequalities.

Bourdieu 1974 (p.37)

Consider the issue of ability grouping (part of the 'ability thinking' discussed by Mark Boylan and Hilary Povey in the previous chapter). It is taken as a given in the UK that in mathematics we must place students in ability groups. Indeed, it is difficult to find schools in which this has not been the accepted practice for years. By contrast, such an approach is uncommon across Scandinavia. Indeed, it is illegal to set by ability in Finland, Denmark and Norway to name but three countries. The PISA (Programme for International Student Assessment) data highlights how countries with a less differentiated attainment range do better in those tests (OECD, 2010).

One of the problems of grouping by ability is that it labels young people from an early age. The problem of labelling goes further; what should we call those students in the 'lower' sets: low attainers, low achievers, low performers? It is the word *low* that is problematic as it positions some students relative to others. In this sense low is a metaphor. Pat Thomson and Barbara Comber (2003), in trying to challenge the language used to describe certain groups of 'deficient' learners, suggest that new metaphors be used to create more positive attitudes and identities. So, for example, in their context they rename 'disadvantaged students' as 'media-savvy meaning makers'. It is worth considering how this could work for mathematics learners.

So why is ability grouping illegal in Finland, Denmark, Norway and other countries? If ability grouping is so good that it is just impossible for most UK mathematics teachers to even conceptualise what teaching would be like without it, why does Finland come top in international comparisons (OECD, 2004)? In Finland, low attainers did better than their compatriots in the UK and the gap between lower and higher attainers was lower than elsewhere.

The challenge is to try and engage young people more effectively with mathematics rather than focus on structural organisational principles. However, it is not just a professional matter, it is a deeply political and ideological one (Gates, 2006). It is also dependent upon the value that young people place on the mathematics that they encounter. In a study of three contrasting schools the relevance of mathematics to young people is understood quite differently (Sealey and Noyes, 2010). In a school serving an ex-mining community the department work hard to make mathematics relevant but here is how two relatively successful students – Nathan and Joe – see it:

Nathan: [looking at the advanced maths on the board] Seriously when am I going to use that when I get a job?

Joe: It's just dead confusing when you look at it. What bit of that do you understand apart from the date?

Nathan: Kids like to learn stuff that they're interested in.

Joe: You need basic mathematics but that's just shit.

Nathan: I can't really see where we're going to use that in our later life. You go to ASDA, you don't use one of them, do you? You don't take a pen and paper and write all of that, do you?

Joe: What's the three point moving average for a tin of baked beans? [laughter from group]

Nathan: Like my mum works the till at ASDA and she's the thickest person you'd ever meet. But she works at ASDA. She uses mathematics but on a calculator thing.

Joe: You only need general mathematics. There's no point in using all of this.

Contrast this with the discussion a few miles away at the suburban school that has some of highest attainment in the area and is full of the children of professional families, many of them of Asian heritage:

Tim: For nearly all the careers you need mathematics.

Andrew: 'Cause like I'm doing music, 'cause I want to do music, but then mathematics and physics and stuff, it's like a back-up. And like most places or jobs you go to they say 'have you got a mathematics degree?' For better jobs.

Affiza: That woman … she had just come out of university … with physics … and she was like 'most people don't do anything that is related to their degree, they do mathematics instead, they go and do accounting or something'. So like everyone uses mathematics as a back-up. … I picked them [subject choices] because I just thought they're all quite academic and I definitely need mathematics and chemistry to go into medicine.

Tim: I want to be a vet. If I don't get the grades then I can always go into something else 'cause like all my teachers are saying that it [mathematics] will open doors rather than close them.

For these students mathematics has exchange value. They need it for what it can do for them. They understand its power to open doors – or to shut them in your face. It all depends on which community you come from. Consider the following question: what is the role of mathematics education in such communities as Nathan's? To even ask that question is to take a political stance though – where do those students struggling with mathematics come from? What backgrounds do they have? What needs do they have? Do you know this of your own students?

Karen Pellino (2007) argues 'the social world of school operates by different rules or norms than the social world these children live in'. She summarises much of the literature on the effects of poverty by drawing our attention to some of the characteristics of children in poverty – and before you read this, think of some 'difficult' students again. She found they experience: high mobility, hunger, repeated failure, low expectations, undeveloped language, clinical depression, poor health, emotional insecurity, low self-esteem, poor relationships, difficult home environment, and a focus on survival.

Socioeconomic disadvantage may have a direct influence on children's development, for example through limited material resources and an increased risk of a range of health and developmental problems, and an indirect influence through parental education, expectations and aspirations. Schools favour middle-class attitudes and expectations – which is why working-class students often get into trouble. Working-class students are too often defined by what they are not or do not have: they have no motivation, have low ability, low aspirations, parents who are not interested.

DIFFERENT STROKES?

There are a small number of careful inquiries into social class. One such is Sarah Lubienski (2000, 2002) who studied mathematical experiences of students with an eye to looking at their backgrounds. Whilst she naturally expected to find SES differences what she actually found were very *specific* differences in two main areas – *whole-class discussion* and *open-ended problem solving*. These are two well-researched pedagogical strategies and classroom practices which at least in professional discourse are held in some esteem. Discussion-based activities were perceived differently by students from different social backgrounds. High SES students thought discussion activities were for them to analyse different ideas whilst low SES students thought it was about getting right answers. The two groups had different levels of confidence in their own type of contributions with the low SES students wanting more teacher direction. Higher SES students felt they could sort things out for themselves. We suspect this is not an uncommon feature of many schools but from where does it emanate? This is an example of social class being an important characteristic that is largely absent from literature on discussion-based mathematics.

A second area where Lubienski noted differences was that of *open-ended problem solving*. The high level of ambiguity in such problems caused frustration in low SES students which in turn caused them to give up. High SES students just thought 'harder' and engaged more 'deeply'. Middle-class students tend to come to school with dispositions and forms of language which gives them an advantage for the reasons outlined above. High SES students have a level of self-confidence very common in middle-class practices whilst working-class practices tend to be located in more subservient dependency modes, accepting conformity and obedience.

Middle-class students tend to live in families where there is greater independence, autonomy and creativity. Studies of parenting suggest that low SES parents are more directive, requiring more obedience whereas high SES parents tend to be more suggestive and accommodating of reason and discussion (Lareau, 2003). One outcome of this is that the middle classes grow up to expect and feel superior with more control over their lives and this sense of agency and control reaches into the mathematics classroom with an affinity with certain pedagogical strategies: 'Researchers and educators should not assume that learning mathematics through problem solving and discussion is equally natural for all students. Instead, we need to uncover the cultural assumptions of these particular discourses' (Lubienski, 2002, p.120).

HOW WILL YOU TEACH?

The thing about social classification is that it goes on all around us all of the time – quietly and powerfully – and it goes on because of us. The challenge we want to give you as a reader is to recognise the part that you play, often unwittingly, in these processes and to consider what might be done in response. So, in this final section we invite those of you who are teachers or student teachers to think of the school in which you are teaching in or aspire to teach in. What it is like? How similar or dissimilar is it than the school(s) you yourself went to? Andy's study of student teachers' decisions about their first teaching posts (Noyes, 2008) highlights the tendency for teachers to take up their first post in a school similar to the one that they themselves attended. Who then will teach in the schools in more deprived areas?

Our experience over many years of teaching mathematics in schools, and of reading and researching around the subject (see Perry and Francis, 2010), suggests the following might be a good place to start to raise the attainment of those more economically and culturally disadvantaged young people:

- Work on encouraging working-class young people to feel engaged in the mathematics curriculum and to feel it has a purpose.
- Find something out about vocational transition routes and pay attention to alternatives in your examples.
- Focus on what students know and can do rather than on what they don't know and cannot do.
- Engender positive, respectful social and pedagogic relationships to explicitly foster self-esteem and resilience in working with mathematics.
- Treat low SES students to the same high expectations, with a demanding and rigorous mathematics curriculum that expects all students to succeed and understand.
- Recognise and embrace the diversity in the student body, valuing the talents and abilities of low SES learners, encompassing a respect for different life worlds and their contributions to mathematics.
- Get to know the families, and provide differentiated support.
- Create and use meaningful tasks involving inquiry and cooperative learning, where low SES learners have some control and responsibility.

Perhaps the greatest challenge for all of us is to see the ways in which school tends to reinforce social *class* differences. More specifically, as mathematics teachers, this is to recognise the influence that SES and poverty has on all aspects of teaching and learning mathematics. Engaging explicitly with class and social differences in learning has been shown to have the potential to open up greater opportunities for higher order thinking (Jorgensen, Sullivan, *et al.*, 2011) and for raising the intellectual quality of student cognition (Kitchen, DePree, *et al.*, 2007). *Class*, in some guise or another, is always a latent variable whose invisibility obscures possibilities for action. We need to not only talk about, but do something about, class.

Further Reading

Boaler, J. (2009) *The Elephant in the Classroom.* London: Souvenir Press. In this book Jo Boaler talks about some of the enduring problems of mathematics teaching and how to acknowledge and use support from home to make mathematics more exciting.

Cooper, B. and Dunne, M. (2004) *Assessing Children's Mathematical Knowledge: social class, sex and problem solving.* Buckingham: Open University Press. This book argues that much mathematical assessment (particularly high stakes external assessments such as the national tests) requires particular cultural ways of reading the questions. Those with the tools (in their virtual school bags) to decode these questions will get the most marks. Students who read the questions too literally will be penalised for not decoding and ignoring the distracting contexts. This speaks to the ongoing tensions between everyday/workplace/vocational mathematics and abstract/generalisable/higher mathematics.

Kitchen, R., DePree, J., Celedón-Pattichis, S. and Brinkerhoff, J. (2007) *Mathematics Education at Highly Effective Schools that Serve the Poor: Strategies for Change.* New Jersey: Lawrence Erlbaum. This book comes from the USA and talks about successful strategies that have been used in several schools that have large numbers of disadvantaged students.

Noyes, A. (2007) 'Mathematical Marginalisation and Meritocracy: inequity in an English classroom', in B. Sriraman (ed), *International Perspectives on Social Justice in Mathematics Education.*

Missoula MT: University of Montana Press. This book chapter presents a detailed account of how two 11-year-olds (Stacey and Edward) experience mathematics together in the same class when they are socially very distant from one another. Their mathematical trajectories are about to diverge quite dramatically and the roots of this divergence can be traced to their social backgrounds and the values and dispositions that have been acquired there.

References

Boaler, J. (1997) 'Setting, social class and the survival of the quickest', *British Educational Research Journal*, 23, 5, 575–595.

Bourdieu, P. (1974) 'The school as a conservative force: scholastic and cultural inequalities', in J. Egglestone (ed), *Contemporary research in the sociology of education*. London: Methuen and Co Ltd.

Bourdieu, P. (1986) 'The forms of capital', in J. G. Richardson (ed), *Handbook of Theory and Research for the Sociology of Education*. New York: Greenwood Press.

Bourdieu, P. (1998) *Practical reason*. Cambridge: Polity Press.

Bynner, J. and Parsons, S. (1997) *Does numeracy matter? Evidence from the national child development study on the impact of poor numeracy on adult life*. London: Basic Skills Agency.

Cassen, R. and Kingdon, G. (2007) *Tackling low educational achievement*. York: Joseph Rowntree Trust.

Connolly, P. (2006) 'The effects of social class and ethnicity on gender differences in GCSE Attainment: A Secondary Analysis of the Youth Cohort Study of England and Wales 1997–2001', *British Educational Research Journal*, 32, 1, 3–21.

Cooper, B. and Dunne, M. (2000) *Assessing children's mathematical knowledge: social class, sex and problem solving*. Buckingham: Open University Press.

Gates, P. (2006) 'Going beyond belief systems: exploring a model for the social influence on mathematics teacher beliefs', *Educational Studies in Mathematics*, 63, 5, 347–369.

Goodman, A. and Gregg, P. (2010) *Poorer children's educational attainment: how important are attitudes and behaviour?* York: Joseph Rowntree Foundation.

Jorgensen, R., Gates, P. and Roper, V. (submitted) 'Structural exclusion through school mathematics: using bourdieu to understand mathematics a social practice'. *Educational Studies in Mathematics*.

Jorgensen, R., Sullivan, P., Grootenboer, P., Neische, R., Lerman, S. and Boaler, J. (2011) *Maths in the Kimberley. Reforming mathematics education in remote indigenous communities*. Brisbane: Griffith University.

Kitchen, R., DePree, J., Celedón-Pattichis, S. and Brinkerhoff, J. (2007) *Mathematics education at highly effective schools that serve the poor: strategies for change*. New Jersey: Lawrence Erlbaum.

Lareau, A. (2003) *Unequal childhoods: class, race and family life*. California: University of California Press.

Lubienski, S. (2000) 'A clash of cultures? Students' experiences in a discussion-intensive seventh grade mathematics classroom', *Elementary School Journal*, 100, 4, 377–403.

Lubienski, S. (2002) 'Research, reform, and equity in U.S. mathematics education', *Mathematical Thinking and Learning*, 4, 2–3, 103–125.

Matthews, A. and Pepper, D. (2007) *Evaluation of participation in A-level mathematics final report*. London: Qualifications and Curriculum Authority.

Noyes, A. (2003) 'Moving schools and social relocation', *International Studies in Sociology of Education*, 13, 3, 261–280.

Noyes, A. (2006) 'School transfer and the diffraction of learning trajectories', *Research Papers in Education*, 21, 1, 43–62.

Noyes, A. (2007) 'Mathematical marginalisation and meritocracy: inequity in an English classroom', in B. Sriraman (ed), *International Perspectives on Social Justice in Mathematics Education*. Missoula, MT: University of Montana Press.

Noyes, A. (2008) 'Choosing teachers: exploring agency and structure in the distribution of newly qualified teachers', *Teaching and Teacher Education*, 24, 3, 674–683.

Noyes, A. (2009) 'Exploring social patterns of participation in university-entrance level mathematics in England', *Research in Mathematics Education*, 11, 2, 167–183.

Organisation for Economic Cooperation and Development (OECD) (2010) *PISA 2009 Results: what students know and can do: student performance in reading, mathematics and science (Volume I)*. Paris: OECD.

Perry, E. and Francis, B. (2010) *The social class gap for educational achievement: a review of the literature*. London: RSA.

Organisation for Economic Cooperation and Development (OECD) (2004) *Learning for tomorrow's world: first results from PISA 2003*. Paris: OECD.

Sealey, P. and Noyes, A. (2010) 'On the relevance of the mathematics curriculum to young people', *Curriculum Journal*, 21, 3, 239–253.

Thomson, P. (2002) *Schooling the Rustbelt Kids: making the difference in changing times*. Stoke-on-Trent: Trentham.

Thomson, P. and Comber, B. (2003) 'Deficient "disadvantaged students" or media-savvy meaning makers? Engaging new metaphors for redesigning classrooms and pedagogies', *McGill Journal of Education*, 38, 2, 305–327.

Wolf, A. (2002) *Does education matter? Myths about education and economic growth*. London: Penguin.

Zevenbergen, R. (2000) '"Cracking the code" of mathematics classrooms: school success as a function of linguistic, social and cultural background', in J. Boaler (ed), *Multiple perspectives on mathematics teaching and learning*. Westport: Ablex Publishing.

Zevenbergen, R. (2001) 'Language, social class and underachievement in school mathematics', in P. Gates (ed), *Issues in Mathematics Teaching*. London: RoutledgeFalmer.

Chapter 5

Mathematics and gender

Mark McCormack

Examining the differences in success at maths between boys and girls is something that we, as a society, seem to find endlessly fascinating. Whether boys or girls are getting more top grades, even by just one percentage point, takes on a special significance, as does the percentage of boys and girls getting a grade C or above in the GCSE examination usually taken by students aged 16 at the end of compulsory schooling in England and Wales. Yet whilst I argue that it is vital to think about gender and maths, it is also worth highlighting the generally small differences in results between boys and girls at mathematics (and, as Peter Gates and Andy Noyes note in their chapter, much smaller than differences by social class). Even so, these results are always seen through a lens of gender difference – of one gender being better than the other.

Highlighting this lens of gender difference sensationalism, despite the marginal differences between boys' and girls' results, 2009 was the first year boys got more of the top two A and A* GCSE grades than girls for several years. It was this that became the media story: for example, *The Guardian* newspaper proclaimed, 'Boys have leapfrogged over girls in maths GCSE results, bagging more of the top grades for the first time since 1997 after the government scrapped coursework last year' (Curtis, 2009). And yet just two years later, a finding that 6.8% more girls than boys were achieving A* and A grades was seen by the Director of the Joint Council for Qualifications as a 'growing divide in performance between boys and girls at the top grades' (Shepherd, 2011). Seemingly, we cannot avoid looking at gender and mathematics as an issue of boys *versus* girls.

Whilst I have been sceptical of gender differences in results at school level, it is important to recognise the importance of gender in other ways. Primarily, gender differences persist in the take-up of advanced mathematics courses, as well as regarding numbers of men and women who pursue maths-related careers (Gunderson *et al.*, 2012). Furthermore, students' experiences of mathematics – as enjoyable, as interesting, as difficult – are also influenced by gender, and the very idea of mathematics has associations with masculinity (Mendick, 2005). These factors will affect students' use of and relationship with mathematics both in school and throughout their lives. This means that even if gender imbalances in maths results at school are minimal, we still have to pay great attention to how we deal with gender in the classroom (McCormack, 2011).

> *It is very difficult to think about the difference that gender makes to our own life. Do you think that your personal relationship with mathematics has been influenced by your gender? Do you ever see this influence in other people's relationships to mathematics?*

WHAT GENDER DIFFERENCES IN MATHEMATICS EXIST?

Early studies found significant gender differences in mathematics performance, which were then attributed to innate 'ability'. For example, by studying boys and girls identified as gifted and talented in mathematics, Camilla Benbow and Julian Stanley (1980, p.1262) argued that there were 'large sex differences in mathematical aptitude' between boys and girls, suggesting that environmental influences are a contributing but not primary factor. In a later study, Benbow and Stanley (1983) argued that gender differences were most pronounced in relation to mathematical reasoning, particularly among more 'able' students. Again, they attributed this 'male superiority' to predominantly biological factors, arguing that social factors were unlikely to be the key issue.

These findings proved both newsworthy and contentious, and have continued to influence debates about mathematical ability ever since. Yet great gains have been made over the past several decades, and more recent research has documented few and marginal gender differences in mathematics performance (Hyde and Linn, 2006). Furthermore, other research has highlighted that gender differences vary across countries (Else-Quest, Hide and Linn, 2010) – suggesting social reasons are the basis of the few remaining differences. Moreover, as discussed in the introduction, significant differences do not exist in GCSE results in England and Wales.

Yet, as mentioned above, results at GCSE are not the whole story. Despite differences in mathematics results at the school level bordering on insignificance, it is still of vital importance to understand the gendering of mathematics. The key reason for this is that despite near-equality in academic test scores at school, there are significant disparities in outcomes further down the line. Specifically, fewer women continue to pursue maths at degree level and the careers requiring scientific or quantitative knowledge are still heavily male-biased (Gunderson *et al.*, 2012). In order to appreciate how these disparities occur, it is first necessary to understand how gender is constructed and regulated in social life.

> *If you are currently working within a co-educational school context, are there gender differences in the results of the mathematics classes? What could be the reasons for these?*

THE SOCIAL CONSTRUCTION OF GENDER

When scholars talk about the social construction of gender, the first thing to highlight is that we are not arguing men's and women's bodies are *literally* created socially. Of course, bodies exist, and no amount of social interaction would change this. But the practices, expectations and meanings ascribed to these different types of bodies *are* socially constructed, and this has great impact on how we live our lives (West and Zimmerman, 1987). The nature/nurture debate is an extremely contentious one and some gender scholars do appear to endorse a view that gender is entirely socially constructed. Such debates have been termed as social determinism versus biological determinism (that is, it is either all social or all biological). In my view, the reality is somewhere between these two poles – society and biology interact to produce these differences (see McCormack, 2012).

In a classic article on the construction of gender, Don West and Candace Zimmerman (1987) explain how people actively 'do' gender. They write that gender is 'not simply an aspect of what one is, but, more fundamentally, it is something that one *does*, and does recurrently, in interaction with others' (p.140). They highlight that even though the essential characteristics thought to constitute our sex (such as genitalia) are hidden, we are always socially perceived as either male or female. Great emphasis is therefore placed on our *gendered* behaviours – that is, on our behaviours that are coded as masculine or feminine. This is because our gendered behaviours are seen to confirm (or alternatively question) the 'true' status of our sex. All our gendered behaviours and the meanings attached to them are thus framed and distilled through this desire to demonstrate a united sexed and gendered self. Combined with our innate need to conform to social norms (Asch, 1951), West and Zimmerman argue that our continual quest to be seen as maintaining the appropriate sex and gender is how we 'do' gender in social interaction.

However, while social interaction is of paramount importance in understanding gender in society, it is also necessary to examine the broader construction of gender. Sociological studies of institutions demonstrate that gender is also a form of power that pervades the social structures of society. Joan Acker (1990) explicates the ways in which organisations are gendered, where 'advantage and disadvantage, exploitation and control, action and emotion, meaning and identity, are patterned through and in terms of a distinction between male and female, masculine and feminine'. As Michael Kimmel (2004, p.102) argues:

> To say that gender is socially constructed requires that we locate individual identity within a historically and socially specific and equally gendered place and time, and that we situate the individual within the complex matrix of our lives, our bodies, and our social and cultural environments.

The notion of gendered organisations also applies to schools. Mairtin Mac an Ghaill (1994) highlighted that schools were 'masculinity-making' institutions, where gender differences between boys and girls are produced and consolidated. From school discourses of sport and competition, to interactions between boys and girls, the meanings and behaviours associated with masculinity and femininity are actively produced within schools. Accordingly, when we are examining the gender differences within mathematics education, and when we examine the gendered experiences of boys and girls learning maths, it is of fundamental importance to consider the social and institutional contexts that shape these experiences and differences.

Think about your experiences of being in a mathematics classroom, as a teacher or a student – did this classroom construct gender in particular ways?

Were there discussions of the uses of maths beyond gendered examples (of finance, shopping, etc)? Phrases like 'listen up guys' applied to both boys and girls? Pictures of famous male mathematicians on the wall, but not female ones?

SOCIAL FACTORS AFFECTING GENDER DIFFERENCES

The initial research that found significant gender differences attributable to biology has been critiqued by feminist scientists. Anne Fausto-Sterling (1993), for example, highlights that this research ignored other scholarship that focused on parental attitudes, teachers' attitudes and experiences of mathematics lessons as reasons for gender differences in maths; scholarship that showed boys' and girls' experiences of learning maths within the same classroom were different (Leinhart, Seewald and Engel, 1987). More recent research has continued to examine these issues. For example, Elizabeth Gunderson and her colleagues (2012) highlight that these differences are not the result of biology, or of one single social factor, but are the result of what they call 'early-developing math attitudes' (p.153). These form from a variety of factors, including aptitude, parental and teacher attitudes, maths-gender stereotypes and expectations of success or failure in maths, among many others.

One of the key ways that girls can be put off maths is through the patronising behaviours of teachers and parents. Sarah Gervais and Theresa Vescio (2012) highlight the detrimental effects of condescending behaviours and attitudes toward women. Distinguishing this 'benevolent sexism' from more overt forms of gender discrimination, they highlight that even well-meaning acts can have negative consequences if they serve to patronise or belittle women. Accordingly, having equal expectations of boys and girls, praising them in similar ways and not using inappropriate gendered language are of vital importance.

It is worth highlighting at this point that patronising behaviours can often be unintentional and occur from even the most well-meaning of trainees. For example, observing a teacher trainee in school, whom I call Eli here, it was evident that he was reproducing gender stereotypes through how he praised students. During one of his question and answer sessions, he praised boys and girls differently: 'Good girl, Jennifer', Eli said after Jennifer answered a difficult question. 'Brilliant Sarah, good girl', he responded to another student. Yet when he praised a male student: 'Brilliant John, good man'. Without realising, and in an effort to encourage the boys in the class, Eli was constructing the boys as adults and the girls as children. When I discussed this with Eli after, he was shocked that he was doing it. Eli had never thought carefully about the *gendered* nature of the language he used, and so did not realise the negative effect his teaching might have (see also Burton, 1986). Similarly, research shows that even when teachers are trying to give more attention to girls than to boys, they still spend greater time interacting with boys (Younger, Warrington and Williams, 1999).

Research also suggests that parental expectations matter a great deal in the desire to pursue maths beyond school. Jacqueline Eccles, Janis Jacobs and Rena Harold (1990) demonstrate that parents of boys had higher expectations of what their child would achieve in mathematics than parents of girls, and that parents of boys also believed their child to be of greater mathematical ability than parents of girls did. In addition to this, they showed that these beliefs were apparent at the age of ten, with these parents also rating mathematics as harder for girls than boys. Crucially, these beliefs were evident despite there being no difference according to test scores.

It is not only other people's perceptions of mathematics that matter, but also how students themselves think of gender within school. In order to understand this, the concept 'stereotype threat' is important. Stereotype threat refers to the phenomenon by which when people are reminded of a stereotype about themselves, they perform in such a way that conforms to it. This has been demonstrated among many groups, including African-Americans who perform worse on intelligence tests when their race is highlighted (Steel and Aronson, 1995).

Ilan Dar-Nimrod and Steven Heine (2006) highlight the importance of people's conceptions of *gender* in mathematics ability. In their study, when young women were told that gender differences were the result of biology, they performed worse on mathematics tests than when women were told that they were the result of societal influences.

Dar-Nimrod and Heine argue that this highlights the importance of discussing the social elements of gender differences: if female students know that there are minimal biological differences, and that women's relative lack of success in mathematics careers is the result of social issues, some of the negative impacts of gender stereotyping will be ameliorated.

> *Do you reproduce stereotypes of maths and gender in your interactions with others inside and outside of classes?*
>
> *Do you*:
>
> – *say 'good man' and 'good girl'?*
> – *give boys and girls equal time in answering questions?*
> – *let a student's gender influence your expectations of them?*
> – *discuss the same possible maths careers with all capable students?*

Unfortunately, however, not all issues are based around social constructions of gender and people's perceptions and stereotypes. There are other profound and structural ways in which gender differences in mathematics are produced – most significantly, this involves the very 'nature' of mathematics itself.

THE SOCIAL CONSTRUCTION OF MATHEMATICS AND MATHEMATICS EDUCATION

Perhaps the prevailing understanding of mathematics in society is that it forms a body of immutable and certain knowledge. Often called the absolutist view of mathematics (Ernest, 1998), it is argued that mathematical logic is fundamentally objective and independent of culture and of social attitudes. However, such a view has been critiqued on both philosophical and social levels. Imre Lakatos (1976), for example, highlighted that mathematics is based on a set of foundational principles (or axioms) that are not themselves provable and thus all mathematical proof rests upon *contingent* foundations. He also showed how even proof itself is negotiable – what counts as a valid proof has varied in different times and places (see the chapter by Leo Rogers for further discussion of this).

Paul Ernest (1991) augmented this rejection of absolutism to develop a 'social constructivist' approach to understanding mathematics. Crucially, it argues that mathematics is situated within the world and is created within particular physical and social realities – that knowledge is created by people rather than discovered. Mathematics has the appearance of objectivity because mathematical knowledge undergoes a process of (scientific) testing to ensure such knowledge is congruent with how reality is experienced; a long process that is subtle and not readily apparent. It is because this process is so slow that the argument is counter-intuitive: like the theory of evolution, it confounds our everyday thinking because the changes are very rarely noticeable in our lives, occurring over much greater time spans.

Despite its counter-intuitive nature, this social constructivist framework has been adopted by most scholars of mathematics education. This approach has particular significance for gender, because it opens up opportunities to explore the relationship between the social construction of mathematics and the social construction of gender. Examining the doing of mathematics as a community of practice, Leone Burton concentrated on the implications of the social and contextual elements of mathematics for the people learning it. About this approach, Burton (1995, p.287) wrote that

> Knowing mathematics would … be a function of who is claiming to know, related to which community, how that knowing is presented, what explanations are given for how that knowing was achieved, and the connections demonstrated between it and other knowings.

That is, the ability to learn mathematics is dependent on the learner and who (in terms of class, ethnicity, gender, sexuality, etc) that person is, as well as how that person is taught. In other words, not only is mathematics constructed, becoming proficient at it is inherently social.

The learning of mathematics as social has been discussed by a number of feminist mathematics educators (notably, Becker, 1995; Burton, 1986; Walkerdine, 1988). One of the key themes within these discussions has been understanding how the method of teaching maths impacts on how it is learned and by whom. Joanne Rossi Becker (1995) emphasises the importance of both making connections between components of mathematical learning as well as presenting mathematics as a process and not a set of facts. In Richard Skemp's (1979) terminology, this would be privileging relational learning over instrumental learning (this distinction is elaborated in the chapter by Gwen Ineson and Sunita Babbar). Becker argues that the ongoing failure to do this has disadvantaged women, writing,

> the imitation model of teaching, in which the impeccable reasoning of the professor as to "how a proof should be done" is presented to students for them to mimic, is not a particularly effective means of learning for women.
>
> Becker (1995, p.169)

Here, she is drawing on ideas that men/boys and women/girls, in general, have different 'ways of knowing' with the former favouring abstract or 'separated' ways of knowing and the latter preferring 'connected' ways of knowing in which knowledge is embedded within human relationships. It is clear that pedagogies supporting women's ways of knowing are more compatible with social constructivist than with absolutist philosophies of mathematics. Developing this theme, Jo Boaler (1997, also discussed in the chapters by Hilary Povey and by Anna Llewellyn) showed that girls performed better when taught using investigative pedagogies than in 'traditional' talk-and-chalk classrooms because they had a 'quest for understanding' that the latter could not satisfy, while boys were content to apply rules without understanding why they worked. While this work by Becker and Boaler has been hugely influential, such approaches in some ways reproduce the oppositional 'girls vs. boys' arguments that we saw earlier. This is because when talking about differences in results between girls and boys, it is difficult to avoid the tendency to see these differences as 'natural' and to avoid generalising about what all boys and all girls are like; ignoring the 'in-group' differences between boys and between girls, and the equally significant overlap between boys and girls.

SOCIETAL CONSTRUCTIONS OF MATHEMATICS AND MATHEMATICIANS

Valerie Walkerdine's (1988, 1990) work invites us to think differently about gender and mathematics. She traces the historical processes through which maths became enshrined in the curriculum as being *equivalent* to reason and those through which rationality became conflated with masculinity. She suggests that mathematics fits into a pattern of oppositions that are deeply embedded within Western thought – objective *versus* subjective, abstract *versus* concrete, rational *versus* emotional, etc. Masculinity and mathematics line up with the terms on the left-hand sides of these oppositions and femininity with those on the right-hand sides (Walkerdine, 1990). Following this logic, setting up oppositions between separated and connected ways of knowing, and between rule-following boys and under-standing-seeking girls can support the reproduction of gender differences in mathematics. Heather Mendick (2006) used these ideas to make sense of gender differences in the take-up of post-compulsory mathematics, showing how the boys she spoke to used mathematics to construct a masculine identity, something which was problematic for girls studying the subject. In addition to the historical patterns Walkerdine analysed, Mendick explored how stereotypes of mathematics and mathematicians in the broader culture reinforce the associa-tions between mathematics and masculinity.

It is necessary to recognise the impact that cultural conceptions of mathematics and mathematicians have on how people experience and learn mathematics. While our own histories shape our conceptions of what a mathematician looks like – for example, my under-graduate degree in maths has left me with the residing image of mathematicians as middle-aged, eccentric Russian men – it is discourses at a *societal* level that have the greatest impact on how we as a general population think of mathematicians.

Stereotypes of mathematicians have tended to be those of white, old men, with grey beards sat alone in offices thinking deep, abstract thoughts. While this image has changed somewhat in recent years, Marie-Pierre Moreau, Heather Mendick and Debbie Epstein (2010, and see the chapter by Heather and Marie-Pierre) highlight that it still remains rooted in a gendered version of mathematics. That is, whether it be Russell Crowe in *A Beautiful Mind* or Matt Damon in *Good Will Hunting*, mathematicians are socially awk-ward, attractive men whose relationships with women are disrupted by their tempestuous love affair with mathematics. Furthermore, these men are always positioned as geniuses, as men who 'just know' how to solve mathematical problems. Here, maths ability is something that is innate (this is the 'ability thinking' that Mark Boylan and Hilary Povey discuss in their chapter). The important point is that the cultural conception among young people remains that maths is something that one either can or cannot do. This reproduces the notion that mathematics is something to be passively learnt (instrumentally) rather than a (relational) set of processes and skills to acquire.

> *What is your philosophy of mathematics and what approach do you use to learn math-ematics? Do you think this impacts on how you teach mathematics?*

Conclusion

In this chapter, I have examined how the social construction of both gender and mathemat-ics results in gendered inequalities. Highlighting the compulsive attention we pay to gender differences in results in mathematics, and noting the rather small differences that exist at GCSEs, I also argued that there are serious and damaging consequences to how gender is currently treated in maths education. These include fewer women taking maths at higher levels and maths-oriented careers continuing to be male-dominated. Furthermore, I have argued that these differences are being reproduced within maths classrooms – at both primary and secondary levels – and that subtle, nuanced expectations, attitudes and behaviours can result in disparities in later life. Accordingly, it is vital that we consider how we talk about maths and gender in order to ameliorate these differences.

Further reading

Fine, C. (2011) *Delusions of gender: The real science behind sex differences.* London: Icon Books. More on the social determinist side, this book offers a powerful critique of biological research. It argues for social factors and presents a critique of the science of gender studies in an accessible manner.

McCormack, M. (2012) *The declining significance of homophobia: How teenage boys are redefining masculinity and heterosexuality.* New York: Oxford University Press. My own research on masculinities within schools examines how boys are becoming more inclusive and less 'anti-school'. The second section of the book is devoted to understanding gender in society, masculinities in school, and social change.

Mendick, H. (2005) *Masculinities in mathematics.* Buckingham: Open University Press. *Masculinities in mathematics* provides book-length treatment of the gendered nature of mathematics. From looking at how gender is constructed within maths to how boys negotiate these issues, it is an important work in understanding the complexities of gender and maths.

Walkerdine, V. (1998) *Counting girls out.* London: Routledge. This book provides a detailed empirical and theoretical account of the myths, prejudices and theorising of the gendered body and mind, and how it intersects with gender in the teaching and learning of mathematics.

References

Acker, J. (1990) 'Hierarchies, jobs, bodies: a theory of gendered organizations', *Gender and Society*, 4, 2, 139–158.

Asch, A. (1951) 'Effects of group pressure upon the modification and distortion of judgements', in H. Guetzkow (ed), *Groups, leadership and men.* Pittsburgh: Carnegie Press.

Becker, J. R. (1995) 'Women's ways of knowing in mathematics', in G. Kaiser and P. Rogers (eds), *Equity in mathematics education: influences of feminism and culture.* London: Falmer.

Benbow, C. P. and Stanley, J. C. (1980) 'Sex differences in mathematical ability: fact or artefact', *Science*, 210, 12, 1262–1264.

Benbow, C. P. and Stanley, J. C. (1983) 'Sex differences in mathematical reasoning ability: more facts', *Science*, 222, December, 1029–1031.

Boaler, J. (2009) *The elephant in the classroom: helping children learn and love maths.* London: Souvenir Press.

Boaler, J. (1997) *Experiencing school mathematics: teaching styles, sex and setting.* Buckingham: Open University Press.

Burton, L. (1986) *Girls into maths can go.* London: Holt, Rinehart and Winston.

Burton, L. (1995) 'Moving towards a feminist epistemology of mathematics', *Educational Studies in Mathematics*, 28, 3, 275–291.

Curtis, P. (2009) 'GCSE results: boys bag top grades in maths' *The Guardian*, 27 August.

Eccles, J. S., Jacobs, J. E. and Harold, R. D. (1990) 'Gender role stereotypes, expectancy effects and parents' socialization of gender differences', *Journal of Social Issues*, 46, 2, 183–201.

Else-Quest, N. M., Hyde, J. S. and Linn, M. C. (2010) 'Cross-national patterns of gender difference in mathematics: A meta-analysis', *Psychological Bulletin*, 136, 1, 103–127.

Ernest, P. (1998) *Social constructivism as a philosophy of mathematics.* Albany, NY: SUNY Press.

Fausto-Sterling, A. (1993) *Myths of gender: biological theories about women and men*. New York: Basic Books.

Gervais, S. J. and Veschio, T. K. (2012) 'The effect of patronizing behavior and control on men and women's performance in stereotypically masculine domains' *Sex Roles*, iFirst, 1–15.

Gunderson, E. A., Ramirez, G., Levine, S. C. and Beilock, S. L. (2012) 'The role of parents and teachers in the development of gender-related math attitudes', *Sex Roles*, 66, 1, 153–166.

Hyde, J. S. and Linn, M. C. (2006) 'Gender similarities in mathematics and science', *Science*, 314, 5799, 599–600.

Kimmel, M. S. (2004) *The gendered society (second edition)*. Oxford University Press.

Lakatos, I. (1976) *Proofs and refutations*. Cambridge: Cambridge University Press.

Leinhart, A. M., Seewald, A. M. and Engel, M. (1979) 'Learning what's taught: sex differences in instruction', *Journal of Educational Psychology*, 71, 4, 432–439.

Mac an Ghaill, M. (1994) *The making of men: masculinities, sexualities and schooling*. Buckingham: Open University Press.

McCormack, M. (2011) 'Queer masculinities, gender conformity, and the secondary school', in J. C. Landreau and N. M. Rodriguez (eds), *Queer masculinities: A critical reader in education*. New York: Springer.

McCormack, M. (2012) *The declining significance of homophobia: how teenage boys are redefining masculinity and heterosexuality*. New York: Oxford University Press.

Mendick, H. (2005) 'A beautiful myth? The gendering of being/doing "good at maths"', *Gender and Education*, 17, 2, 89–105.

Mendick, H. (2006) *Masculinities in mathematics*. Maidenhead: Open University Press.

Moreau, M.-P., Mendick, H., and Epstein, D. (2010) 'Constructions of mathematicians in popular culture and learners' narratives: a study of mathematical and non-mathematical subjectivities', *Cambridge Journal of Education*, 40, 1, 25–38.

Shepherd, J. (2011) 'GCSE results 2011: girls widen their lead' *The Guardian*, 25 August.

Skemp, R. R. (1976) 'Relational understanding and instrumental understanding', *Mathematics Teaching*, 77, 20–26.

Steele, C. M., and Aronson, J. (1995) 'Stereotype threat and the intellectual test performance of African Americans', *Journal of Personality and Social Psychology*, 69, 797–811.

Walkerdine, V. (1988) *The mastery of reason*. London: Routledge.

Walkerdine, V. (1990) 'Difference, cognition, and mathematics education' *For the Learning of Mathematics*, 10, 3, 51–56.

Younger, M., Warrington, M. and Williams, J. (1999) 'The gender gap and classroom interactions: reality and rhetoric?', *British Journal of Sociology of Education*, 20, 3, 325–341.

West, C. and Zimmerman, D. (1987) 'Doing gender', *Gender and Society*, 1, 2, 125–151.

Chapter 6

Made for mathematics?

Implications for teaching and learning

Patricia George

BACKGROUND AND FOCUS

In this chapter, I discuss teachers' expectations as these relate to their students' achievement in mathematics. I will focus on the Caribbean island state of Antigua and Barbuda. In Antigua and Barbuda and across the Caribbean, like in many other countries, there has been and still is a perception that student performance in mathematics is poor. Newspaper headlines over the years have borne out some of these concerns, for example:

- Poor regional pass rate in CXC maths (*Jamaica Gleaner*, August 30, 2001).
- Why are so many of us not good at maths? (*Jamaica Observer*, February 15, 2004).
- Math remains CXC's weakest link (*Antigua Observer*, August 31, 2005).
- CXC Math results below par (*Antigua Observer*, August 17, 2011).

Concerns about poor student performance are usually made in reference to pass rates in the Caribbean Examinations Council (CXC) Certificate of Secondary Education (CSEC) examinations typically taken at the end of compulsory schooling at age 16. These examinations replaced the former GCE O-Level examinations in the late 1970s. Candidates in 19 Caribbean territories take the examinations; in 2010 approximately 90,000 candidates across the Caribbean took the May/June examinations in mathematics. Results from these examinations over the years show mathematics to be the subject in which candidates were often least successful, with usually fewer than 40% of candidates being successful.

There are a number of factors that impact on student performance and success in mathematics, and the picture of influence is undoubtedly complex. However, in this chapter I want to focus on what has long been acknowledged as an important factor in facilitating students' learning, that is, the views and expectations of their teachers. I want to show how teachers' views and expectations become embodied in what the students themselves say about their own performance and expectations of success in mathematics. At times in this chapter I use the terms views, beliefs and expectations relatively interchangeably; the purpose is not to disentangle these constructs but to see them as falling under a general umbrella of dispositions as related to mathematics teaching and learning.

That teachers' views of mathematics could interact with their views about the mathematical possibilities and potential of their students is not far-fetched. Teachers' views of mathematics are not formed in isolation, but in a context of having themselves had long years of experience in classrooms as learners of mathematics. In these classrooms, mathematics teaching and available ways of learning were modelled before them as well as societal beliefs about mathematics and expectations of what is possible in it and with whom these possibilities lie. Ideally, it is hoped that teachers would have developed more sophisticated and informed beliefs of mathematics and thus expectations for their students too. It is important that teachers (both in-training and in-service) be given space and opportunity to reflect on and examine their mathematical beliefs and expectations of students, considering how they may impact their classroom practice.

Reflect on your school-days experience as a learner of mathematics. How far do you think this experience is reproduced in your own teaching practice of mathematics?

WHAT TEACHERS SAID

In the study, a sample of secondary school mathematics teachers (27 senior mathematics teachers across 11 secondary schools) along with a sample of their students who were nearing the end of their secondary school experience (265 Form 4/Year 10 students, aged 14–15, across the same secondary schools representing about a quarter of that year's cohort of Form 4 students) were asked the closed questionnaire item: *Do you think every secondary school child can do maths to CXC level?* with a follow-up open item asking them to give reason(s) for their response. The question could be interpreted as addressing two issues wrapped up as one, namely, whether every secondary school child could *do* mathematics (this question related to having some 'ability' or 'aptitude' for mathematics) and the extension of the question to CXC level. This feature doubtless directed the responses of both teachers and students. That said, both teacher and student responses to the question yielded insights into a prevailing view of mathematics with implications for how it is taught and whether it is learnt. This is the pervasive 'ability thinking' discussed in the earlier chapter by Mark Boylan and Hilary Povey.

For the teachers, 14 (52%) responded *Yes* to the question, with two inter-related reasons being the most frequent responses. These reasons were, first, that all students were fundamentally able (given by seven teachers), e.g. 'Yes, even though students work at different rates or working levels, through the use of different strategies, they can all learn' and, second, that with proper teaching any student could (given by four teachers) e.g. 'with proficient teaching and sufficient motivation any secondary school student can do mathematics to any level', as well as 'if mathematics is properly taught anybody can learn it'. Notably however, 13 (48%) of the teachers responded *No*, that is, gave a view that every secondary school child could not do mathematics to CXC level. The two most frequent reasons given here had to do with a view that students had to be 'made for maths' (given by seven teachers) and a view related to students having been previously subjected to poor mathematics teaching with some teachers going on to give as consequence the futility of efforts to redeem that situation (given by five teachers), e.g. 'most students do not receive a solid foundation in the concepts or in some cases are taught incorrectly' and 'some students get lost in primary school and also in the lower forms of secondary school. It is extremely difficult for them to catch up in the upper forms'.

It is specifically the 'made for maths' view that is the focus of this chapter, and how such expectations see ability in mathematics and hence success in it as pre-determined. The following are some of the reasons given by teachers whose *No* response was associated with this 'made for maths' view:

- Some students were just not made for maths.
- Some students will never be able (no matter what) to handle mathematics at CXC level because of their interests and 'make up'.
- Mathematical abilities are not uniformly distributed throughout the population.
- Not everyone is mathematically inclined.

As well as their responses to the questionnaire item, teachers elaborated their views during interviews. One teacher noted that they [teachers] were being expected to 'perform miracles' in getting all students up to a level which would allow them to be successful in mathematics at CXC, and that there was not in fact a problem with the country's pass rate in mathematics as it was 'a good reflection of the best that can be done with what is given' further going on to say that 'we are beating ourselves with a wooden stick trying to get all students to [pass] mathematics, when it is not needed, is impractical, and is impossible'.

Relatedly, one mathematics educator who worked with teachers in schools noted a perception of mathematics she found amongst teachers at the primary level, going on to describe the consequences for students by the time they reached secondary school:

> mathematics was perceived as a subject that was difficult, and only something that people with a rare brain could do ... that is what I think I had to work on first of all to make certain that we could alleviate this fear of teaching mathematics, and change the perception ... and especially the professionals who would meet youngsters and tell them things like, 'Oh, when I went to school mathematics was a difficult subject ... so I'm not expecting anybody to be able to do mathematics' ..., by the time these children [reach] secondary school they're so traumatized by the experience in the primary school ... we get some of these people's children in first form, and it's as if, you're asking them a very simple question, but what, they hear the word 'mathematics'. And you get them outside, outside of maths class, and you can ask them that ... same question again, and they answer. And you say, 'So how come you couldn't answer me that?' – 'Because it's a maths class, you know'.

The educator brought out a number of issues here, including the existence of the 'made for mathematics' view among teachers. She also referred to an apparent stupor which seemingly overtook students, affecting what mathematics they can(*not*) do in the formal setting of a mathematics classroom *versus* the mathematics they *can* do in more informal out-of-school settings *and specifically* when what they are doing hasn't been labelled *mathematics*. This, according to the educator, is in part a consequence of early trauma in experiences of learning in-school mathematics – inarguably a strong emotion to associate with the outcome of mathematics teaching.

Yet, there were teachers who recognised the role their expectations could play in student mathematics performance, for example, as noted by one 'If we the teachers enter the classroom thinking that everyone can succeed, then we can improve outcomes'. Other mathematics educators spoke of students' untapped mathematical potential due in part to early labelling as failures, rather than being presented with opportunities to learn and come to know mathematics. One spoke of students 'waiting to be stirred, waiting to be challenged' throughout their whole school mathematics experience as, in his view, many students had not yet been given opportunities to like mathematics due to the way it was presented to them. In his words:

> Instead of saying many of them don't like the subject, because, for you to like the subject, for you to like Joseph then, I have to be introduced to Joseph in such a way that Wow! I begin to see places in Joseph, I begin to see castles in him, I begin to see potential in him. Saying that I don't like Joseph really is probably not a precise enough description. … It is better then to say that I am yet to be given opportunity, maybe I was introduced to Joseph by someone who didn't even really know Joseph, or was excited about Joseph, and so on, all his intricacies and the rest of it … [there is a need for mathematics teachers to] open up avenues and environment[s] for students to really dance in the classroom, see connections, see worlds, and we need to tap into their potential, and to really basically … [allow students] to navigate, to meander, to dream, to dance, to really see what they're capable of, to break down those walls and begin to set up environments that attract students to the subject.

This view of mathematics brings out two main ideas related to its teaching and learning. Firstly, there is a suggestion that perhaps students are being introduced to mathematics by persons who themselves are yet to be introduced to mathematics, who do not yet know of its beauty and possibilities, nor can see the variations, connections, powerfulness it allows. Effectively then, in many cases students had not been (and are not being) introduced to *mathematics*. Secondly, and connected to this first, opportunities for allowing students a (sense of) freedom in mathematics to explore, to enjoy, to have fun with/in it, to lose their way and (importantly) find it back again were not readily available in many classrooms. For the interviewee, these more progressive views of mathematics and its teaching and learning are ways to bring students in, entice them even, to a different and arguably 'truer' form of mathematics.

Are there different forms/types of mathematics? Does in-school mathematics differ markedly from out-of-school mathematics? If so, in what ways? Is this difference okay, needed?

What are/should be mathematics teachers' expectations on entering a classroom? How do the realities of these expectations play out in the classroom? Are these expectations more or less inflexible for mathematics (i.e. is there a characteristic of mathematics versus other subjects that constrains flexibility in expectations)?

WHAT STUDENTS SAID

Moving to look at what students said, 124 (47%) responded *Yes* and 141 (53%) responded *No* to the question. As the question was asked in a general way, it could well be that students in their responses were referring to others of their peers, as well as they could be referring to themselves. That said, in coding their responses to the open adjunct of the question, the most frequent code was assigned to students who responded *No*, and had to do with their perception of the nature of a 'mathematical ability' and how a person might 'have/get' it, essentially they thought that mathematical ability was some pre-fixed characteristic that a student either had or didn't have, so that a student had to be 'made for maths'. Eighty-eight students (33% of the sample or 62% of those responding *No*) gave this as reason for their answer. The following are some of the reasons students gave as to why they thought not all students could do mathematics (to CXC level):

- Not everybody has the aptitude.
- Everyone is not mathematically inclined.
- Some people just can't do maths.
- Everyone is not smart in that subject area. For e.g. me.
- Some students were not made for maths.
- Maths uses a lot of common sense and some of us just lack it.
- Because maths was not cut out for everybody.
- Everyone does not have the capacity to produce good maths work.
- Because not everybody is capable of doing maths.
- Not everyone is made for it.
- Some people just don't have the skill for maths.
- Not everyone has the brains for it.

As mentioned, there were students who felt that all students could do mathematics to CXC level, with the most frequently given (and inter-related) responses here having to do with its possibility if students made the effort (24 students), e.g. 'with focus and determination you can do anything' and the view that all students had the potential (22 students), e.g. 'every child has the potential to perform'. However, the similarity of teacher and student responses for those responding *No*, both in the proportions who responded *No*, as well as in the more qualitative aspects of *why* they responded *No*, was striking. For both teachers and students, reasons for their responses related to being made for mathematics were the most frequently given reasons whether teachers and students responded *Yes* or *No* to the question. On the ground, messages of whom mathematics was for translated into some schools specifically re-grouping students for mathematics teaching based on a notion of 'ability' in the subject. Although most schools did stream students generally based on performances across all subjects, it was only in mathematics that some schools carried out further ability grouping for teaching. These ability grouping practices specifically for mathematics only further served to buttress the idea that students had to fit some pre-determined mould in order to be able to successfully *do* mathematics.

> *How might you determine students' views of and expectations in mathematics? How important is it to know these for each new group of students, and before beginning to teach them?*

Discussion

It would be unfair to cite mathematics teachers as being solely responsible for the mathematics views of their students and specifically for the 'made for maths' view; this perception runs deep through society and so would also explain why some students thought as they did (see the chapter by Heather Mendick and Marie-Pierre Moreau for examples of this view within popular culture). It would though seem that an important responsibility of mathematics teaching would be to lessen, if not eliminate such student views, to create an environment in classrooms where *all* students come to believe and demonstrate that they *can* do mathematics. This is a crucial starting point of teaching, and especially for the teaching of mathematics, if that teaching is in any way to effect learning, and further, to begin challenging otherwise dominant cultural norms. While you cannot deny the wider social and cultural context in which mathematics teaching rests and the concomitant influences of these on classroom practices, it cannot be too idealistic to think that there can be some outward direction to the flow of influence; that what happens in the classroom can (begin to) redefine *what* the cultural views and expectations are for mathematics.

> *What could, or should, be some of the responsibilities of teacher education in getting at and reshaping teachers' views of mathematics?*

Teachers' expectations of their students' capacity to achieve in *mathematics* are likely to be formed *inter alia* by their own years of experience as learners in mathematics classrooms. These school-days experiences can be powerful directing forces on how teachers are prepared to see possibilities in and for their students – essentially, how they allow their students to dance. As noted in the National Council of Teachers of Mathematics Standards:

> Teachers' own experiences have a profound impact on their knowledge of, beliefs about, and attitudes towards mathematics, students, and teaching … years as learners of … mathematics provide them with images and models – conscious or unconscious – of what it means to teach and learn mathematics.
>
> NCTM (1991, p.124)

These school-days experiences are undoubtedly part of the basis for teachers' views of the nature of mathematics itself. According to Alba Gonzalez Thompson (1984, p.105) whatever the level of consciousness of these views, they do guide teaching practice. Thus, teachers' views about the nature of mathematics can guide expectations for their students in the subject and shape how they present and represent mathematics to these students. These expectations can set the stage for the targets teachers set their students, the work they give, how they challenge students (or not) in the tasks given, and how they may interact with male and female students based on gendered expectations, among other things (see the earlier chapters by Mark McCormack and by Peter Gates and Andy Noyes). According to Christine Rubie-Davies (2009), research findings show that teachers with high expectations of their students were more facilitative in their teaching approach, used more mixed-ability grouping, provided students with more challenging tasks, set known goals and targets for their students, and gave students more responsibility for their own learning. On the other hand, teachers with low expectations of their students were more directive and procedural in their teaching approach, more often placed students in groupings based on ability, often did not set or share goals with students, and effectively controlled what and how learning was 'available' to students. Ultimately, these expectations lead to differential opportunities for learning, which, as noted by Christine Rubie-Davies (2009, p.694), is 'the crux of the teacher expectation issue' as expectations become 'operationalised' in classrooms.

Differences in these types of learning opportunities may facilitate or stand in the way of student learning. Whether consciously or not, such views, both about the nature of mathematics and what teachers' expectations are, are conveyed to students and become part of the students' own belief system about mathematics; potentially perpetuating and strengthening the cycle of such views. According to Reuben Hersh (1998, p.13) teachers' beliefs about the nature of mathematics form a stronger basis for how they present the subject than their own notions about the best way to teach.

Attempts at changing or modifying teachers' views should formally recognise the 'baggage' (Ball, 1988, p.41) they bring in terms of the views of mathematics they may hold, and how these may form the basis for expectations of their students. Teachers though are not always aware of their views much less to the soundness of some of these for their teaching practice, and so are oblivious as to how these views might get in the way of the learning opportunities they create for their students. Where views are ill-formed, teachers need to be brought to a point of seeing: the disjuncture in their mathematics views and expectations of their students with desirable practice; the implications for teaching; and the potential disservice these views may operationalise and engender. Without an awareness of this disjuncture, attempts at changing beliefs may result in a rejection of the new ideas, or a modification of those ideas to fit their pre-existing ideas. In a very true sense some beginning (and some other) mathematics teachers may have to 'unlearn' how to teach mathematics (ibid, p.40). The baggage must be unpacked, and its contents examined to determine appropriateness for mathematics teaching. Teacher education should serve as a forum for initiating the process of teachers becoming aware of what beliefs they do hold about mathematics and its teaching, and challenge these as needed.

> *What is your philosophy of mathematics?*

Jo Boaler (2009) identified this 'made for mathematics' view as the 'elephant in the room' of mathematics classrooms. She noted that some mathematics teachers took as part of their responsibility being able to sort students into groups of those who can and those who can't do mathematics. She further specifically identified *mathematics* as being used in schools as a tool for the sorting, tracking and labelling of students. It might be that mathematics presents more fertile ground for the impact of such expectations on practice than most other subject areas, given the pervasiveness of the practice of ability grouping specifically for this subject. And the practices as identified by Christine Rubie-Davies (given earlier) that play out in classrooms of teachers with low expectations of their students have long been used to characterise much of what mathematics teaching looks like in schools. Could it then be that mathematics teaching has unwittingly long had low expectations of students? Peter Gates and Catherine Vistro-Yu (2003) asked the poignant question 'Is mathematics for all?'. That question needs to be thoughtfully considered and answered by every teacher who would step into a classroom to teach mathematics. If the answer is anything other than *yes*, then there is a danger that their students will be taught mathematics 'accordingly', i.e. making it so that the mathematics taught is not accessible by all. Then Peter Gates and Catherine Vistro-Yu's (2003, pp.53–54) position that the perceived poor performance of some students in mathematics is 'more apparent than it is real', that is that the 'apparent' poor performance of some students in mathematics has been in some ways contrived to be so, does not seem so far-fetched. Many different issues set the stage for a complex picture impacting students' mathematics, so that their performance in the subject is very often not a 'real' reflection of an inability to do it. These issues include poor grounding in the fundamentals, low teacher expectations, and certain ways of doing things in education – for example, the fact that 'ability' regrouping practices are regularly carried out, especially in mathematics, supposedly to make *teaching* (not *learning*) easier.

In an ideal world, the 'made for maths' view ought not to have any place in schools, nor should it have so long made its home in mathematics classrooms. The view, whether on the part of teachers or students, stifles potential and robs students of opportunities for success. My view is that being able to do and make sense of mathematics is not a gift, a talent bestowed on persons with a 'rare brain'. It is not something one 'inherits' from parents (although parental support is key in student educational success), nor do students have to be mathematically inclined or 'made for mathematics' in order to be able to do it and enjoy success in it. If taught properly, any student – especially those who have persisted and survived in schools to still be there to a stage where they are taking certifying examinations – should be able to do it. It might be the case that mathematical abilities are not uniformly distributed throughout a population, but then, what is? If mathematics is taught in such a way that it is made accessible to all students, then students will be able to learn it. This cannot be a 'one size fits all' mathematics, as is too often the case in classrooms. What is needed is more equity rather than equality in the way mathematics is taught. This would involve fitting its teaching to the needs of individual learners, rather than trying to fit learners into a pre-conceived mould for mathematics, and so seeing greater equality in the quality of mathematics outcomes for individual learners.

Although this chapter has been written based on research findings in a Caribbean context, the literature presented in the discussion suggests that the 'made for maths' view is relatively pervasive, at least in western countries. Further, there is also some evidence that low expectations of students' mathematics are influenced by such factors as students' social class, gender and ethnicity, among others (Gates and Vistro-Yu, 2003; Ladson-Billings, 1997). It is vital that the issue of the low mathematical performance of *any* student be addressed. Despite perceived views about the importance of mathematics, its teaching and learning continue to suffer in classrooms; a situation which is at best paradoxical. Global advances in technology have, if anything, added to the importance of mathematics and so given the subject much valued currency in the world beyond school (e.g. Boaler, 2009). There is also research suggesting that qualifications in mathematics increase an individual's earning potential. Thus increasingly an individual's life and life chances after secondary school, be this tertiary education and/or the world of work, *demand* a level of numeracy as well as literacy. Qualifications in mathematics can serve to offer a more unrestricted worldview to an individual beyond school. Students' access, or lack thereof, to quality mathematics education and the qualifications that may result too often come to 'stand in the way' of their life chances. Robert Moses (in Moses and Cobb, 2001) in writing about the low mathematics performance of black students in the USA argued that access to quality mathematics education is a civil rights issue, so that it is no longer 'enough' to highlight the poor performances of black students in the subject area. It is time to move beyond this to further investigate possible contributing factors to this observation, and to invest in intervention strategies which would mitigate the loss in human resources being suffered in this area. The idea is to *make* mathematics accessible *for* all students rather than fitting students into mathematics. It is possible and the next section of the book focuses on ways that teachers can do this in their classrooms.

Further reading

Boaler, J. (2009) *The Elephant in the Classroom: Helping Children Learn and Love Maths*. London: Souvenir Press Ltd. This book offers practical suggestions on approaches to teaching mathematics which make it more accessible to students. It sets about bridging what it sees as the huge gap between what research has shown to work in students learning mathematics and what actually happens in classrooms.

Gates, P. (2006) 'Going Beyond Belief Systems: Exploring a Model for the Social Influence on Mathematics Teacher Beliefs', *Educational Studies in Mathematics*, 63, 347–369. More specifically centred on mathematics, this article provides a good follow-on to the Christine Rubie-Davies article (see below). It puts a focus on the social construction of the individual teacher and so on how their views of mathematics – and how it is taught – cannot look only within mathematics but should include wider considerations of the social and cultural context.

Gates, P. and Vistro-Yu, C. (2003) 'Is Mathematics for All?', in A. J. Bishop, M. A. Clements, C. Keitel, J. Kilpatrick, and F. K. S. Leung (eds), *Second International Handbook of Mathematics Education (Part One)*. Dordrecht: Kluwer Academic Publishers. This article provides a good overview of issues that have long remained current in mathematics having to do with socio-cultural-political agendas in its teaching and learning. Among other things, it also foregrounds the plight of marginalised student groups in mathematics classes, groups made so by processes that often pass unquestioned in how schools *do* mathematics.

Rubie-Davies, C. (2009) 'Teacher Expectations and Labeling', in L. J. Saha and A. G. Dworkin (eds), *International Handbook of Research on Teachers and Teaching*, 21, 5, 695–708, Dordrecht: Springer. Though not specifically about mathematics, this provides a good review of the literature on the impact of teacher expectations on student performance, which shows that at times teacher expectations can become enacted as self-fulfilling prophecies in student outcomes. She concludes by noting that issues to do with teacher expectations are ultimately issues to do with quality education for students, so that it is important for teachers to set high expectations for all students.

References

Ball, D. L. (1988) 'Unlearning to teach mathematics', *For the Learning of Mathematics*, 8, 1, 40–48.

Boaler, J. (2009) *The elephant in the classroom: helping children learn and love maths*. London: Souvenir Press Ltd.

Gates, P. and Vistro-Yu, C. (2003) 'Is mathematics for all?', in A. J. Bishop, M. A. Clements, C. Keitel, J. Kilpatrick, and F. K. S Leung (eds), *Second international handbook of mathematics education (part one)*. Dordrecht: Kluwer Academic Publishers.

Hersh, R. (1998) 'Some proposals for reviving the philosophy of mathematics', in T. Tymoczko (ed), *New directions in the philosophy of mathematics (revised and expanded edition)*. New Jersey: Princeton University Press.

Ladson-Billings, G. (1997) 'It doesn't add up: African American students' mathematics achievement', *Journal for Research in Mathematics Education*, 28, 6, 697–708.

Moses, R. P. and Cobb, C. E. (2001) *Radical equations: civil rights from Mississippi to the Algebra Project*. Boston: Beacon Press Books.

NCTM (National Council of Teachers of Mathematics) (1991) *Professional standards for teaching mathematics*. Virginia: NCTM.

Rubie-Davies, C. (2009) 'Teacher expectations and labeling' in L. J. Saha and A. G. Dworkin (eds) *International handbook of research on teachers and teaching*, 21, 5, 695–707. Dordrecht: Springer.

Thompson, A. G. (1984) 'The relationship of teachers' conceptions of mathematics and mathematics teaching to instructional practice', *Educational Studies in Mathematics*, 15, 2, 105–27.

Part II

Debates in the teaching and learning of mathematics

Introduction to *Debates in the teaching and learning of mathematics*

Jo Boaler has coined the term 'relational equity' to describe relationships in classrooms which promote children treating each other with respect and taking responsibility. Her work has highlighted inequities in students' performance and participation that correlate with gender, social class and ethnicity and has identified critical issues that teachers face in making mathematics (and indeed other subjects) equitable (Boaler *et al.*, 2011). Two of the key messages that emerge from her recent work are that:

- Good teaching – which engages students actively; links the subject to the 'real world'; and 'encourages all students to a high level and communicates positive messages of malleable intelligence and hard work rather than fixed intelligence and ability' (p.480) – is equitable teaching.
- In many cases, teaching in the mathematics classroom is 'narrow, procedural, based on fixed rather than changing notions of intelligence and examination driven' (p.480).

In other words, inequities concern the teaching environment.

This second section of this book explores some of the debates in the teaching and learning of mathematics related to these imperatives. In the opening chapter, Gwen Ineson and Sunita Babbar identify the debate between the current UK government and the mathematics education community with regards to increasing the level of 'challenge' in the content of the primary national curriculum versus the importance of developing flexible approaches to calculation in primary school children. They consider the way in which mathematical capabilities are developed in the primary school setting, look at the difference between thinking *with* the head and thinking *in* the head, and investigate the approach to teaching mental calculation in primary schools, comparing it to that taken in secondary schools, raising issues of transition.

Does the use of calculators in primary schools restrict a child's ability to think? Is this just the case in primary education? Should we only grant the use of calculators once learners have become proficient in mental calculation? Do those raising such questions understand how calculators are *really* used in schools? These are questions taken up in the next chapter by Kenneth Ruthven, which investigates the debates surrounding the use of digital technologies in the mathematics classroom. The use of calculators is a debate which has been ongoing for some years, but this is now compounded by the availability of a range of digital technologies to maths teachers. Indeed, just how valuable are interactive whiteboards as mathematical and indeed pedagogical tools? As Ken(neth) identifies, it is not so much a matter of good and bad technologies but rather a question of how they are used.

The role of examples in the teaching of mathematics is considered in the next two chapters in this section, contributed by Tim Rowland and Leo Rogers respectively. Tim points out that 'many concepts grow out of familiarity with a procedure'. We're sure you'd agree, it is commonplace when teaching to draw upon examples to illustrate concepts, but how do we use these examples? Where do they come from (us or our students)? And, what do we do with them? In his chapter, Tim presents particular cases of three teachers which will hopefully prompt you to consider your own practice by demonstrating the impact of using examples in teaching, highlighting some potential problems along the way.

As Jo Boaler identified, a feature of 'good teaching' is making mathematics relevant to the real-world context. This is picked up in Leo's chapter. He points out that this use of examples can be extended to investigate the relationship between mathematics and our heritage and culture, and can draw on how mathematics has evolved over time. Indeed, to quote Leo, 'there is a range of reasons why they [disaffected students who do not continue with mathematics after sixteen] have negative perceptions of mathematics: it is irrelevant to their lives, tedious, disconnected, elitist and de-personalised'. Indeed he reminds us that even successful students often move away from mathematics to pursue subjects which they experience as more 'interesting and creative'. The idea that learning mathematics is not only important for its practical applications, but also for its power to open the mind to the development of ideas and to enable us to realise its connections with other areas of human experience is a powerful one. Leo shows us ways in which the history of mathematics can offer a different approach to learning and teaching, to understanding where the contemporary curriculum comes from and how its key concepts have evolved. Indeed, he identifies a whole host of opportunities that incorporating the history and heritage of mathematics as an integral part of mathematics teaching can provide. Could this be one way of showing the 'human face of mathematics'?

So, teachers – as Gwen and Sunita stress in their chapter – probably hope that using examples to elucidate concepts and explain procedures might promote 'teaching for understanding'. However, in her chapter, Anna Llewellyn challenges us to consider not just what we mean by 'understanding' but what our desire to bring this about does. Her starting point is that rather than being descriptive, 'language creates meaning'. Anna critically revisits a classic study by Jo Boaler using it to exemplify how mathematics education research has a 'romantic' conception of understanding. Anna also discusses the presence (or absence) of understanding in policy, arguing that here it is reduced to functionality. Furthermore, she discusses the impact of the tensions between these conceptions of understanding on student teachers. By calling into question things that have become 'truths' of mathematics education, she helps us to appreciate that we need to consider more widely the effects of what we do.

'Current practices in the teaching of mathematics in secondary schools in the UK do not promote attainment for all'. This is the opening line of Hilary Povey's chapter – the final one in this section. We should refer back to the chapter entitled 'Ability Thinking' in the first section of the book, which she wrote with Mark Boylan, in which they discuss how students' prior attainment informs setting practices and how these affect students' progress. In her chapter in this section, Hilary investigates ways in which contemporary pedagogies operate to limit the attainment of some and narrow the range of attainment for all. However, rather than dwelling on 'what doesn't work that we currently do' she positively presents four case studies which illustrate various 'pedagogical possibilities' for doing things differently and in ways that have been shown to work in real classrooms. She ends by introducing the notion of 'transformability': the firm commitment that change *is* possible for *all* students.

Transformability draws together and underlies all the chapters in this section, which are engaged in developing pedagogies that realise this commitment.

Reference

Boaler J., Alterndorff, L. and Kent, G. (2011) 'Mathematics and science inequalities in the United Kingdom: when elitism, sexism and culture collide', *Oxford Review of Education*, 37, 4, 457–484.

Chapter 7

Mental maths

Just about what we do *in* our heads?

Gwen Ineson and Sunita Babbar

Introduction

In England, as we write this, the launch of a new primary school national curriculum is upon us, a draft version having been released in June 2012 (DfE, 2012a). In a letter to the National Curriculum Expert Panel, UK Education Minister Michael Gove (2012) wrote:

> In mathematics there will be additional stretch, with much more challenging content than in the current National Curriculum. We will expect children to be more proficient in arithmetic, including knowing number bonds to 20 by year 2 and times tables up to 12 × 12 by the end of year 4. The development of written methods – including long multiplication and division – will be given greater emphasis, and children will be taught more challenging content using fractions, decimals and negative numbers so that they have a more secure foundation for secondary school.

Michael Gove claims to be determined to have a primary curriculum in place, which demands the highest of standards and which has gleaned best practice from the most successful schools, both in this country and abroad. However, his plans have been met with strong opposition from the mathematics education community who have stressed the importance of developing flexible approaches to calculation. Where to place the balance between teaching algorithms (for everything from addition to the oft-dreaded but symbolically important long division) and teaching such flexible approaches has been an ongoing debate within mathematics education.

   Indeed, just a year prior to Gove's comments, the England schools inspectorate Ofsted (2011, p.1) advocated a very different approach that identified the key aim of the teaching of calculation as developing mathematical understanding:

> It is … of fundamental importance to ensure that children have the best possible grounding in mathematics during their primary years, number, or arithmetic, is a key component of this. Public perceptions of arithmetic often relate to the ability to calculate quickly and accurately – to add, subtract, multiply and divide, both mentally and using traditional written methods. But arithmetic taught well gives children so much more than this, understanding about number, its structures and relationships, underpins progression from counting in nursery rhymes to calculating with and reasoning about numbers of all sizes, to working with measures and establishing the foundations for algebraic thinking. These grow into the skills so valued by the world of industry and

higher education and are the best starting points for equipping children for their future lives.

Here we see a distancing from Gove's and the public's focus on calculation (evident in the debate about calculator use discussed by Kenneth Ruthven in his chapter). And, although we might want to argue for purposes of mathematics education beyond preparing students for industry and higher education, clearly it is important that we give young people access to these fields. Also, research by Laurie Buxton (1981) and others on maths anxiety shows what a damaging long-term impact not feeling comfortable with numbers can have on people.

These two positions on calculation, represented here by Gove and Ofsted, reflect different underlying philosophies on mathematics education. Paul Ernest (1991) identified five such positions: industrial trainers, technological pragmatists, old humanists, progressive educators and public educators. Gove is typical of the 'industrial trainers' following a New Right ideology that sees mathematics as a set of absolute truths and rules to be learnt and so prioritising a drill and practice pedagogy that aims for '"Back-to-Basics" numeracy and training in social obedience' (p.139). Ofsted, along with many mathematics education researchers, represent a 'progressive educator' position that sees mathematics as a set of absolute truths but 'with great value … attached to the role of the individual in coming to know this truth' (p.182) and so advocating a child-centred process-oriented pedagogy that aims for creativity and self-realisation. Our own sympathies lie with this position based in connection, care and empathy between humans. Thus, in this chapter, we will argue for an informal approach to mental mathematics as a way of developing what Skemp (1978) defines as 'relational understanding' of mathematics. We begin by unpacking what we mean by relational understanding.

WHAT DO WE MEAN BY UNDERSTANDING MATHEMATICS?

Consider the problem 2047 ÷ 23. Take a moment to solve this problem. How did you do this? Did you use the long division algorithm to solve this? Consider the steps that you took – how would you explain these to someone else? Do you feel that you understood what you did?

The problem in more traditional classrooms would be written as in Figure 7.1 and the mantra heard would go something like this:

23 into 2 doesn't go
23 into 20 doesn't go
23 into 204… Hmm, how many 23s are there in 204? [and would then proceed to write down multiples of 23 discretely on the back of a piece of paper].

An alternative approach which has been used in schools is that of chunking. This encourages teachers to promote conceptual understanding as there is no defined approach – students are encouraged to relate division to repeated subtraction where 'chunks' (multiples of the divisor) are subtracted from the dividend. The size of the chunks subtracted are not predetermined, unlike the formal long division algorithm where the largest multiple of the divisor

```
              8   9
2   3 | 2   0   4   7
        1   8   4   ↓
            2   0   7
            2   0   7
                    0
```

Figure 7.1 Long division algorithm for 2047 ÷ 23.

must be subtracted. The number of chunks subtracted are totalled to find the solution. Figure 7.2 illustrates two different approaches to using chunking for long division. The first is a rather cautious approach, subtracting relatively easy multiples of 23. However, what is formally recorded in this illustration is what is often surreptitiously recorded on scraps of paper. The second is slightly more sophisticated in that larger chunks are subtracted. The numbers in bold are the number of chunks being subtracted from the dividend, which are totalled at the end.

Figures 7.1 and 7.2 illustrate some familiar (and maybe some unfamiliar!) strategies for 'long division'. As indicated in Margaret Brown's chapter, some people (including industrial trainers like Michael Gove) would consider this approach long-winded, ineffective with potential for errors, and resulting from 'vague generic statements of little value'. However, although we too feel that there is a significant difference between Figures 7.1 and 7.2, we disagree. For us, the first appears to treat numbers as digits, rather than holistically, and operates algorithmically. The second figure builds on a knowledge and understanding of mathematical relationships, for example the relationships embedded in place value, and those between multiplication and division and between division and subtraction.

```
              8   9                                    8   9
2   3 | 2   0   4   7                        2   3 | 2   0   4   7
      −   2   3   0     (10 × 23)                  −   2   3   0     (10 × 23)
        1   8   1   7                                1   8   1   7
      −   2   3   0     (10 × 23)                −   1   1   5   0   (50 × 23)
        1   5   8   7                                    6   6   7
      −   2   3   0     (10 × 23)                  −   4   6   0     (20 × 23)
        1   3   5   7                                    2   0   7
      −   2   3   0     (10 × 23)                  −   2   0   7     (9 × 23)
        1   1   2   7                                            0
      −   2   3   0     (10 × 23)
            8   9   7
      −   2   3   0     (10 × 23)
            6   6   7
      −   2   3   0     (10 × 23)
            4   3   7
      −   2   3   0     (10 × 23)
            2   0   7
      −   1   1   5     (5 × 23)
                9   2
          −   6   9     (3 × 23)
                2   3
          −   2   3     (1 × 23)
                    0
```

Figure 7.2 Using chunking for long division.

It is useful to draw on the distinction that Richard Skemp made between instrumental understanding of mathematics and relational understanding. He wrote about students developing an 'instrumental' understanding of mathematics who would follow 'rules without reasons' (Skemp, 1978). The alternative approach is to develop 'relational' understanding which encourages students to know *both* what to do with a calculation *and* why. A useful analogy that has been used by Liping Ma (1999) to illustrate the difference between these two types of understanding is a comparison between a tourist visiting London and a London taxi driver. Let's say that a tourist is attempting to navigate between Buckingham Palace and the Science Museum. They would be able to use the underground (tube) map to get themselves between the two but they would struggle if the tube trains weren't running. The London taxi driver, however, would be aware of numerous possible routes between the two landmarks and, further, would be able to cope with finding alternative routes due to traffic restrictions or jams. The tourist visiting London is like the student with instrumental understanding; able to follow rules to go between different concepts within mathematics – for example, able to follow an algorithm to solve long division. The London taxi driver on the other hand, is the student with relational understanding – able to navigate in a multitude of ways between different mathematical concepts. Using the long division example – a student with relational understanding would be able to solve the problem in numerous ways, make a reasonable estimate of the solution and know how to check it.

Do we always have to teach so that students have relational understanding? Consider some examples, such as multiplication of negative numbers, division of fractions and the angle sums of polygons. What does relational understanding mean to you in each case?

Deciding what constitutes relational understanding of any aspect of mathematics is a complicated (perhaps impossible) business. But we're not trying to claim that there's a clear-cut distinction between relational and instrumental understanding. For example, in Ma's analogy, the taxi driver has probably acquired their knowledge of London through 'rote learning' while the tourist's understanding of the underground network is functional and likely to be based on a deeper understanding of urban transportation. However, just as the taxi driver and tourist have different relationships to space and different feelings about navigating London, we would suggest that how a student understands mathematics affects their relationship with the subject, and the distinction between relational and instrumental understanding is helpful in discussing this.

Recently, we conducted a study to compare the approaches to long division of primary and secondary trainee teachers (Babbar and Ineson, 2013). Secondary trainee teachers were found to be more secure in the approaches that they used themselves, but struggled to think of alternative ways to support students in developing approaches for long division. Their favoured approach was that of an algorithm, even when the numbers involved were near multiples of 10. The example we used was $207 \div 23$. Although most secondary trainee teachers recognised that $23 \times 10 = 230$, which is near 207, their initial response was to write down the algorithm. Primary trainees on the other hand were found to be less likely to be able to find the accurate solution but could suggest alternative approaches for supporting learners. This raises questions about the kind of understanding these secondary trainee teachers had and how they would teach division. These are questions that we explore through focusing on mental mathematics in the rest of this chapter.

WHAT IS THE PLACE OF MENTAL MATHEMATICS IN THE MATHEMATICS CURRICULUM?

> *Think back to your own experiences of mental mathematics. What memories do they con-jure up? Do you remember mental mathematics tests? What impact did these have on you? Do you remember any other aspect of mental maths? Whilst considering these ques-tions, how would you define mental mathematics and what does this mean to you?*

Before we consider current explanations of mental mathematics, it is useful to first provide some background. For over a century there has been concern over the 'standards' achieved by school leavers in the UK and less than favourable international comparisons. In addition to this, educationalists have been alarmed by the apparent over-reliance on formal algorithms for relatively simple problems. For example, when faced with problems such as 1001–999, students tended to write these numbers out vertically then laboriously use formal written methods involving decomposition to find the solution (illustrated in Figure 7.3). Because of this over-reliance on formal strategies (sometimes described as 'comfort blankets') students failed to consider the numbers involved and whether, therefore, there was another more effective strategy.

$$
\begin{array}{r}
0\ \ 9\ \ 9 \\
\cancel{1}\ \cancel{0}\ \cancel{0}\ \ {}^1 1 \\
-\quad\ 9\ \ 9\ \ 9 \\
\hline
2
\end{array}
$$

Figure 7.3 Using decomposition to solve 1001–999.

A Task Group was set up in 1997 to explore the possibilities of raising mathematical achievement through the review of research and theory and although concerns were expressed in professional corners about the range and scope of the Task Group's review, it led to the establishment of the National Numeracy Strategy (NNS) in 1998. This strategy emphasised the development of mental calculation in primary schools and the approach advocated in this document was radical. Prior to the implementation of the NNS, the basis of teaching about calculation in primary schools was the formal written approach illustrated in Figure 7.3. This in itself gives rise to another question: why the need to change and focus on mental calculation? The new emphasis placed on mental computation was therefore of considerable significance. For example, the NNS stated that students should not be taught a standard method of written calculation until they could reliably use addition and subtrac-tion mentally for any pair of two digit numbers. This flexibility in using mental calculation strategies is what is lost in Gove's proposed new primary mathematics curriculum.

In the previous primary framework, teachers were asked to focus on encouraging these skills in their students:

- Remembering number facts and recalling them without hesitation.
- Using the facts that are known by heart to figure out new facts: for example, a fact like 8 + 6 = 14 can be used to work out 80 + 60 = 140, or 28 + 6 = 34.
- Understanding and using the relationship between the 'four rules' to work out answers and check results: for example, 24 ÷ 4 = 6, since 6 × 4 = 24.

- Drawing on a repertoire of mental strategies to work out calculations like 81–26, 23 × 4 or 5% of £3000, with some thinking time.
- Solving problems like the following mentally: 'Can I buy three bags of crisps at 35p with my £1 coin?' or 'Roughly how long will it take me to go 50 miles at 30 mph?' (DfEE, 1998, p.6).

Following the establishment of the NNS in 1998, the Secondary National Strategy was developed to support the progression from primary to secondary. In the secondary framework, the following examples are given as ways of building opportunities to develop mental mathematics skills:

- Remember number facts and recall them without hesitation.
- Use known facts to figure out new facts: for example, knowing that half of 250 is 125 can be used to work out 250–123.
- Draw on a repertoire of mental strategies to work out calculations such as 326–81, 223 × 4 or 2.5% of £3000, with some thinking time.
- Understand and use the relationships between operations to work out answers and check results: for example, 900 ÷ 15 = 60, since 6 × 150 = 900.
- Approximate calculations to judge whether or not an answer is about the right size: for example, recognise that 1⁄4 of 57.9 is just under 1⁄4 of 60, or 15.
- Solve problems such as: 'How many CDs at £3.99 each can I buy with £25?' or 'Roughly how long will it take me to go 50 miles at 30 mph?' (DfEE, 2001, p.10)

Consider the progression in mental maths in the primary phase to the secondary phase – does this list seem appropriate?

Liping Ma (1999) carried out some research to explore the way in which effective mathematics teachers understand mathematics. She came up with the term Profound Understanding of Fundamental Mathematics (PUFM) to describe the type of understanding that effective teachers had. This included seeing the connections between different mathematical concepts (for example, the relationship between decimals and fractions, or the number operations), the ability to be flexible when calculating and recognising the coherence of the mathematics curriculum. So, in considering the place of mental mathematics in the maths curriculum, we suggest that almost all of mathematics could be described as 'mental' in the sense that engaging in a mathematical task involves thinking. Mental mathematics is about more than the recall of facts; it is about having the confidence and competence to deal with numbers. Ma would emphasise the teacher's ability to be flexible when calculating in order to encourage flexibility in their students. Many of the examples of skills listed above for both primary and secondary students are about developing flexible strategies for calculating. This reflects the views of those Paul Ernest called 'Progressive Educators', that mathematics education should allow students to gain confidence and not rely solely on formal procedures.

As research shows, mental mathematics is not without dangers (Beishuizen, 1999; Denvir and Askew, 2001). On the one hand, the NNS suggests that the development of mental capability is more than drill and practice, procedural understanding and memorising number facts; teachers are also encouraged to promote students' understanding. On the other hand, research studies also consistently show that there is a tendency, when carrying out daily mental work (as encouraged in the NNS) for teachers to emphasise the procedural at the expense of understanding (Gray and Tall, 1994; Denvir and Askew, 2001). Denvir and Askew (2001) explored the behaviour of students during numeracy lessons and found that teachers tended to emphasise the need for speed and accuracy, rather than mathematical thinking. They suggested that these students were 'participating' rather than 'engaging' in the mathematical activities. In these and similar contexts, an emphasis on rote memory to recall number facts often has a negative effect, compounding the problems faced, in particular, by lower achieving students who were unable to use these facts flexibly (Gray and Tall, 1994).

Another issue in the English context is that all teachers (regardless of age phase or subject) have to pass a numeracy skills test which includes a mental mathematics element prior to gaining their teaching qualification. This consists of twelve oral questions where candidates have 18 seconds in which to respond. These tests are prerequisites for obtaining a place on a teacher training programme and if after three attempts a candidate is unsuccessful, he or she will have to wait a further two years before attempting the tests again. It is suggested that this 'is considered a reasonable time during which candidates can become proficient at the skills assessed in the tests before further attempts' (DfE, 2012b).

> *How do you feel about mental maths being tested in this way? What kind of understanding do you think this promotes?*

We feel that this promotes the industrial trainer approach, seeing mathematics as a fixed body of knowledge which is best tested in this way. It also reflects the status of mathematics and its power to act as a gatekeeper to teaching in largely unrelated subjects such as art and history. However, we feel that there is a distinction to make when working mentally and in this situation the emphasis is on working in the head, rather than with the head. So, for example, focusing on quick recall or memorising of number facts focuses on *in*-the-head thinking, whereas some of the strategies that were discussed earlier such as using facts (for example, 20 times a number to solve 19 times a number) encourage *with*-the-head thinking. This would not be a 'known fact' but we could use our heads to find the solution, without reliance on an algorithm. Whilst there are clearly benefits of quick recall of number facts (for example times tables and number bonds, and passing the numeracy skills test) it is also important to focus on the importance of developing strategies – *with* the head (Beishuizen, 1997). This has parallels with Skemp's concern over instrumental understanding which has a tendency to focus on *in*-the-head work. Research has shown that students who have a large bank of known facts (i.e. those that they can instantly recall) are able to make use of these to derive more facts (Gray, 1991). Conversely, the same researchers found that students who rely heavily on counting strategies (usually because they don't have a bank of known facts) are likely to be slower and less accurate in their solutions (Gray, 1991).

We end this chapter by using the example of the empty number line to illustrate this tension between the *in*-the-head and *with*-the-head ways of thinking.

The empty number line: model *versus* tool

As mentioned previously, mental mathematics is not just about what is done *in* the head. In both primary and secondary settings informal jottings are very much encouraged and these usually draw on visual images that students have built up from an early age. You may have come across the hundred square in a primary setting. This ten-by-ten grid starting from one and ending with one hundred, commonly found in primary classrooms in England and Wales, was seen by some mathematics educators as restricting, particularly in terms of mental calculation. The Empty Number Line (ENL) was introduced as a model in schools in the Netherlands, which helped students visualise the quantity value of numbers. Ian Thompson (1999) makes the useful distinction between the *quantity* value of numbers and the *column* value of digits. He suggests that it is important for students to understand the relative size of numbers, rather than focusing on which column the digits are in. The ENL replaced the practice of partitioning using base ten that encouraged students to concentrate on the column value of numbers.

The ENL is exactly what its name describes; a line which is empty. The emptiness is significant because it discourages students from counting in ones (which we identified above as unhelpful) and provides the scope for flexible approaches. It is also a useful image on which to record calculation steps. Figure 7.4 uses the ENL to solve 53–26.

In this example the 'take away' approach to subtraction is illustrated (rather than the approach which would focus on the 'difference' between the two numbers). The student has started with 53 and counted back first 20, then a further 6. Beishuizen (1999) explains that the benefits of this approach in terms of general mathematics competence are that this supports students' understanding of number and operations: 'dealing with whole numbers supports pupils' understanding and insight into number and number operations much more than the early introduction of vertical algorithms dealing with isolated digits' (p.159).

Other benefits of the ENL as opposed to the hundred square have been identified by Anton Klein and Meindert Beishuizen (1998) as:

- Involving a higher level of mental activation.
- Being a more natural and transparent model for number operations.
- A model open to informal strategies and also providing support for children to develop more formal and efficient strategies.
- A model enhancing the flexibility of mental strategies.

In an earlier study by Gwen (Ineson, 2011) primary trainee teachers were encouraged to use the Empty Number Line to solve simple numerical problems in a variety of ways in preparation for teaching in primary schools. They were encouraged to use the ENL as a

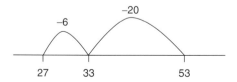

Figure 7.4 One way of using the ENL to solve 53–26.

model to visualise the relationship between the numbers involved in specific calculation problems and as a tool to note steps in their calculations – so that they were working *with* their heads. Initially many trainees were sceptical about the benefits of such an approach as they felt comfortable and confident using the more traditional methods of calculation that they had grown up with. However, after spending time in school, many reported that they found that students were using the ENL well to support their approach to calculation and were beginning to change their opinion about it. Some even claimed to be using the ENL to support their own calculations. However, during one activity focusing on using the ENL for different approaches of subtraction one trainee was heard to say, 'I'm confused, which numbers do I write on the line?' This suggests that the trainee was beginning to use the ENL approach as a procedure, or algorithm, rather than as a conceptual model and was focusing on working *in* the head. This may have been because he was so unfamiliar and uncomfortable with an alternative approach to calculation that his only way to embrace it was to 'learn' it as an algorithm. However, it may be that even fresh approaches become algorithms for many because that's how they have become used to operating within mathematics. Given the level of anxiety that mathematics creates for people, it is not surprising that they will seek the apparent security of algorithms.

> a) *Have you seen the empty number line being used in the primary classroom? Can you think of alternative ways to use the ENL to solve 53–26? Can you think of examples where it could be used to support calculations in secondary classrooms? What alternative jottings have you seen secondary students use to support their calculations?*
>
> b) *How would you solve 2001–999? It was students' perceived over-reliance on formal written methods for problems such as this that was one of the prompts to a focus on mental calculation. Thinking about the arguments in this chapter, how important is it that teachers emphasise alternative approaches to formal written methods?*

Summary

In this chapter, we have investigated some of the debates surrounding mental mathematics, including what it is, its place in the curriculum and how students might be encouraged to engage with it. We offer the viewpoint that it is important for secondary teachers of mathematics to understand and build on the approaches taken to calculating in primary settings. Furthermore it is important for them to be fluent in the strategies that students are likely to make use of so that they are able to encourage students to adopt a more flexible approach, ultimately enabling them to develop relational understanding without an over-reliance on formal written algorithms. Being taught, and subsequently being able to use, specific strategies for mental calculation equips students with the ability to make choices and have a 'toolkit' at their fingertips. So even if they have learnt facts and can recall them (*in* the head), they feel sufficiently confident that they are able to apply what they have learnt to unknown situations (*with* the head).

To conclude, we would like to bring the debate back to where we started, with Gove's new primary curriculum. The emphasis on rote learning times tables and particular procedures for dealing with fractions in primary school suggests a move towards industrial training. Primary and secondary mathematics teachers are tasked with the job of ensuring that children and young people leave with relational understanding of at least some concepts through an emphasis of what they are doing *with* their heads.

Further Reading

Ma, L (1999) *Knowing and Teaching Elementary Mathematics.* Mahwah, NJ: Lawrence Erlbaum. This book has quickly become a classic in mathematics education. Through a comparative study of Chinese and North American primary school teachers, Liping Ma develops her theory that they need a Profound Understanding of Fundamental Mathematics.

Murphy, C. (2011) 'Comparing the use of the empty number line in England and the Netherlands'. *British Educational Research Journal*, 37, 1, 147–161. This article explores the reason for introducing the ENL as a model to support mathematics education in the Netherlands as part of the Realistic Mathematics Education programme. Carol Murphy critiques the way in which this has been adopted in England and suggests that this has led to an algorithmic approach to teaching mental calculation.

Plunkett. S. (1979) 'Decomposition and all that rot', *Mathematics in School*, 8, 3, 2–5. Ever thought about how/why we teach decomposition? A classic article querying the teaching of algorithms.

Skemp, R. R. (1978) 'Relational understanding and instrumental understanding' *Mathematics Teaching*, 77, 20–26. This provides further distinction between these two different ways of understanding mathematics from the originator of the terms.

Thompson, I. (2010) 'Subtraction in Key Stage 3: Which algorithm?' *Mathematics in School*, 39, 1, 29–31. Ian Thompson has written prolifically about mental mathematics but this article continues the debate started in this chapter about algorithms and instrumental understanding.

References

Babbar, S. and Ineson, G. (2013) 'Mental mathematics: a comparison between primary and secondary trainee teachers' strategies', paper presented at British Society for Research into Learning Mathematics. Bristol University, UK. March 2013.

Beishuizen, M. (1997) 'Mental arithmetic: mental recall or mental strategies?', *Mathematics Teaching*, 160, 16–19.

Beishuizen, M. (1999) 'The empty number line as a new model', in I. Thompson (ed), *Issues in teaching and numeracy in primary schools*. Buckingham: Open University Press.

Denvir, H. and Askew, M. (2001) 'Pupils' participation in the classroom examined in relation to "interactive whole class teaching"', *Proceedings of the British Society for Research into Learning Mathematics (BSRLM)*, 21, 1, 25–30.

Department for Education (DfE) (2012a) *National curriculum for mathematics key stages 1 and 2 (Draft)*. London: DfE.

Department for Education (DfE) (2012b) 'Skills Tests FAQs'. Available at: http://www.education. gov.uk/schools/careers/traininganddevelopment/professional/b00211225/skills-test-faqs/faqs-general (accessed 9 August 2012).

Department for Education and Employment (DfEE) (2001) *Framework for teaching mathematics: years 7, 8 and 9*. London: DfEE.

Department for Education and Employment (DfEE) (1998) *The NNS framework for teaching mathematics from reception to year 6*. London: DfEE.

Gove, M. (2012) Secretary of State letter to Tim Oates regarding the National Curriculum review. Available at: http://media.education.gov.uk/assets/files/pdf/l/secretary%20of%20state%20letter%20to%20tim%20oates%20regarding%20the%20national%20curriculum%20review%2011%20june%202012.pdf (accessed 27 January 2013).

Gray, E. M. (1991) 'An analysis of diverging approaches to simple arithmetic: preferences and its consequences', *Educational Studies in Mathematics*, 22, 6, 551–574.

Gray, E. M. and Tall, D. O. (1994) 'Duality, ambiguity and flexibility: a proceptual view of simple arithmetic', *Journal for Research in Mathematics Education*, 25, 2, 115–141.

Klein, A. S. and Beishuizen, M. (1998) 'The empty number line in Dutch second grades: Realistic Versus Gradual program design', *Journal for Research in Mathematics Education*, 29, 4, 443–464.

Ma, L. (1999) *Knowing and teaching elementary mathematics: teachers' understanding of fundamental mathematics in China and the United States*. Mahwah, NJ: Lawrence Erlbaum Associates.

Macintyre, T. and Forrester, R. (2003) 'Strategies for mental calculation', *Proceedings of the British Society for Research into Learning Mathematics (BSRLM)*, 23, 2, 49–54.

Murphy, C. (2004) 'How do children come to use a taught mental calculation strategy?', *Educational Studies in Mathematics*, 56, 1, 3–18.

Office for Standards in Education (Ofsted) (2011) 'Good practice in primary mathematics: evidence from 20 successful schools (Report Summary)'. Available at: http://www.ofsted.gov.uk/resources/good-practice-primary-mathematics-evidence-20-successful-schools (accessed 7 January 2013).

Skemp, R. R. (1978) 'Relational understanding and instrumental understanding', *Mathematics Teaching*, 77, 20–26.

Thompson, I. (1999) 'Implications of research on mental calculation for the teaching of place value', *Curriculum*, 20, 3, 185–191.

TMM (2005) *Teaching mental mathematics from level 5: number*. London: DfES.

Treffers, A. and Beishuizen, M. (1999) 'Realistic mathematics education in the Netherlands', in I. Thompson (ed), *Issues in teaching numeracy in primary schools*. Buckingham: Open University Press.

Chapter 8

System error?

Debating digital technologies in mathematics education

Kenneth Ruthven

One debate dominates all others when it comes to the place of digital technologies in mathematics education: the controversy surrounding the acceptability of calculator use. Whenever the public discusses school standards, or politicians broach revision of the national curriculum, the same sound-bites surface about the 'danger of producing a "Sat-Nav" generation of students overly reliant on technology', who 'reach for a gadget every time they need to do a simple sum'. The opinions that public and politicians express about this all too familiar tool indicate the preoccupations that they bring to any wider consideration of the place of digital technologies in school mathematics. Thus the first half of this chapter will explore the terms of the public debate over calculator use, and then examine the educational reality in more depth. In view of the trend that will emerge in which digital technologies are valued more as pedagogical than mathematical tools, the second half of the chapter will examine how teachers' classroom technology use links to their broader pedagogical orientation. Here, the chapter will consider the continuing debate around the use and value of interactive whiteboards; then it will examine contrasting approaches to the classroom use of dynamic geometry.

THE CALCULATOR IN POPULAR QUESTION

Let's look more closely at a discussion on 'Should the use of calculators be restricted in primary schools?', conducted on the website of the *Guardian* newspaper in December 2011 (Guardian, 2011). Many contributors see the issue as extending as much to secondary schools as primary:

> They should not be used until secondary level and even then their use should be controlled.

> Calculators should be banned throughout school all the way up to A-Level.

Frequently contributions depict the use of calculators by students as antagonistic to thought and subversive of intelligence:

> One of the most important things that a child learns is the ability to think. If you give them a tool that discourages that at such a young age, that aspect of their thinking will be stunted.

> A child's mind needs exercise just as their body does.

Indeed, some comments portray the use of calculators not only as developmentally debilitating but as a morally iniquitous avoidance of mental effort:

> Using a calculator ... rots the brain, not to mention the poor ethic it instils in [students] if they don't work out the answers with hard graft.

> Going straight for the answer is the easy, cheap and wrong way to go.

Where contributions concede that using a calculator does involve a degree of skill, this tends to be presented as distinct from mathematics itself:

> Learning to work a calculator is only learning to work a calculator, not learning how to do maths.

A common suggestion is that access to calculators should be granted students only once they have become confident with number and proficient in mental or written calculation:

> They should learn how basic arithmetic works first, which means doing it either in their head or on paper.

Occasionally, reasons for permitting such use are acknowledged:

> There is an argument for the use of calculators at later levels when the method is more important than the ability to be able do the sum in your head.

> Once the arithmetical capability has been developed, then a calculator can be used as a device which can save time, but until then, ban them entirely.

Some of the contributions are salutary in showing how deeply opposition to calculators is embedded in contributors' sense of personal worth, grounded in their own educational experiences. One such narrative is positive about self, conveying a sense of personal accomplishment associated with mastery of mental and written calculation, expressed in a continuing proud refusal of 'dependence' on the calculator:

> I learned arithmetic the old-fashioned way, using a sums book, following the methods demonstrated by the teacher on the blackboard. By six, I could add and subtract up to a hundred, by eight I had long division and multiplication, and all the tables to ten ... My mathematical skills took me all the way through A-level into degree-level statistics, and then a (boring) first job in Health Service data analysis. I have never owned a stand-alone calculator, and I don't use the one in Mac OS X.

One does wonder how the presence or absence of computer tools, or perhaps an incapacity or reluctance to use them, helped to make that first job in data analysis quite so boring!

Another narrative tells a contrasting story, conveying a sense of personal inadequacy associated with lack of competence and confidence in mental and written calculation, accompanied by regret at 'reliance' on the calculator even for simple computations:

> I grew up not being very competent at maths and even now I tend to rely on calculators for quite basic sums. I very much wish I had that ability to do long division in my head

and that I'd had a good teacher early on in life, because it can be a struggle in the supermarket if you're rubbish at adding and you only have a £10 note on you!

The poignancy here is only sharpened by a suspicion that, in 'the ability to do long division in my head', someone is aspiring to a misconceived notion of arithmetic proficiency.

A last narrative conjures up a very different type of personal history, offering a sense of how, for some students at least, calculators might serve as a catalyst for developing interest and capability with numbers:

> I am really good at mental arithmetic, but as a child abhorred rote learning of times tables, couldn't see the point as I could work them out in an instant. It almost alienated me completely from maths. Luckily, playing with calculators ... rekindled my interest in number games. So when I was older and scientific calculators starting coming in ... I used to play with it, especially the functions that worked out means and standard deviations. That set me up well for the types of maths I used in later life, inferential statistics.

Nevertheless, even this positive narrative of a beneficial experience of calculator use hardly challenges the common criticisms. First, this story relates to someone already capable in mental arithmetic, who has thus passed the threshold where calculator use is considered by many to become acceptable. Second, talk of 'playing' with calculators and the focus on rekindling 'interest' in numbers will, for those so minded, tend only to confirm the association of calculators with an insufficiently serious approach to learning mathematics.

The main thrust of those contributions that reject an oppositional stance to calculators is less to argue for their use than to minimise their significance, suggesting that current school practice continues to emphasise mental and written calculation, and makes only sparing use of calculators which is carefully guided:

> I work in a primary school and have to say the children there do far more mental arithmetic than I ever did. We sometimes use calculators to check answers or play mathematical games. There is a heavy emphasis on developing mental arithmetic and written forms of calculation. We also do a lot of investigative based work as well as using and applying mathematical knowledge. This has been the case in all of the primary schools I've seen mathematics taught in.

What seems to be missing here is any more positive argument; for example, along the lines that access to a calculator can enable students to tackle more challenging investigations and problems, allowing them to focus on strategic and conceptual matters by removing some of the burden of computation, while still calling for intelligent cross-checking of results.

Another contribution of this type concludes in less defensive mode, arguing for the importance of preparing students to use a range of mathematical tools, including calculators:

> Primary school children are currently taught a range of 'mental maths' techniques which allow them different methods to work out calculations in their heads very quickly ... Calculators are not used on a day-to-day basis and children have to work things out either in their heads or with pencil and paper. Teaching children how to use a calculator should be included in the curriculum. It is just another tool that children can use.

Indeed, some comments do make a positive case based on the ubiquity of computational technologies such as the calculator in most workplaces:

> Calculators are an integral part of working life for those who work in figure-related jobs so why pretend to children that they are not an acceptable part of maths?

And this same contribution continues in a way that challenges the popular idea that use of calculators in school entails the abandonment of learning to calculate mentally:

> But that doesn't mean that kids should not be taught how to do mental arithmetic, nor that they should be dispensed from practicing and improving their abilities regularly. On the contrary, those skills are very important in all our daily lives. Just ask those who can't do any mental arithmetic.

> *If you were participating in this online discussion of calculator use in schools, which contributions would you recommend? What response would you make to contributions that you disagree with?*

The debate around calculators is particularly instructive because they are the first type of digital mathematical tool to become available in a form and at a cost that makes it feasible for them to become part of the standard mathematical toolkit of every student. As such, the fate of calculators may well prefigure that of other mathematical technologies as these become more readily and widely available, particularly in forms that makes them suited to becoming personal tools for students. An important weakness, however, of public discussion is that it is generally poorly informed about how digital technologies are actually used in classrooms, and what educational considerations underlie such use. The next section, then, will provide a fuller and deeper analysis of the educational use of calculators, informed by professional literature and relevant research.

THE CALCULATOR IN EDUCATIONAL ACTION

As far as England, at least, is concerned, a suitable starting point for a history of serious attempts to think through calculator use in schools might be 1977, the year in which one of Her Majesty's Inspectors of Schools proposed that basic numeracy should be redefined as 'the ability to use a four-function electronic calculator *sensibly*'. Studies of workplace mathematics, initiated around the same time, reported that calculators had dramatically reduced the use of traditional written methods for all kinds of calculations, and indeed that the computerisation of work processes was increasingly automating any calculation required. Findings of extensive use of informal mental strategies by both adults and children led to a suggestion that: 'With mental methods ... as the principal means for doing simple calculations ... calculators ... are the sensible tool for difficult calculations, the ideal complement to mental arithmetic' (Plunkett, 1979, p.5).

Such ideas and findings, and the practical experiments that they stimulated, laid the ground for a pioneering government-supported project which piloted a 'calculator aware' number curriculum for primary schools, during the late 1980s (Shuard *et al.*, 1991). Key principles of this curriculum included:

- Tackling a challenging range of practical and investigational tasks.
- Encouraging a spirit of exploration of 'how numbers work'.
- Emphasising the importance of mental calculation, and treating it as first resort.
- Treating use of a calculator as the normal fall-back means of calculation.
- No longer teaching traditional written methods of calculation.

Research found that, at the end of primary education, students who had followed such a curriculum were more willing to calculate mentally, and more capable of doing so, employing relatively powerful and efficient strategies (Ruthven, 1998).

This same body of research showed how using a calculator is far from being the unthinking process of popular repute: it is not simply a matter of operating the machine, but one of formulating computations and interpreting their results, understanding how these are expressed in the specific terms of the device (Ruthven and Chaplin, 1997). For example, using the calculator to carry out 'division' involves grasping the relationship between other forms of division operation and number representation and the particular form privileged by calculators. Moreover, using the calculator to solve a problem may depend on carrying out a chain of computations, interpreting each result and formulating the next step accordingly. Consider, for example, the 11-year-olds in Figures 8.1 and 8.2, each talking through their use of a calculator to solve the problem: *313 people are going on a coach trip. Each coach can carry up to 42 passengers. How many coaches will be needed? How many spare places will be left on the coaches?*

What are the strengths and weaknesses of the approaches to solving the problem shown in Figures 8.1 and 8.2?

How feasible would these approaches be without access to a calculator, and how does using a calculator affect the form that they take?

The example shown of calculator quotient-and-remainder division (Figure 8.1) illustrates a situation in which the result from the particular type of division carried out by the calculator has to be interpreted by the user and reformulated in terms of the type of division sought. Indeed, you might find it surprising that the English national curriculum for mathematics expects students to learn a written method of quotient-and-remainder division but not a calculator one. However, what that national curriculum did come quickly to recognise is the value of technology in pursuing iterative trial-and-improvement strategies: the example of calculator trial-and-improvement multiplication (Figure 8.2) illustrates how the low 'cost' of calculator computation makes this type of approach much more feasible; offloading the burden of computation allows the calculator user to focus attention on monitoring the result of each trial and revising the estimate accordingly. (Interestingly, a few minutes prior to tackling this task the student had multiplied a two-digit number by 10 mentally, suggesting that keying 42×10 here was a matter of maintaining a pattern of working with the calculator rather than of not being able to do such a calculation mentally.) In modifying

"313 divided by 42"
Keys 313 ÷ 42 = 7.452380952
"About 7 and a half coaches"
Keys 7 × 42 = 294
"So we'd need one more coach"
Keys 294 + 42 = 336
"8 coaches"
Keys 336 – 313 = 23
"23 spares"

Figure 8.1 Calculator quotient-and-remainder division.

Keys 42 × 12 = 504
"42 times any number but
 it was a bit high"
Keys 42 × 10 = 420
Keys 42 × 8 = 336
"They'd need 8 coaches and
 they'd have" (calculating
 mentally) "23 places left over"

Figure 8.2 Calculator trial-and-improvement multiplication.

Keys 313 ÷ 42 = 7.452380952
"Not that many coaches
 I can't read it."
Keys 313 × 42 = 13146
"No, you need to know how
 many 42s there are in 313"
Keys 42 ÷ 313 = 0.134185303
"No"

Figure 8.3 Difficulty in interpreting result of calculator division.

estimates downwards when they produce excessive results, the student displays understanding of how the number of places will vary with the number of coaches. Likewise, in view of the quick recognition of when an optimal value has been reached, it seems that the student is also monitoring proximity to a solution.

Nevertheless, this same low cost of computation means that students are also more able to follow through superficial and misconceived strategies with an ease that mental and written calculation rarely permit. One example is shown in Figure 8.3, where a student, unable to interpret the calculator output from a correctly formulated division, pursues two variations which, while they are not wholly unreasonable, are superficial: using the inverse operation and reversing the operands. This provides the teacher with a greater insight into the student's thinking, thanks to the calculator enabling that thinking to be expressed more fully. Likewise, while we might like students to be able to successfully carry out a

"I'm trying to work out how
many 42s in 313 but I don't
know how many"
Keys 313 ÷ 42 = 7.452380952
"Well you'd probably get 7
coaches but you'd have
some left"

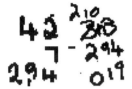

"7 coaches and 19 spare seats"

Figure 8.4 Calculator 'repair' of written computation.

written division with a two-digit divisor (although experience indicates that many struggle to learn to do so), having a calculator to hand enabled the student in the example shown in Figure 8.4 to 'repair' the 'breakdown' in their use of the written algorithm, only to fall at the final hurdle of interpreting the results. This emphasises the distinction between carrying out a computation procedure – whether mental, written or calculator – and interpreting the results; here it is all too easy to jump to associating the quotient with the number of coaches and the remainder with the number of seats left over. Weak interpretation, then, can be as much associated with written calculation as with calculator use (see the chapters by Richard Barwell and Hamsa Venkat for discussions of the complexities of 'interpretation').

These examples give an indication of how using calculators makes some powerful ways of mathematical thinking possible for students. They also show how less intelligent use of calculators by students can still give their teacher distinctive insights that can help diagnose and develop their mathematical thinking.

I have focused on the arithmetic calculator because it illustrates, in an accessible way, key issues that recur when more sophisticated but less-known and -used technologies for mathematical computation such as graph plotting, computer algebra, dynamic geometry and statistical analysis are brought into play in mathematics teaching. The calculator remains the popular archetype of a mathematical technology; and the ideas and attitudes that surround it provide templates for the thinking that emerges around the educational use of other mathematical technologies.

Over the late 1980s and early 1990s, the trend was towards an expectation that students should become effective users of calculators – not just arithmetic and scientific but graphic, even symbolic (i.e. handheld computer algebra systems) – and that this should be taken as a central element of an enlarged notion of mathematical proficiency. However, as it became clearer how such developments touched directly on prized skills that had long been taken as basic components of school mathematics, government intervention pressed curriculum and examinations to become more 'calculator beware' than 'calculator aware'. In particular, when calculator use was still permitted in examination papers, questions were rarely framed in ways that required such use, let alone rewarded capability in it; this gave little encouragement to teachers and students to become thoughtful and effective users of the technology. This retrenchment over the late 1990s positioned digital technologies less as tools underpinning new forms of mathematical proficiency, more as pedagogical aids supporting the development of proficiency along largely traditional lines; as the capability of an individual working independently of any technology, rather than as the capacity of the combined human/machine system.

Choose another mathematical technology that you are familiar with (for example, a spreadsheet, graphing or geometry package), and which you have some experience of in educational use.

What parallels can you see with the discussion here of calculators? What differences do you think need to be taken into account?

'INTERACTIVE' TEACHING AND 'INTERACTIVE' TECHNOLOGY

From the 2000s onwards then, the drive in English schools has been towards viewing digital technologies more as pedagogical than mathematical tools. Concern has shifted towards harnessing technology as a support, typically as a dynamic visual aid or a rapid feedback provider, in teaching towards a traditional mathematical proficiency quite independent of technology use. A widespread development has been to equip classrooms with a touch-sensitive 'interactive' whiteboard (IWB), or, failing that, with a digital projector, connected to a school network or teacher laptop.

The introduction of IWBs coincided with a national programme of school improvement, the National Strategies (see the chapter by Gwen Ineson and Sunita Babbar), which promoted a model of direct 'interactive' whole-class teaching that emphasised the role of the teacher in demonstrating, explaining and questioning. Although the pamphlet produced to promote use of IWBs in teaching secondary mathematics (DfES, 2004) did make some connections between the contrasting technological and pedagogical notions of 'interactive', the term has become an underexamined buzzword. The pamphlet suggested that, by enabling teachers to demonstrate and present ideas in exciting and dynamic ways which actively engage students, IWBs could improve their motivation and involvement, and their understanding of new concepts. The pamphlet also recommended preparing lessons around a single IWB file to support smooth retrieval and seamless use of resources by the teacher, improving the flow and pace of lessons.

The main debate has been around whether the very substantial investment of schools in IWBs has been pedagogically beneficial. The health-of-the-system reports produced periodically by the Office for Standards in Education (Ofsted) have described the main types of use that have developed in mathematics classrooms, identifying both positive and negative features. On the credit side:

> Good practice included the use of high-quality diagrams and relevant software to support learning through, for example, construction of graphs or visualisation of transformations. Pupils enjoyed quick-fire games on them.
>
> Ofsted (2008, p.27)

On the debit side:

> However, many of the curricular and guidance documents seen did not draw sufficient attention to the potential of interactive whiteboards. Additionally, too often teachers used them simply for PowerPoint presentations with no interaction by the pupils.
>
> Ofsted (2008, p.27)

It seems, then, that classroom use of electronic whiteboards has often been barely interactive in either the technological or pedagogical senses. Moreover, the emphasis on whole-class teaching through interactive whiteboards appears to have led to a reduction in students' experience with other potentially valuable types of educational resource:

> A negative effect of interactive whiteboards was a reduction in pupils' use of practical equipment: software is no replacement for hands-on experience, for example in measuring angles and lengths.
>
> Ofsted (2008, p.28)

Evidence from Australia, based on comparing lessons in which IWBs were used with those in which they were not, suggests that these perverse patterns are not peculiar to the English situation. Far from supporting pedagogical interactivity, it seems that the electronic whiteboard often diminishes it.

> [T]he technologically impressive features of the IWB can lead to it being used to close down further the possibility of rich communications and interactions in the classroom as teachers are seduced by the IWB's ability to capture pupils' attention. We suspect, also, that teachers' advance preparation for using the IWB, often via the ubiquitous PowerPoint package or pre-prepared lessons for the IWB, means that they will be less likely to deviate from their planning in response to pupils' needs and indeed might notice pupils' needs less frequently through the possibility to increase the pacing of mathematics lessons.
>
> Zevenbergen and Lerman (2008, p.124)

In the debate about the educational value of IWBs, then, positions tend to reflect broader pedagogical preferences (as Margaret Brown elaborates in her analysis of curriculum policy in her chapter). Many teachers prize the IWB as an efficient support for fast-paced, objectives-driven, teacher-led lessons, but often use it in a restricted way. Some teachers appreciate the IWB as a means of supporting whole-class experimentation and discussion, but see this as complementary to forms of technology which support students in working more independently, either individually or in small groups.

> *Think back to mathematics lessons that you have seen in which interactive whiteboards have been used.*
>
> *What are more, and less, productive examples of an interactive whiteboard in use?*
>
> *In your overall experience, what (if any) are the main ways in which the use of interactive whiteboards in mathematics teaching is beneficial?*

PEDAGOGICAL ORIENTATION AND TECHNOLOGY INTEGRATION

There is, then, a more fundamental pedagogical debate underlying the question of how best to integrate use of digital technologies into the mathematics classroom. This extends to the use of digital mathematical tools such as spreadsheets, graphing and geometry packages. Consider two lessons, both employing dynamic geometry software to examine the sum of the interior angles of a polygon (Ruthven, Hennessy and Deaney, 2008).

In one lesson, a single computer is projected to the whole class with dynamic figures manipulated only by the teacher. In his view, 'it would take a long time … for [students] to master the package' and 'the return from the time investment … would be fairly small', so that 'the cost benefit doesn't pay'. For him, the payoff from using this technology is a faster-paced lesson that holds the attention of students.

> [It] keeps the lesson moving at a good pace. It holds their attention, because its movement is dynamic, the numbers come up. So they're not sitting there for a long time doing nothing, while I'm standing drawing and measuring on the board.

As well as the ease of displaying prepared figures, and the attentive response of students to dynamic manipulation, the teacher attributes this faster pace to the ready comprehensibility of material presented this way.

> I was able to change the shape of each of the shapes … to drag the triangle around, to make different triangles … so the students could actually see that happening in a dynamic way.

He accompanies his presentation with questioning intended to maintain students' attention and regulate progression through the lesson.

> In terms of paying attention … [I] asked students around the classroom, at random almost, what the answers were, not necessarily the ones with their hands up, just to make sure that they were always keeping on their toes and thinking and not drifting through the lesson.

In another contrasting lesson, students work with the software in small groups around shared laptops (and later discuss their work as a class through the IWB). Their teacher is concerned about potential technical demands on students, often choosing 'to structure the work so [students] just have to move points [on a prepared figure]', so that 'they don't have to be complicated by that, they really can just focus on what's happening mathematically'. On this occasion, however, she feels that asking students to work from scratch to create dynamic figures would give them a better appreciation of the geometric relations defining the figure.

> The package is geometry-based, and it is from-first-principles geometry ... One of the main parts of this lesson was that they could learn the software, and have some idea of how shapes and points relate to each other, and to see that the software works geometrically.

The teacher recognises that students are likely to encounter some difficulties but sees resolving these as productive for their mathematical learning.

> I wanted to draw attention to ... how the software measures the smaller angle, thus reinforcing that there are two angles at a point and they needed to work out the other ... Because a lot of them had found that they'd got the wrong answers, and [that] it measured the obtuse angle rather than the reflex angle.

Indeed, the most significant contrast between the lessons is the form of mathematical thinking expected of students. A crucial difference lies in how the respective teachers handle the apparent mathematical anomalies which arise when dynamic figures are dragged to positions where an angle becomes reflex (with the associated measurement problem), or where rounded values obscure an arithmetical relationship between measures (Figure 8.5). The first teacher takes great care to avoid exposing students to apparent anomalies of these types, through vigilant dragging to avoid 'possibilities where students may become confused, or things that might cloud the issue'. The second teacher actively wants students to encounter such anomalies so as to become more critical in their mathematical thinking.

> For me, success is when the kids produce something and then say 'This can't be right because it's not what I expect' ... [That] was one of the key things that the kids learned, that you can't assume that what you've got in front of you is actually what you want, and you have to look at it ... and question it.

This approach reflects a pedagogical orientation that views analysis of such discrepancies as supporting deeper learning and developing more flexible mathematical thinking. This

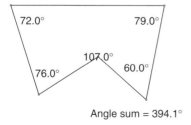

Angle sum = 394.1°

Figure 8.5 Dynamic geometry figure for establishing the angle sum of a pentagon.

discussion of the pedagogic use of examples is taken up by Tim Rowland in the next chapter.

What types of classroom use of technology do you particularly value? How does this reflect your views on teaching and learning mathematics?

Relate this, if possible, to your own experience of planning and conducting lessons in which technology is used.

Conclusion

In this chapter I have focused on issues and examples that are particularly relevant to the current state of English schools. Given the fairly conservative policy on technology integration now found there, it has become necessary to look to other educational systems for more adventurous uses of mathematical technology. In recent years, much of the further-reaching investigation of the integration of dynamic geometry and computer algebra has taken place in French secondary schools, and latterly in the Netherlands. Relevant references feature in the further reading for this chapter.

There is one simple conclusion that can be drawn from the examination of students' and teachers' mathematical and pedagogical use of digital tools in this chapter: it is all too easy to underestimate or overlook the expertise required to make effective use of such tools. Time and again, experience has shown that, however apparently simple and straightforward the technology, effective use depends on developing appropriate expertise, well coordinated with other mathematical and pedagogical knowledge: this is the central idea of the theory of 'instrumentation'. All too often, however, students and teachers are expected just to pick new technologies up and go, with little opportunity to learn about, and to develop further, powerful uses and techniques.

Further reading

Artigue, M. (2002) 'Learning mathematics in a CAS environment: The genesis of a reflection about instrumentation and the dialectics between technical and conceptual work', *International Journal of Computers for Mathematical Learning*, 7, 3, 245–274. Theoretically oriented overview, from France, of the challenges of developing a pre-calculus course around use of symbolic calculators in the face of established approaches to the topic. A classic exposition of the idea of instrumentation.

Drijvers, P. and Gravemeijer, K. (2005) 'Computer algebra as an instrument: examples of algebraic schemes', in D. Guin, K. Ruthven and L. Trouche (eds), *The didactical challenge of symbolic calculators: Turning a computational device into a mathematical instrument*. New York: Springer. Detailed analysis, from the Netherlands, of how students use a symbolic calculator to handle algebraic expressions and equations, particularly those involving a parameter or multiple variables. An accessible introduction to the idea of instrumentation.

Laborde, C. (2001) 'Integration of technology in the design of geometry tasks with Cabri-geometry', *International Journal of Computers for Mathematical Learning*, 6, 3, 283–317. Careful exemplification, from France, of the progressive rethinking of geometry teaching at lower-secondary level. Teachers exploit dynamic software to redesign curricular tasks so as to enhance student learning and support new forms of reasoning.

Ruthven, K., Deaney, R. and Hennessy, S. (2009) 'Using graphing software to teach about algebraic forms: A study of technology-supported practice in secondary-school mathematics', *Educational Studies in Mathematics*, 71, 3, 279–297. Detailed analysis, from England, of the mathematical and pedagogical reasoning guiding experienced teachers' use of graph-plotting software in lower-secondary mathematics.

References

Department for Education and Skills (DfES) (2004) *Use of interactive whiteboards in mathematics*. London: DfES.

Guardian (2011) Should the Use of Calculators be Restricted in Primary Schools? Available at: http://www.guardian.co.uk/commentisfree/poll/2011/dec/02/should-calculators-be-restricted?INTCMP=SRCH (accessed 11 January 2013).

Office for Standards in Education (Ofsted) (2008) *Mathematics: understanding the score*. London: Ofsted.

Plunkett, S. (1979) 'Decomposition and all that rot', *Mathematics in School*, 8, 3, 2–5.

Ruthven, K. (1998) 'The use of mental, written and calculator strategies of numerical computation by upper-primary pupils within a "calculator-aware" number curriculum', *British Educational Research Journal*, 24, 1, 21–42.

Ruthven, K. and Chaplin, D. (1997) 'The calculator as a cognitive tool: Upper-primary pupils tackling a realistic number problem', *International Journal of Computers for Mathematical Learning*, 2, 2, 93–124.

Ruthven, K., Hennessy, S. and Deaney, R. (2008) 'Constructions of dynamic geometry: a study of the interpretative flexibility of educational software in classroom practice', *Computers and Education*, 51, 1, 297–317.

Shuard, H., Walsh, A., Goodwin, J. and Worcester, V. (1991) *Calculators, children and mathematics*. London: Simon and Schuster.

Zevenbergen, R. and Lerman, S. (2008) 'Learning environments using interactive whiteboards: new learning spaces or reproduction of old technologies?', *Mathematics Education Research Journal*, 20, 1, 108–126.

Chapter 9

The role of examples in mathematics teaching

Tim Rowland

This chapter is about some of the ways that teachers use examples in mathematics teaching, and aims to raise your awareness of the importance of choosing and using them with care. Contrasting but complementary approaches to examples in mathematics are explored in the chapters by Richard Barwell, Heather Mendick and Marie-Pierre Moreau, Hilary Povey, Leo Rogers and Hamsa Venkat.

> *Imagine that you are planning a lesson on pie charts as a way of representing relative frequency. Your objective is that the students will be able to construct pie charts from a frequency table. You decide to explain with a worked example; but which one? The options available to you are limitless. What will you choose? Why choose these numbers for your data? Perhaps a second worked example would be good as well – what will it be?*

For the last ten years, together with various colleagues, I have been observing and analysing mathematics lessons to see how teachers make use of their mathematical knowledge as they teach. We identified about 20 general factors connecting this knowledge to what teachers do in the classroom. It turned out that the most prevalent factor, present many times in every lesson, was the choice and use of examples. But different examples play different roles, and are used for different purposes. The aim of this chapter is to describe and explore these roles and purposes.

WAYS OF USING EXAMPLES

Quite a few teachers introduce the focus of the lesson by asking for a definition: 'What is a pie chart?', 'What is a fraction?', 'What is symmetry?'. Sometimes, rather than asking for a definition – of a fraction, for example – it can be more productive to invite students to offer *examples* of fractions, to see what variety they produce. A fruitful approach is to ask for one example, then another, and another … each one being in some way different from the last one. This teases out the range of things that they would count as fractions, and what they believe can be varied while remaining within the concept of fraction. Does anyone offer an integer (e.g. 3)? Or a decimal number (e.g. 0.137)? What do you think about these two examples? Do they 'count' in your opinion? Why? This discussion could go a long way – if you do allow decimal numbers, then what about infinite decimals?

Teachers mainly use examples in mathematics teaching in two ways. The first is in connection with teaching mathematical concepts and procedures. The second is the provision of exercises for students. These two kinds of use are different, and may require different choices. Most of this chapter is focused on these two purposes, but examples fulfil two more important roles: as counterexamples and 'generic' examples. These will be discussed towards the end of this chapter.

Teaching concepts and procedures

In order to teach something, we often provide students (or ask them to provide) examples *of* the thing to be learnt. The 'thing' is *general* in character (e.g. the notion of rotational symmetry, or a procedure for solving a quadratic equation); the examples are *particular* instances of the generality. The fractions example was chosen to illustrate an approach to *teaching a concept*. When Jason began a Year 2 lesson by asking 'What is a fraction?', George replied 'It's a number, a line and then another number'. You might think about the adequacy of George's definition, and about alternative definitions. For example, do you want to distinguish between rational numbers and fractions? Do you consider $\frac{2}{3}$ and $\frac{4}{6}$ to be equal fractions, or the same fraction? Do you want to emphasise particular *representations* of fractions in your definition (a number of equal parts of a whole, say), or fraction *notation* (which is also a representation) referring to numerator and denominator (as George did)? Do you want to restrict to 'vulgar' fractions, or include decimal fractions?

In any case, as indicated earlier, some of these considerations would arise if you asked for examples of fractions. Likewise, if the target concept were 'factor', you would want to find examples of pairs of whole numbers such that one is a factor of the other, like 7 and 21. The pair 13, 611 might be less helpful as an introductory example, because the effort to determine whether 13 divides into 611 'exactly' might become a distraction. On the other hand, the same example might be ideal as an assessment or practice exercise.

Similarly, we *teach a general procedure* by a particular demonstration of that procedure. For example, if we were going to teach solving two simultaneous linear equations by elimination, we could choose two linear equations (in two variables), and demonstrate how to construct equivalent linear equations sharing one variable with the same coefficient. Typically, if we want students to see *why* the procedure works (to gain 'relational understanding', as Gwen Ineson and Sunita Babbar discuss in their chapter), we build in a kind of commentary with the demonstration, to explain what is going on, and to draw attention to potential difficulties and pitfalls. If you started with this example:

$$3x + 10y = 22$$
$$x + 2y = 6$$

you would probably realise that it fails to demonstrate what to do in some other cases, and feel that you ought to do one or two more before setting exercises for the class. In your earlier consideration of examples of pie charts, you may have considered that 4 or 5 categories (sectors) would keep an introductory example reasonably simple; and that having the sum of the frequencies equal to a factor of 360 will assist understanding to begin with.

Eddie Gray and David Tall (1994) pointed out that the learning of concepts and the learning of procedures are not unrelated. Many concepts grow out of familiarity with a procedure. They capture this duality in the word '*procept*': a procept is both an abstract mathematical 'thing', or concept, and also a procedure intimately associated with the concept. Anna Sfard (1991, 2008), using different language, observed that abstract mathematical notions can be viewed both *operationally*, as processes; and *structurally*, as objects. She uses the word *reification* to describe the mental transition from process to object. When we speak of addition and subtraction being 'inverse operations', we have certainly reified both addition and subtraction.

The second major use of examples in teaching is usually directed towards familiarisation and practice, *after* a new idea or method has been introduced. Examples in this instance are often called *exercises*. Exercises *are* examples, usually selected from a wide range of possible examples. Suppose you had taught a class how to solve simultaneous linear equations in two variables, by elimination. After your introduction, you might well want the students to try some exercises themselves, perhaps in groups, and a few more for homework, to assist retention of the procedure by repetition, then to develop fluency with it. Sometimes such exercises are also a means of assessment, from the teacher's perspective (see the discussion of Assessment for Learning in the chapter by Rachel Marks and Alice J. Onion). Practice does not need to be drudgery: sometimes it can lead to different kinds of awareness and understanding. Again, the selection of such examples is neither trivial nor arbitrary. Why choose some of them in preference to others?

> *Propose about five examples of simultaneous linear equations, in sequence, which you could use when introducing solution by eliminating variables.*

Summing up, my main point is that examples are used all the time in mathematics teaching, and for several different reasons. But whatever their purpose, the examples provided by a teacher ought, ideally, to be the outcome of a careful process of *choice*, a *deliberate* and informed selection, because some are simply 'better' than others. Now I want to introduce and consider in detail one particular lesson, thinking about the teacher's choice of examples, and setting out some principles for choosing.

John's lesson: quadratic functions

John was in the later stages of an initial teacher education (PGCE) secondary mathematics course, and a participant in a research project looking at how teachers use their mathematical knowledge in the classroom. For this lesson, John was teaching a Year 9 class (age 13–14) in a non-selective state school.

The focus was on quadratic functions (polynomials), and finding equivalent expressions by completing the square (CTS). The aim was to apply CTS, which they had met in a previous lesson, in two ways: to solve quadratic equations, and to find the minimum point of quadratic functions. These two techniques were then to be used to sketch graphs of quadratic functions. CTS is not usually introduced this early in the UK, but these students were following an accelerated mathematics course, and John judged that they were 'ready'.

John began by reminding the class about the procedure for CTS by working an example, showing that $x^2 + 6x + 8 = (x + 3)^2 - 1$. Then he gave the students these five expressions to try CTS for themselves:

$x^2 - 8x + 14$, $x^2 + 2x - 8$, $x^2 + 6x + 5$, $x^2 + 3x - 1$, $2x^2 + 4x - 2$.

Later he worked through each example on the board, interacting with ideas from the students.

Following this introduction, John demonstrated solving the equation $x^2 + 8x + 14 = 0$ by CTS, then asked the students to find the zeros of the original expressions. While they were busy, he attempted to activate a graphing package on his laptop, but without success, so later he reviewed some of the examples 'manually', without the graph-sketching software.

John then proceeded to explain how to sketch $y = x^2 + 6x + 8$, finding the minimum value using CTS. The zeros of the function, –2 and –4, had been found earlier, and these were used to identify where the graph intersects the x-axis.

He set the students $y = x^2 + 6x + 5$ to sketch as an exercise, and 'went over' it later. The lesson concluded with sketching $2x^2 + 4x - 2$, when John invited as many students as possible to contribute to a collaborative solution.

> *Look at John's examples. Do you think they were well-chosen? Why? In what ways might you have chosen differently, and why?*

John's choice of examples

John used six expressions as examples. I knew that John had selected them in advance, because they were listed in his lesson plan. So why these examples? After school, the same day, we looked at some episodes from a video of the lesson with John, and I asked him:

TR: What made you pick those six examples?

John was able to articulate reasons for his choices.

JOHN: They all have real solutions was the first thing, umm, so that when sketching them they can use the whole "oh I have got two solutions, it crosses twice, it's a U-shape" … got one odd coefficient of x, cos they had had a bit of practice of that and if the focus was going to be on sketching there's no need to have sort of overly complicated, umm, squaring point fives and stuff in there cos they can already do that.

Umm, and the bottom example [$2x^2 + 4x - 2$] was chosen because you can take a factor of 2 out, and I thought that might be good for when we were talking about the difference between an expression and an equation; because if you are solving that you'd say "I'll divide both sides by two", whereas if you're just putting it into a completing the square form as an expression, you can't say that and so you have to take 2 out as a factor.

TR: So if you like, you kind of invented these, with those factors in mind.

JOHN: Yes.

TR: OK. So what, what made you pick on the $x^2 + 6x + 8$ for this particular …

JOHN: That's the only one, the only one that factorises, I think. Well I know it factorises but I'm not sure if any of the others do. That factorises so that you get the solutions −1 and −5, which means that they will be able to draw the graph more easily, sketch it more easily, rather than getting a daft surd, to try and draw on their *x*-axis, just to make … ease the drawing on their own for the first time.

> *How does John's explanation of his choice of examples compare with your own analysis of them? Did he consider any factors in addition to the ones that you identified? Did you take into account any factors that John doesn't mention?*

Dimensions of variation

Before continuing with John's lesson, I want to introduce a way of thinking about examples proposed by Ference Marton. Marton's Theory of Variation proposes that humans learn by becoming aware of the different ways in which things can vary, and therefore variation needs to be experienced by the learner. In essence, we learn from discerning variation, and what varies in our experience influences what we learn. The provision of examples must therefore take into account the 'dimensions of variation' (Marton and Booth, 1997) inherent in the objects of attention. Anne Watson and John Mason (2005, p.108) explore this position, from the perspective of mathematics teachers:

> Marton proposed that we learn from discerning variation in simultaneous situations. What varies in a lesson is an important influence on what is learnt. The provision of examples becomes an exercise in deciding how to vary the examples so that learners will learn what we hope they will learn, and trying to minimise other variations which are irrelevant or distracting.

Learning the concept of 'square', for example, is marked by growing awareness of the various ways that squares can vary (dimensions of variation, such as side length, orientation and colour), and the variants that do not qualify as squares (beyond permissible change, such as number of sides, relative side-lengths and angles).

John's examples

Now look at John's six quadratic functions again, and his reasons for the choice, this time through the lens of variation theory. We can think about a quadratic function in various representations, principally its symbolic expression (the 'formula') $ax^2 + bx + c$, but also its visual representation as a Cartesian graph – a parabola of some sort. In the symbolic form, the 'parameters' a, b, c correspond to dimensions of variation.

The choice of the variable 'a' contributes to the complexity, or otherwise, of CTS. When $a > 1$, the factor a needs to be taken out, rewriting the expression as $a[x^2 + b'x + c']$ first. In fact all of John's examples have $a = 1$, except the one they did together at the very end. He probably judged that in their very first encounter with CTS, this dimension of variation would best be left fixed, but doesn't comment on it in the interview. Permissible variations for 'a' also include $a < 0$ and a not an integer, both probably best delayed to another lesson.

Notice that John also comments on his last example, $2x^2 + 4x - 2$, in terms of the students' learning to distinguish between *expressions* (formula for functions) and *equations* (statements satisfied only by the zeros of the function). When he divides $2x^2 + 4x - 2$ by 2, the expression changes but the solutions of the equation stay the same.

Suppose, like John, we fix $a = 1$, and consider the variable 'b'. The complexity of CTS is significantly reduced when b is even. When b is odd CTS involves, in John's words 'squaring point fives and stuff', and the arithmetic is just a bit more messy. The first four of John's examples have even values of b. The sign of b is another dimension of variation, and his second example introduces a negative (but even) value.

In the final example, when $a = 2$, b is chosen to be 4. This has the advantage that the coefficient of x remains an even integer after the factor 2 has been taken out of the expression.

The choice of the variable 'c' does not affect the complexity of CTS so much, but John includes positive and negative values of c in any case.

In the interview, John begins by referring to the *graphical* representation of the quadratic functions when explaining his choices. He is thinking about the dimensions of variation of the graph, and how these affect the complexity of the task of sketching it. His approach to sketching quadratics in the lesson was: (a) decide whether the parabola is a 'U' or an upside-down 'U', by reference to the sign of the coefficient 'a'; (b) find where the graph intersects the x-axis, corresponding to the solutions of the quadratic equation; (c) find the minimum (or maximum, if $a < 0$) value of the function by CTS, and check that the x-coordinate of this point is half-way between the x-intercepts. John's first concern, in the interview, was that the roots of the equations should be real, so that the x-intercepts could be found and used in the sketch. He also says that he chose $x^2 + 6x + 8$ for the first sketch because it factorises, and so the x-intercepts will neatly be at integers on that axis, 'rather than getting a daft surd'. You may have observed that his roots of -1, -5 in the interview are incorrect, and that two more expressions factorise, but this does not undermine his reasoning.

Heidi

We make a brief visit to a Year 8 (age 12–13) class taught by Heidi, another secondary PGCE participant in the same project as John. Heidi was revising simultaneous equations, and started by asking the class how they would solve

$$2x + 3y = 16$$
$$2x + 5y = 20$$

She expected the students to eliminate x by subtraction, but to her surprise they preferred to eliminate y (one suggestion was to multiply the equations by 10 and 6, respectively, and subtract). Later, in a meeting with us, Heidi remarked that the class often seemed to prefer to eliminate y, but she didn't know why. Now, Heidi had given them a rule to help them decide whether to add or subtract the two equations (once the coefficients of one variable had been made equal), and the rule depended on whether the coefficients of the variable to be eliminated had the same sign or not. Later in the interview, Heidi realised that the sign of the coefficients of y would always be *explicit* whereas, in the examples they had encountered so far, the coefficients of x were always positive, and their signs therefore *implicit* (e.g. $2x$ rather than $+2x$). Heidi then realised that restricting the x-coefficients to positive values (and emphasising the 'rule') could explain the preference for eliminating y, even when eliminating x would appear to be simpler.

Examples to avoid

A 'dimensions of variation' analysis of a concept or process identifies a few key, independent variables in any mathematical situation (such as the three coefficients in a quadratic expression). When choosing examples to *introduce* a topic, it is usually wise to keep the values of these different variables *distinct* in one example.

Kirsty was reviewing the topic of Cartesian co-ordinates with her Year 7 (age 11–12) students. She began by asking the children for a definition of co-ordinates. One student volunteered that 'the horizontal line is first and then the vertical line'. Kirsty then checked the students' understanding of this convention by asking them to identify the co-ordinates of some points on a grid.

Kirsty's first example was the point $(1,1)$, which would seem to be entirely ineffective in assessing the students' grasp of the significance of the order of the two elements of the pair. This is an example of 'confusing the role of variables', and it happens surprisingly often, though not as blatantly as in Kirsty's co-ordinates. It is useful to be aware of the possibility of confusing the role of variables in your own choice of examples (for some other types of best-avoided examples see Rowland, 2008).

> *By reference to dimensions of variation, give a sequence of about five examples that might have worked well for Kirsty.*

INTERLUDE: WHOSE EXAMPLES?

In discussing the lessons of John, Heidi and Kirsty, my emphasis was on the examples that *they*, the teachers, chose, why they choose them, and whether they chose them well. As I remarked earlier, teachers *do* choose and use examples a great deal in mathematics teaching. However, I also began by speculating what responses would be forthcoming if *students* themselves were invited to offer examples (of fractions, in that case), what their responses might reveal, and what opportunities for teaching these responses might afford. In their book, Anne Watson and John Mason (2005) develop both the theory and the practice of such *learner-generated examples* (LGEs), building on the variation theory (Marton and Booth, 1997) mentioned earlier. So is it better to develop a 'student-centred' pedagogy based on LGEs rather than a 'teacher-centred' approach in which the teacher chooses the examples? I would say that this implied association between pedagogies and the sources of examples is unhelpful, and that both approaches are valuable, depending on the intended purpose. As I have already demonstrated, and as Watson and Mason explain at length, the LGE approach is especially valuable in exploring the scope and limitations of concepts with students. On the other hand, if (like Heidi) we set out to teach solution of simultaneous equations by substitution, it is almost certainly better to have prepared a sequence of examples in advance, progressively introducing the variety of possible complexities that arise. This is more or less what John did in his selection and sequencing of quadratic expressions. This is not to be confused with a 'didactic', transmission-type teaching style, however. Whatever tasks we offer students to do, they often respond in ways that we had not expected or planned for – witness the case of Heidi earlier – and student-centred (and mathematically-comfortable) teachers investigate students' thinking by following up such responses as they occur.

PROVING AND DISPROVING: COUNTEREXAMPLES AND GENERIC EXAMPLES

There are two additional uses of examples, which support and challenge students' mathematical reasoning in important ways.

Sometimes a mathematical enquiry leads to an interesting and/or unexpected finding. Take this one, for example. Try it yourself first.

> How many ways are there of ascending a flight of stairs if you can take one or two stairs at a time? For three stairs, for example, there are 3 ways: 111, 12 and 21.

Students can soon find how many ways there are for one stair (one way!), two stairs, four stairs, and so on. The sequence of numbers-of-ways is 1, 2, 3, 5, 8, 13, … Students usually readily see 'a pattern', and point out that $1 + 2 = 3$, $2 + 3 = 5$, and so on. This is the Fibonacci sequence, of course. If they have listed all the possibilities for the first five cases, they usually predict that there are 13 ways for six stairs, and may check that this is correct. By then most students are convinced that it continues, 21, 34, …, and have no appetite for further checking. But at this point, the belief that every term is the sum of the previous two, has the status of a *conjecture*. In mathematics we never know general truths – in the sense of being completely sure that there are no exceptions – on the basis of examples, no matter how many we try.

To establish that a conjecture like the one above is true, we need to *prove* it. To show that it is false, we need a *counterexample* i.e. one case where the conjecture turns out not to be true. If the number of ways for eight stairs turned out to be 35, not 34, then the claim about always summing the previous two terms could not be true in general.

Applying this to the 'stairs' Fibonacci-conjecture: we don't have a counterexample yet, so could we show that it is always true, i.e. explain *why* each term is the sum of the previous pair? I find that very often a student volunteers an explanation, and that a feature of these accounts is that they are invariably grounded in a particular value of *n*. Following some group discussion, one student, Jenny, expressed it something like this.

> Suppose we've done flight-lengths one to five by listing all the ways. Now consider ascending six stairs. The first step must be one or two. If it is one, then five stairs are left, and we know that there are eight ways to ascend them. If it is two, then four stairs are left, and we know that there are five ways to ascend them. This exhausts all the possibilities, so there are five plus eight ways of climbing the six stairs.

This particular example then became a window through which other students could see what would happen in other cases (say from eight, nine stairs to ten stairs), and indeed beyond particular cases to the general. Jenny's example, with four, five and six stairs, is called a generic example, and her argument, displayed above, is a *proof by generic example*.

This kind of explanatory insight, achieved by 'talking through' a *single* example, needs to draw attention to the *structure* of that example, in the way that Jenny did. This helps others to see why the same, or analogous, reasoning would work just as well in other cases. This kind of 'seeing' is seeing *through* the particular example, as if it were a window onto a world of things analogous to it.

> *Suggest a generic example to show why the sum of any three consecutive integers is a multiple of 3.*

You can read more about proof by generic example in Rowland (2001) and the NRICH March 2012 issue (see the further reading, below).

Conclusion

This chapter has been about the ways in which examples are used in mathematics teaching. Examples play an essential role in the teaching of concepts, in the teaching of procedures, and as exercises through which students become familiar with new ideas, and fluent in the use and application of procedures. Through consideration and careful examination of some actual lessons, I have argued that the examples used in mathematics teaching should be chosen with care, keeping in mind their intended purpose, and the possible dimensions of variation within a particular example. I concluded with two rather different uses of examples, in determining the truth or falsehood of some general mathematical claim. A suitable *counterexample* can demonstrate that such a claim is false, thereby disproving or refuting it. The normal procedure for establishing mathematical truth is by general proof, but insight into the nature of such a proof can often be achieved by means of a carefully structured argument based on a *generic example*. Thoughtful choice of examples, in advance of teaching where possible, pays dividends.

Further reading

Bills, L., Dreyfus, T., Mason, J., Tsamir, P., Watson, A. and Zaslavsky, O. (2006) 'Exemplification in mathematics education', *Proceedings of the 30th Psychology of Mathematics Education (PME) Conference*, Prague, Czech Republic, July. A readable and useful insight into the scope of the topic, including a historical overview of the way examples have been seen in mathematics education, and accounts of issues relating to teachers' and learners' use of examples.

Chick, H. L. and Harris, K. (2007) 'Pedagogical content knowledge and the use of examples for teaching ratio', *Proceedings of the 2007 conference of the Australian Association for Research in Education* (available at: http://www.aare.edu.au/07pap/chi07286.pdf). The authors of this paper relate teachers' choice and use of examples to the topic of 'teacher knowledge' i.e. the different kinds of knowledge that teachers bring to and mobilise in the classroom. The focus here is on the place of exemplification in this field of knowledge.

NRICH Issue on Generic Examples, March 2012 http://nrich.maths.org. Every teacher and student should know this great website, a resource of interesting mathematical problems for students of all ages. The March 2012 edition features generic examples, with problems, notes for teachers, an article by myself, and a link to Rowland (2001).

Rowland, T. (2008) 'The purpose, design and use of examples in the teaching of elementary mathematics', *Educational Studies in Mathematics*, 69, 2, 149–163. This research paper has a section on some classroom situations in which examples were not well chosen by teachers, and analyses why this was so. Three types of examples are identified which, for different reasons, do not achieve the intended pedagogical purpose. The conclusions apply equally well to secondary teaching.

Special Issue 69, 2 of *Educational Studies in Mathematics* on exemplification. In this collection of papers, researchers from the UK, North America and Israel consider the use of examples from several perspectives and within different mathematics topics. The majority of the papers relate to secondary mathematics.

Watson, A. and Mason, J. (2005) *Mathematics as a constructive activity: the role of learner generated examples.* Mahwah, NJ: Lawrence Erlbaum Associates. This book brings together many years of reflection and enquiry by the authors into ways that teachers can work with students with a focus on examples. It is an eminently 'practical' resource for teachers, securely underpinned by theory, and probably the next thing you should read if you found this chapter relevant and helpful.

References

Gray, E. M. and Tall, D. O. (1994) 'Duality, ambiguity, and flexibility: a proceptual view of simple arithmetic', *Journal for Research in Mathematics Education*, 25, 2, 116–140.

Marton, F. and Booth, S. (1997) *Learning and awareness.* Mahwah, NJ: Lawrence Erlbaum.

Rowland, T. (2001) 'Generic proofs: setting a good example', *Mathematics Teaching*, 177, 40–43.

Rowland, T. (2008) 'The purpose, design and use of examples in the teaching of elementary mathematics', *Educational Studies in Mathematics*, 69, 2, 149–163.

Sfard, A. (1991) 'On the dual nature of mathematical conceptions: reflections on processes and objects as different sides of the same coin', *Educational Studies in Mathematics*, 22, 1, 1–36.

Sfard, A. (2008) *Thinking as communicating. Human development, the growth of discourse, and mathematizing.* New York: Cambridge University Press.

Watson, A. and Mason, J. (2005) *Mathematics as a constructive activity: the role of learner generated examples.* Mahwah, NJ: Lawrence Erlbaum Associates.

Chapter 10

History of mathematics in and for the curriculum

Leo Rogers

Introduction

We teach mathematics because it is part of our common heritage that has endured for generations. It is important for managing our lives, from the daily actions of individuals and communities to corporations and governments. Mathematics has evolved in many contexts, but whatever form it may have taken in the past, or may assume in the future, it has been and will continue to be, a tool for the solution of human problems. These problems come in many forms, and touch on the whole range of human experience, from the earliest social organisations and ritual practices, to managing the contemporary global economy. Mathematics is about ideas and their development, and it is also about people, societies, and cultures, and the History of Mathematics traces the genesis and development of these ideas that have had a major impact on our society.

For many students, studying mathematics is like learning English grammar without having any experience of the literature. In learning our language, we study the contexts, authors, literature, plays and poetry, and we can compare, contrast and relate past literature with its relevance to contemporary problems. History has a similar function, giving different perspectives to our culture. But what do we know about the culture of Mathematics? Few students ever experience anything of the variety and extent of mathematics, of its styles, its contexts, the people who made it, their problems and achievements. It is a tragedy that such an important part of our culture is unknown to many of our school students.

Few people realise that most of the mathematics taught up to KS4 was developed by other cultures and not brought into Western Europe until the late 15th century. Probability and statistical techniques began as rules of inheritance in Jewish and Arabic legal practices, while Mediaeval Arab scholars completed most of A-level trigonometry. Even some basic ideas of the Calculus are found in 14th-century China, India and Arabia. Our 'Western' school curriculum is the result of a transmission of ideas whose origins have been completely hidden. We live in a multicultural society, and students deserve to know about the contribution that past cultures played in the development of school mathematics.

The decline in the number of students applying for courses in Science, Technology, Engineering and Mathematics (STEM) subjects is apparent. Recent research on disaffected students who do not continue with mathematics after sixteen shows a range of reasons why they have negative perceptions of mathematics: it is irrelevant to their lives, tedious, disconnected, elitist, and de-personalised. Apart from the organisational problems of curriculum and the pressures of regular testing, students complain about uninteresting teaching, lack of perceived connections between different areas of mathematics, and meaningless rote application of formulas. Even successful students decide to leave for other subjects that are more interesting and creative. (See the chapter by Cathy Smith for an analysis of students' choices to opt into or out of mathematics at A-level). With curriculum and textbooks based on assumptions that mathematics is entirely hierarchical and students' progress has to be linear, and where schools readily categorise students, many of them think it is unfair to assume they are unable to succeed, or that they are not capable of more challenging work (Brown, Brown, and Bibby. 2008).

Many of these perceptions were attributed to the emphasis on teaching to the test, and not enough on engaging and inspiring students. The common element to these investigations is that *mathematics teaching is not addressing the affective, personal, needs, beliefs, attitudes and emotions* of students and the lack of any affective dimension and social context to the opportunities for learning. For many students, mathematics has lost its human face. Students' beliefs, attitudes and emotions towards mathematics are an inextricable component of general mathematical performance. These aspects are known to increase confidence and self-efficacy, and encourage positive learner identities with respect to our subject. (Nardi and Steward 2003, Lange and Meaney 2011).

Teaching mathematics requires particular attention to the *quality of pedagogy* and to *student engagement* throughout secondary school, and student achievement at any level requires engaging the learners. Engagement requires motivation and in mathematics it is necessary to go beyond mere procedure following to make connections and engage with concepts in active discussion and argumentation. Recent studies of attitudes of 11–14-year-olds show that *interest* is a key aspect of effective mathematics teaching. The NRICH website enables engagement in interesting and significant contexts where mathematics has regularly contributed to our scientific, and cultural well-being. We can engage students' interests and provide a wealth of accessible, meaningful problems by enabling access to historical material that is directly related to the curriculum we teach. If we are going to have an opportunity to introduce the history and culture of mathematics as part of a new approach to the curriculum, we have to produce good educational material so that history of mathematics becomes part of this enterprise.

HISTORY AND HERITAGE

We cannot teach history of mathematics as an extra subject, and very few of us have either the time or the energy to become an expert. However, there is an important distinction between the *history* and the *heritage* of mathematics.

- *History* addresses the question, 'what happened in the past?' and focuses on detailed research to provide evidence, so far as we are able to tell, of what, why, and how things happened. Such accounts are always open to debate, to alternative views, and comparison with other versions.
- *Heritage* on the other hand, refers to the impact of a theory on later work and address the question, 'how did we get here?'. This is where previous ideas are seen in terms of contemporary explanations, and we look for similarities with present ideas.

Presenting Euclid's work as 'geometrical algebra' is not *history*, but as *heritage* is legitimate because it is the form in which Arab mathematicians interpreted the *Elements* as the logical justification for their algebra, and this is how it becomes justified in the classroom.

With this view we do not have to be experts. We can make links between the mathematics of the past and our present contexts, but *we must be aware that the mathematics of the past is not the same as mathematics today*, even though it may appear so when described in contemporary notation. As teachers we can pass on our *heritage* by exploiting links between the content of the curriculum and what we know of the history of mathematics. So it becomes possible to describe events in the history of mathematics in terms that students can understand without making impossible demands on our own capabilities or teaching time.

CULTURE AND HERITAGE

Knowledge from the stars

Mathematics has arisen wherever people have begun to settle and deal with production of food, measuring land, building storage facilities, irrigating fields, and so on. Not only did they deal with their basic needs, but they also organised their activities with ceremonies based on the movement of the sun, moon and stars. The constellations rotating about a fixed point in the sky led to more precise regulation of the seasons and the establishment of important events. Linking the natural with the supernatural established ritual practices, and timing these was crucial, so the need for precise observation was born. The evolution of astronomy has been the most powerful motivation for developing a wide range of mathematics from earliest times.

By 2300 BCE Egyptian priests had divided the ecliptic into 36 sections of 10 degrees each. Detailed Babylonian astronomical records began about 1600 BCE where they adopted 360 days for the length of the year and established 360° in a circle by calculating that the sun moves relative to the fixed stars about one degree each day. From about 700 BCE they developed a mathematical theory of the motion of the planets, and the twelve-constellation zodiac appeared about 500 BCE, corresponding to their year of 12 months of 30 days each. The earliest Chinese calendars appear about 2000 BCE showing a 12-month year with an occasional 13th month. Over long periods of observation they were aware that their calendar became unreliable every 300 years and in the fifth century CE the scholar Zu Chongzi created the first calendar that corrected this problem.

From about 1500 BCE the Vedic people in Northern India developed simple geometrical constructions with peg and cord that enabled them to build their altars aligned in special

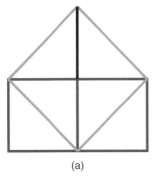
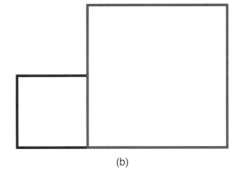

(a)   (b)

Figure 10.1 Hindu Squares

directions. Their instructions contain transformation rules for preserving areas, and these provided the basis for much of the geometry that appears in *Euclid* Books II and III.

It is easy to combine the equal small squares to make the large square equal to their combined areas as in Figure 10.1a. For the unequal squares in Figure 10.1b, can you draw one line in the diagram to show the side of a square equal to the combined areas of these two squares?

Construct a square and draw a diagonal. Through any point on the diagonal draw perpendiculars to its sides. What do you observe about the areas created as your point moves along the diagonal?

Now move the point of intersection of the perpendiculars in Figure 10.2 along the diagonal. What do you observe about the areas created? Are there other points on the diagonal where a square and rectangle become equal in area?

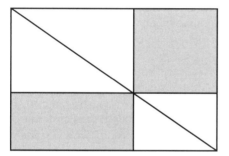

Figure 10.2 Euclid Book II Proposition 4

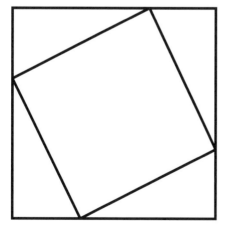

Figure 10.3 Bhaskaracharya's Pythagoras Proof

In the 12th century CE, Bhaskaracharya gave his well-known proof-diagram for the Pythagorean Relation shown in Figure 10.3. *How can this be justified?* Activities like these provide students with the essential experiences of visualisation and justification before we attempt more formal proof.

The desire for precision drove development of astronomical observation. Careful division of the circle and precise timing devices became paramount and, in the 8th century CE, Arabian emissaries went 'as far as China' to collect knowledge from the known world for the House of Wisdom in Baghdad. By this time, both the Chinese and Hindus had begun the investigation of infinite series for the calculation of sines by using differencing techniques, and the evaluation of the ratio *perimeter:diameter* for the circle. The Arabs inherited both Babylonian and Greek traditions, improved Ptolemy's *Almagest* and, in the 10th century, Abul Wafa produced new trigonometric tables to an accuracy of five sexagesimal (eight decimal) places.

The skills of navigation profited from data gained by the astronomers. Navigation within the Mediterranean was relatively easy compared with the voyages of the Portuguese to Africa and India in the 15th century. Finding one's way across the open ocean was a much more difficult task, but by the early 15th century the Chinese had established trading posts in Atlantic and Pacific America and in 1421–1423 had circumnavigated the globe. Expansion of empires, the lust for gold, spices, and other materials drove improvements in navigation and technology, supported by mathematics. This steady development by many ordinary sailors and merchants resulted in more sophisticated instruments to support the management of trade and the prosecution of war.

From algorithms to algebra

The algorithms developed in Mesopotamia from simple land measurement came to us through the discovery of the scribal tablets. However, by about 500 BCE these procedures were standardised in Middle Eastern oral tradition for solving various problems. Typically, 'given a *sum* of two numbers and their *product*, find the two numbers involved'. The algorithm is:

> Take half the sum, square it, from this square subtract the product, find the square root of the result, and add or subtract this result to half the sum, to find the two numbers.

For some simple arithmetical values, (such as sum, 7 and product, 12), using this 'Babylonian Algorithm', we can illustrate the procedure as in Figure 10.4.

$$\frac{7}{2}; \left(\frac{7}{2}\right)^2; \left(\frac{7}{2}\right)^2 - 12; \sqrt{\left(\frac{7}{2}\right)^2 - 12}; \frac{7}{2} \pm \sqrt{\left(\frac{7}{2}\right)^2 - 12}$$

Figure 10.4 The 'Babylonian Algorithm'

Here, 7 represents the semi-perimeter of a rectangle, and 12, its area. This algorithm reappears in various forms over the years and is the basis of the quadratic equation today. The Hindus had solved this problem geometrically (see Figure 10.5), and a Euclidean solution uses a special case of the intersecting chords theorem and the concept of the 'mean

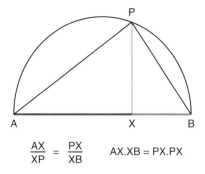

$$\frac{AX}{XP} = \frac{PX}{XB} \qquad AX.XB = PX.PX$$

Figure 10.5 Euclid Book VI, 13 The Mean Proportional

proportional' where, given two quantities (A, B), we look for a third quantity lying between them such that the ratio A:X is the same as X:B.

In contrast to the arithmetic approach, this geometrical construction is quite general and can reveal the non-rational situations that Euclid dealt with in his Book X. The ratios show that AX.XB is a rectangle, and PX.PX is the square equal in area.

This information was adopted in the early days of the Arab empire, where scholars were preoccupied with the possible *combinations* of word-forms in standardising the language for a new nation, and debating the religious meaning of the 'knowable unknown' (Rashed, 2009, pp.16–30). These influences led to Al-Khowarizmi's proposal for finding the 'knowable unknown' and the six classical forms of algebraic equations, given the three elements *mal* (x^2), *jidhr* (x) and *'adad* (n):

$$ax^2 = bx \qquad ax^2 = n \qquad bx = n$$
$$ax^2 + n = bx \qquad ax^2 + bx = n \qquad ax^2 = bx + n$$

Figure 10.6 Al-Khowarizmi's Equations

Using the Babylonian Algorithm from Figure 10.4, develop a series of 'sum' and 'product' examples for use in the classroom. Compare these with the equations in 10.6 above. What opportunities can you find for developing solutions to your problems and what variations are possible? (You may find it helpful to look back to the discussion of variation in the chapter by Tim Rowland.)

Impressed by Euclidean logic, scholars sought to demonstrate the consistency of this algebra geometrically. By the 9th century CE, Thabit ibn Qurra had shown that each algebraic form could be modelled by a consistent geometrical proof.

Fibonacci's Book of the Abacus, a compendium of the mathematical knowledge of the 12th-century Middle East, contains practical problems used for training merchants, but also

$$\left(\frac{10}{2}\right); \ \left(\frac{10}{2}\right)^2; \ \left(\frac{10}{2}\right)^2 - 40; \ \sqrt{\left(\frac{10}{2}\right)^2 - 40}; \ \frac{10}{2} \pm \sqrt{\left(\frac{10}{2}\right)^2 - 40}$$

Figure 10.7 Cardano's Solution

$$\left(5 + \sqrt{-15}\right)\left(5 - \sqrt{-15}\right)$$

Figure 10.8 Cardano's Factors

holds the traditional recreational puzzles and the mathematical problems that became the basis for the development of number theory and algebra. However, Mediaeval algebra lacked a notation, and dealt only with special cases that gave solutions within an integral-geometric context. Dealing with surd numbers was possible but extremely awkward, resulting in a number of clever but disparate techniques. In the Renaissance, when algebraic notation was beginning to appear, breaking out of the geometric mould was difficult. In 1545 Cardano followed the Babylonian Algorithm and showed that (in spite of serious misgivings) square roots of negative numbers could give a sensible answer. Without any algebraic notation, he demonstrated that '*if the sum of two numbers is 10 and their product is 40*', as in Figure 10.7, then the result yields the two parts of 10 which, when multiplied together confirm the product, as in Figure 10.8.

He drew a geometric diagram to explain, and asked his readers to imagine a negative side of a square, *but he had achieved the result by following the algorithm into unknown territory.*

Arts, sciences and engineering

There is considerable scope for making connections between the arts and the sciences. As practical mathematics supported building and technology, so these arts demanded advances in the search for more sophisticated technical solutions.

The invention of the crane in the 6th century BCE by Greek engineers and the introduction of the winch and pulley led to the theoretical mechanics of Archimedes, and by the 1st century CE, Hero's *Mechanica* described the mathematical basis for many ingenious machines. In 1901, a remarkable object constructed by some unknown technician was recovered from an ancient shipwreck. Dated about 150 BCE the 'Antikythera', is a mechanical model of the geocentric planetary system, with over 30 gears. It demonstrated the position of the planets with respect to the Earthly observer – something we can now discover by an App on an iPhone.

The creation of depth in paintings led to the ingenious devices of Renaissance practitioners, while architects like Brunelleschi and artists like Piero della Francesca, were involved in developing perspective that evolved into projective geometry in the 17th century.

Figure 10.9 from Piero's *De Prospectiva Pingendi* (c. 1480), the first treatise on perspective, shows his important converse of Euclid's theorem which established the transitivity of similarity (*Elements* VI. 21):

Figures which are similar to the same rectilinear figure are also similar to one another.

Euclid

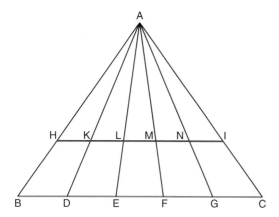

Figure 10.9 Piero della Francesca's 'Vanishing Point Theorem'

> If above a straight line divided into several parts a line be drawn parallel to it and from
> the points dividing the first line there be drawn lines which end at one point, they will
> divide the parallel line in the same proportion as the given line.
>
> Piero

Thus, for a pair of unequal parallel segments divided into equal parts, the lines joining corresponding points converge to a vanishing point. Later, comparing the number of points on parallel lines is considered by Galileo in his *Two New Sciences* of 1638. The theory of the real line may have its roots in Euclid and Piero, but does not begin to appear formally until the middle of the 19th century.

Theo van Doesburg, an important figure in the Avant Garde movement, created his *Arithmetic Composition*. Figure 10.10 is an extension of his theme, and has many interesting possibilities for classroom exploration. Careful analysis of this picture shows that there is a connection with the principles of proportion in *Euclid* Book V.

Explore the picture in Figure 10.10. What arithmetic and geometric investigations could be devised for students in Y7 and Y10?

Mechanical problems have inspired artists like Alexander Calder to develop kinetic sculptures. Salvador Dali's hypercube crucifixion is a representation of four dimensions and 'L'Arche', constructed at La Défense in Paris is a construction of a four-dimensional hypercube (see Figures 10.11 and 10.12).

Efficient technology requires good design, and good design has aesthetic appeal and lasting value. There is much potential in exploring the connections between mathematics and the history of technology.

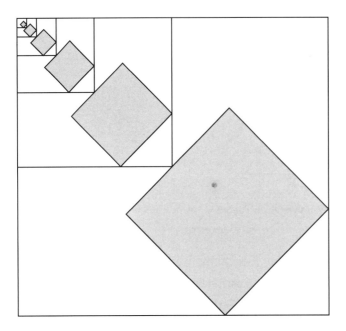

Figure 10.10 Arithmetic and Geometry: © Leo Rogers after Theo van Doesberg

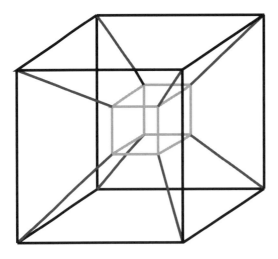

Figure 10.11 Tesseract

Figure 10.12 Le Grand Arche © Lyndon Baker - SumImages

MATHEMATICS: EVOLUTION AND ACTION

The relativity of mathematical rigour

A common belief about mathematics is that our subject consists of certain, abstract, indisputable truths. Only later do we realise that 'truth' and 'certainty' are slippery ideas to be regarded with caution. We insist that mathematical proof rests on logic, but this is an idealisation. Actually, it rests on a series of common understandings, generally accepted within a limited cultural group.

What has changed? The Greek axiomatic method developed a procedure in a discussion where the starting points were made clear and agreed by the protagonists. The objects (points, lines etc.) were simply defined, and the basic principles of the system (axioms) taken as understood and agreed. However, the statement of the condition for straight lines to be parallel immediately caused problems. The quest for a simpler statement continued until mathematicians in the 18th century accepted the alternative logical possibilities and 'non-Euclidean' geometries were discovered that opened a new world of theory and applications. Logical argument necessarily involves clarification of ideas and the ways we use them. Imre Lakatos demonstrated the difficulties involved in his *Proofs and Refutations* (1976) where 'proofs' of Euler's formula (shown in Figure 10.13), describing the relation between the faces, edges, and vertices of a polyhedron, are disputed.

$f + v = e + 2$

Figure 10.13 Euler's Formula

Lakatos showed that in successive attempts, anomalies arose and choices had to be made. Exceptions were either excluded, or if accepted, the concepts involved changed. Bringing different tools to the problem suggests different results, and changes the conceptual basis of what we are doing. Each generation sees problems differently, and consequently finds it necessary to re-define, re-justify or reject earlier hidden assumptions.

> *During problem-solving activities, how often do we help students to bring out hidden assumptions, extend ideas and generate their own examples?*

Those who have taken on this challenge have built up a repertoire of examples and techniques based on classroom experience that encourage teachers to emulate the heuristic process and to develop students' learning with tools that mathematicians employ regularly. See, for example, Anne Watson and John Mason's (2005) *Mathematics as a Constructive Activity*.

Cognitive and affective opportunities

Recent research shows that other cultures had a very different approach to justifying mathematical processes, and that 'Euclidean-style proof' is not the only way to show the consistency, validity and generality of mathematical procedures. The writing of mathematics began with explaining the work of an earlier mathematician by critically examining the older text. This tradition of commentaries was the normal way that ideas were interrogated, extended and improved. The process is not much different today: peer review is similar to the interrogation, and we question, accept, or develop the idea.

There is now a better understanding of the reasoning behind the mathematical arguments of Indian and Chinese mathematicians that has provided evidence of new perspectives on the concepts of proof, truth and validity. There was no single set of rules for logical demonstration of mathematical statements. Instead, we find a style of reasoning quite different from that of Euclid. This idea is just as important and fundamental because it aims for deeper understanding rather than 'proof' and generalisation rather than abstraction.

Figure 10.14 below is adapted from the commentary on the *Nine Chapters* by Liu Hui written during the 3rd century CE. Here is a circle touching all three sides of a right triangle. This is taken as the starting point for an exploration of the properties of the figure that might then be extended to cover the general case.

Regarding Figure 10.14a, what are the simplest properties of the figure you can deduce from the information given in the diagram?

Assuming the circle is tangent to all three sides of the triangle, we arrive at Figure 10.14b. From the symmetries in the object we deduce Figure 10.14c. Now other properties can follow. We can use the radius of the circle as a common measure. By rearranging the smaller triangles into rectangles, we see they all have one dimension in common, and so can find an expression for the area of the original triangle.

By using Figure 10.14a as a generic example in this way, a teacher can gradually help students to discover, confirm, extend and establish new properties.

If the dimensions of the triangle are integers, does this property apply to all Pythagorean triangles? Can this idea be extended to isosceles and other triangles?

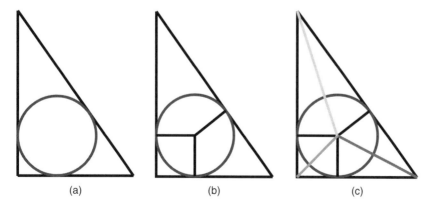

(a)   (b)   (c)

Figure 10.14 Liu Hui Triangles

CLASSROOM PRACTICE: MAPS, NARRATIVES AND ORIENTATIONS

Concept Maps are graphical multi-layered tools for organising and representing knowledge. They have considerable advantages over linear text, to support the collaborative development of knowledge, the sharing of vision and understanding, and the enhancement of higher levels of mathematical thinking (Rogers, 2011). This is in contrast to most curriculum texts that are presented as a linear sequence of facts, procedures and exercises, restricted to some arbitrary levels of students' competence. Given a *Concept Map*, a user would need a guide (the *Narrative*), that provides information on the general context and background of the Map, and an *Orientation* that describes the activities proposed for students to find their bearings among the ideas presented.

Software today enables us to consider a map as a *virtual environment* where the arrangement of concepts, objects, events, proposals and actions may be partially ordered and multi-layered, thus breaking up a linear sequence and juxtaposing different ideas. No Map is ever complete. The principal concept(s) chosen at one stage can be rearranged according to the needs of the learning process, and the individuals involved. To be relevant and useful, Maps are best developed collaboratively where a group of teachers, or a teacher and students, can share knowledge and combine their visions. In this way both students and teachers can be offered Maps to be explored and interpreted. By organising ideas in a particular way, and examining the possible links between them in a visual display, Maps can be used as plans for teaching and scaffolding for learning, leading us to new connections between ideas.

Visualisation is important in these activities. Representing objects, manipulating them physically and simultaneously in the mind, brings out hidden properties and relations. Adapting a Map to explore links through the curriculum to historical contexts can act as part of a developable knowledge structure available for integrating aspects of our mathematical heritage into a teaching programme. The history then becomes integral to the exploration of the mathematics. A Map enables teachers to have the freedom to develop their own Narrative. It can throw light on problems, suggest different approaches to teaching, and generate new questions.

A practical example

One of the most fundamental concepts in mathematics with a wide range of applications in mathematics, science and daily life is ratio and proportion.

Figure 10.15 shows a Concept Map with some of the main ideas in their historical contexts. It is constructed to relate to the school curriculum, and an important exercise is for teachers to make their own map of the relevant contents of their school curriculum.

> *Where does the knowledge and use of ratio and proportion occur in the school curriculum? How could these interconnections appear in a curriculum plan? Where and how are they placed in the textbook? What, if any, is a necessary sequence for learning these ideas? How can these be realised in practice?*

Historical narrative

The mathematical definitions are found in *Euclid* Book V, but the experiences leading to this idea arose when people began to appreciate a relation between the shadow of a stick,

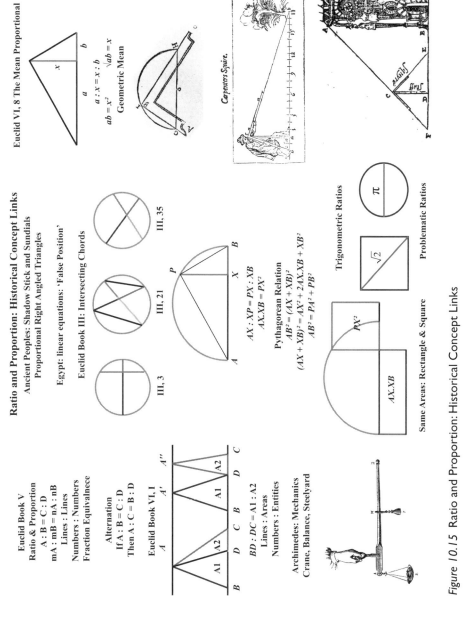

Figure 10.15 Ratio and Proportion: Historical Concept Links

and the time of day. Once a proportional relationship between sides of similar right-angled triangles was formalised, new developments became possible. Pyramids symbolise engineering achievements, but the proportional relationship is also found in the solution of linear equations in problems 24–29 of the Rhind Papyrus. As the relation between numerical and geometrical measures was quantified, the techniques of inverse proportion and alternation appear. Thus we see mathematical relations enabling advances in practical life, long before any theoretical basis emerged.

The Pythagorean relation was common practical knowledge for ancient peoples, and independently shown to be theoretically true by Indian and Chinese mathematicians, while the intersecting chord theorems stating relationships between segments and angles led to the family of trigonometric ratios. The Mean Proportional (Figure 10.5) was used by Viete in the 16th century in his formulation of quadratic equations, and the same construction shows how it is possible to transform a rectangle into a square of equal area, now easily achieved using algebra. However, the algebra conceals the problem of *precisely measuring the side of the square*. The *existence of the square and its diagonal* is obvious; but a common measure is impossible and symbolising the diagonal by √2 omits a great opportunity to discuss an approximation made some 4,000 years ago.

Similarly the ratio of the diameter of a circle to its perimeter become problematic. The statement that 'Archimedes' value for π was 3.1429' neglects a wealth of opportunities for engaging with important mathematical ideas. These examples show how ratio and proportion underlie the most essential ideas and techniques in elementary mathematics. They demonstrate equivalence relations, links between arithmetic and geometry, algorithms evolving into algebra, fundamental ideas of linear and quadratic equations, trigonometric functions, infinite division of the real line, and the existence of irrational numbers.

Starting points using historical material from occasional reference to a fact, to raising questions about some fundamental ideas, can be brought into a teaching plan. Awareness of the possibilities is important, but so is the teacher's judgement of the ways ideas may be introduced.

THE HISTORY OF MATHEMATICS AND CLASSROOM RESEARCH

Educational research derived from investigations into the use of history in mathematics teaching is no less significant than research from other areas. Many results reinforce conclusions from psychology-based theory because investigating the process of how knowledge grows, through looking at historical materials and through their use directly or indirectly in the classroom, reaches similar understandings and valid results as 'mainstream' educational theory (Clark, 2012; Kjelsden and Blomholj, 2012).

Our mathematical heritage and its use in teaching and learning contributes to the mainstream of concerns about the cognitive, affective and operative functioning of students, and evidence of all these benefits is found in the ICMI Study, *History in Mathematics Education* (Fauvel and van Maanen, 2000) and other published research at the History and Pedagogy of Mathematics (HPM) website (see 'Further reading' below).

For students, a range of possibilities exists using suitably-edited historical situations and problems as assignments, encouraging investigation and comparison of sources, producing and analysing data, and discussing the contexts in which ideas arose. This is possible at virtually any level, with any age group.

Viewing the heritage of mathematics as part of mathematics:

- Provides opportunities for students' affective and cognitive engagement.
- Indicates connections between areas of mathematics.
- Links mathematics with science, technology and the arts.
- Explores cultures, contexts, individuals and groups.
- Shows how mathematics evolved from social, economic and political situations.
- Demonstrates how mathematics changes with contexts and time.
- Provides evidence for a critical evaluation of mathematical processes.

I hope these remarks have shown that the history of mathematics and its use in teaching and learning contributes to the mainstream of concerns about students' engagement with cognitive and affective functioning, and can easily provide a variety of rich tasks for use in the classroom.

Further reading

Clark, K. M. (2012) 'History of Mathematics: illuminating understanding of school mathematics concepts for prospective mathematics teachers', *Educational Studies in Mathematics*, 81, 1, 67–84. This paper uses the case of the quadratic equation to show how history of mathematics contributes to a person's mathematical knowledge for teaching.

Fauvel, J. and van Maanen, J. (eds) (2000) *History in Mathematics Education: The ICMI Study*. London: Kluwer. This book, from the International Study Group on the History and Pedagogy of Mathematics (HPM), contains a wide range of studies on the practical implementation and educational benefits of integrating the history of mathematics into school curricula.

Kjelsden, T. H. and Blomholj, M. (2012) 'Beyond Motivation: history as a method for learning meta-discursive rules in mathematics', *Educational Studies in Mathematics*, 80, 3, 327–349. This analysis of students' project reports on historical topics shows how reflecting upon the actual historical process contributes to the development of their own understanding and ways of managing mathematical reasoning in the classroom.

Lakatos, I. (1976) *Proofs and Refutations: The Logic of Mathematical Discovery*. Cambridge: Cambridge University Press. This is the classic text on the evolution of mathematical concepts in the pursuit of proof, and the pitfalls of attempting precise definitions.

Rashed, R. (2009) *Al-Khwarizmi: The Beginnings of Algebra*. London: SAQI. This is the new translation and commentary on Al-Khwarizmi's original text.

Rogers, L. (2011) 'Mapping our Heritage to the Curriculum: Historical and Pedagogical Strategies for the Professional Development of Teachers', in V. Katz and C. Tzanakis (eds), *Recent Developments on Introducing a Historical Dimension in Mathematics Education*. Washington: M.A.A. This text describes in detail the philosophy, educational approach and practical principles of using of Concept Maps in the classroom.

Watson, A. and Mason, J. (2005) *Mathematics as a Constructive Activity*. London: Lawrence Erlbaum. Here, teachers and students together develop mathematical creativity. This is an outstanding contribution to practical, effective, pedagogy.

History and Pedagogy of Mathematics (HPM) at http://www.clab.edc.uoc.gr/HPM. This is the site of the International Study Group on the Relations Between the History and Pedagogy of Mathematics. There are copies of many Newsletters with accounts of teachers using history of mathematics in their classrooms.

The MacTutor History of Mathematics Archive at http://www-history.mcs.st-and.ac.uk/history. This is the principal website in the UK where you can find biographies of mathematicians and histories of many mathematical topics.

The Mathematical Society of America provides a wealth of resources to help teach mathematics using its history e.g. Congruence at http://mathdl.maa.org/mathDL/23.

NRICH is a mathematics enrichment website. Teachers Experiences of using NRICH at http://nrich.maths.org/6537 offers pedagogical principles, advice and project work by teachers. Some of my own relevant NRICH topics, created for teachers and students and accompanied by notes and pedagogical discussion, are:

A Brief History of Time Measurement: http://nrich.maths.org/6070

Development of Astronomy and Trigonometry: http://nrich.maths.org/6843

Development of Algebra 1: http://nrich.maths.org/6485

Development of Algebra 2: http://nrich.maths.org/6546

References

Brown, M., Brown, P. and Bibby, T. (2008) '"I would rather die": reasons given by 16 year olds for not continuing their study of mathematics', *Research in Mathematics Education*, 10, 1, 3–18.

Clark, K. M. (2012) 'History of mathematics: illuminating understanding of school mathematics concepts for prospective mathematics teachers', *Educational Studies in Mathematics*, 81, 1, 67–84.

Fauvel, J. and van Maanen, J. (eds) (2000) *History in mathematics education: the ICMI study*. London: Kluwer.

Kjelsden, T. H. and Blomholj, M. (2012) 'Beyond Motivation: history as a method for learning meta-discursive rules in mathematics', *Educational Studies in Mathematics*, 80, 3, 327–349.

Lakatos, I. (1976) *Proofs and refutations: the logic of mathematical discovery*. Cambridge: Cambridge University Press.

Lange, T. and Meaney, T. (2011) 'I actually started to scream: emotional and mathematical trauma from doing school mathematics homework', *Educational Studies in Mathematics*, 77, 1, 35–51.

Nardi, E. and Steward, S. (2003) 'Is mathematics T.I.R.E.D.? A profile of quiet disaffection in the secondary mathematics classroom', *British Educational Research Journal*, 29, 3, 345–367.

Rashed, R. (2009) *Al-Khwarizmi: the beginnings of algebra*. London: SAQI.

Rogers, L. (2011) 'Mapping our heritage to the curriculum: historical and pedagogical strategies for the professional development of teachers', in V. Katz and C. Tzanakis (eds), *Recent developments on introducing a historical dimension in mathematics education*. Washington: M.A.A.

Watson, A. and Mason, J. (2005) *Mathematics as a constructive activity*. London. Lawrence Erlbaum.

Chapter 11

Should 'teaching for understanding' be the pinnacle of mathematics education?

Anna Llewellyn

> I know that you believe you understand what you think I said, but I'm not sure you realise that what you heard is not what I mean.
>
> (Robert McCloskey)

What does the above quotation mean to you? It reminds me of the frequently heard question in the classroom 'do you understand?'. Whilst looking rather innocent, this can be a problematic question – for instance, how valid is the answer? If you ask this to a student and they answer 'yes', what have you learnt? That they are compliant? That they have heard you? Or that they think they understand you? Perhaps the question you are really asking is 'do you understand in the manner that I understand?' or 'do you understand in the manner that I want you to understand?' but of course the student may not always know if they do. Even if you can establish that they have understood in the way you intended, what do you mean by understanding? Do you mean that you want them to understand how to do the work or are you hoping for something else mathematically; a spark that suggests something 'deeper'?

By asking these questions we have begun to problematise the concept of understanding. We have questioned the amount it is used and the way it is used. We have queried what people mean when they use that word; we have even begun to consider the value it has and what it does to the classroom. We have also suggested that language, in general, is not transparent, meaning is subjective and created in context. This is essentially what this chapter is about; I want to question an accepted good of the mathematics classroom – teaching for understanding. One key way in which I do this is to examine the subjectivity of language and how it can create meaning.

Teaching for understanding seems to be viewed as the crème de la crème of mathematics education. Indeed it features as a topic on most teacher education programs. But why is this? Do we believe this creates better mathematicians or people, or do we believe this is the correct, and only, way to learn mathematics? If we do suppose these things what does that mean for the classroom? Should we blindly pursue teaching for understanding and assume there are only good consequences for all? My opinion is we should not. Instead, we should question the truths we are told and examine what effects they have in the classroom. Specifically whether they include or exclude people from mathematics. In addition, truths are not absolute, they change over time. For instance, forty years ago many people would have thought that boys were better than girls at mathematics. Indeed, some people may still do so. How can this idea be damaging? It could be that teachers holding such beliefs deliberately exclude girls or conversely they may praise girls more as they think they need more encouragement, which could exclude boys.

Another example is the idea/notion that 'girls prefer pink'. This is actually a modern concept that has only been around since the 20th century. But how can it be bad to think that girls prefer pink? Well, what if you are a boy who likes pink, does that mean that there is something wrong with you and perhaps you are not a 'real' boy? (See the chapter by Mark McCormack for more on the problem with dominant ideas about gender). So somewhere, and at some point, this 'truth' was created. I don't mean that someone sat down and thought, 'Hey, I know what would be good marketing, let's produce everything for girls in pink and for boys in blue'. Instead, I mean that through time and the use of language and practice, we have come to accept something as having meaning. We have internally accepted it as the truth.

Hence to engage with this chapter, I need you to do a few things. Firstly, I acknowledge that many people reading this chapter will probably be committed to working with teaching for understanding. If this is the case then I ask you to put this on a placeholder and allow some space for other ideas. Next I want you to look beyond the idea that language describes meaning and instead consider that language creates meaning. Of course, and as discussed, creating meaning is about more than language, it is about the way we act towards something and about how it acts with us. Thus instead of language I am going to use the word discourse and state that discourses create meaning; they are constructive rather than descriptive (Heather Mendick and Marie-Pierre Moreau use the word 'story' to capture the same idea in their chapter).

Discourse is a term I borrow from the work of Michel Foucault; he contends that some discourses are more easily heard than others. For example, what would happen if a teacher acted like they did not want their students to pass their exams? This way of acting and speaking would not be permitted; instead the teacher may be ignored and/or branded abnormal or incompetent. A key theme of this chapter, is to unpack what we take for granted as 'normal' with regards to teaching for understanding and show how it is not natural but instead constructed by systems, structures and society; Foucault calls this process normalisation (Foucault, 1978). I argue that normalisation thrives in education; the conformity of the classroom is constructed to propagate it.

> *Do you agree with me that normalisation thrives in the classroom? What do you think are the positive and negative aspects of this?*
>
> *Think about the perfect classroom. What would it look like and hence what would be normalised? Think of three things you place importance on, and list the reasons why these things are important. Finally, consider where those ideas come from and hence consider why some things are important and others seemingly not?*

In an attempt to unpack the concept of understanding, I examine it with/in two key contexts: educational research and educational policy. It is important to recognise the role the government has in shaping education in England. Decisions are often made hastily and sometimes it seems without support. Recently, the New Labour government (from 1997–2010) introduced a wealth of policies and initiatives that have had a significant impact upon English education generally and the maths classroom specifically. At the time of writing, schools in England are attempting to adjust to the Govian desires of the new education minister that are slicing through the system at an even more manic speed.

I use the next sections of this chapter to look at how government policy and educational research work to normalise the mathematics classroom. Specifically, I argue that mathematics education research is preoccupied with exploring teaching for understanding and more often than not develops a blinkered, romantic approach to this concept. I compare this to educational policy which views understanding as more functional. Then I use an example of a primary education student teacher to show how these positions (or discourses) can be problematic for the teacher, the students and the classroom. Although based around primary education, these arguments are transferable to secondary education.

UNPACKING UNDERSTANDING

Discourses of understanding within educational research

In the first instance, though understanding is often presented as a uniform and self evident concept, different forms are found within academic literature. This includes: hierarchical constructs such as (Benjamin) Bloom's taxonomy (1956), which has enjoyed recent popularity in schools; Richard Skemp's (1976) value-laden oppositions of instrumental and relational understanding (discussed in the chapter by Gwen Ineson and Sunita Babbar); and Jean Piaget's influential stages of development. More recently Patrick Barmby and his colleagues (2009) have constructed understanding as a process of connections and representations. These different constructs are not mutually exclusive; in particular they all rely on one key concept – the 'normal', 'naturally developing' child. This enlightened, naturally curious child has much in common with Rousseau's romantic child as a 'state of nature'. However, Valerie Walkerdine (1997, p.63) argues that in 'child-centred pedagogy, "the child" is deferred in relation to certain developmental accomplishments … the very practices that claim to discover them actually produce them'. Hence this natural child cannot be found, as they are what is being sought; this child is always already a normalised developing child.

This position is problematic as it can create a divide, where these 'developed' children are given status as they are deemed to produce 'real' understanding and 'real' attainment (Walkerdine, 1998). As Walkerdine points out, this is a seductive fantasy and one that is generally accepted as commonsense wisdom. However, I (and Walkerdine) argue that this naturally curious child, where understanding organically develops from experience, is a romantic fiction. Instead the child is more than this; the child has a context, including (amongst other things) gender, sexuality, culture and race.

To illustrate how this romantic discourse can be persuasive I focus on an influential and seductive piece of research. In the 1990's Jo Boaler carried out a comparative ethnography of two secondary schools with contrasting styles of teaching. In unsophisticated terms one school employed an 'open' (or child-centred) approach to mathematics pedagogy whilst the other adopted a 'closed' (or transmission) approach. Boaler's conclusions drew attention to differences between mathematics results and attitudes to mathematics between each school. In short, she argued that open classrooms were more equitable and the closed classrooms disadvantaged certain groups of students. In particular she identified that girls, had a 'quest for understanding' and were alienated from the transmission-based classrooms. Her arguments are in many ways typical of other research in mathematics education so it is useful to unpack them, which I do from three angles (Hilary Povey offers an alternative take on Boaler's research in the next chapter).

Firstly, I contend that Boaler creates an unnecessary divide between knowledge and understanding; giving value only to the latter. Such use of binary divisions is prevalent within language, however, it is not natural and should not be left uncontested. In this case it suggests there is a right way to acquire mathematics, which stigmatises those who acquire mathematics otherwise. It suggests that understanding should come before and be held in higher regard than knowledge when in fact the relationship between the two is more complex. Indeed 'for many people the acquisition of information both excites and liberates' (Alexander, 2010, p.247). This leads onto my second critique, the concept of the 'natural' child.

The child within Boaler's classrooms is not only 'free' but is naturally inquisitive, working furiously in social groups demanding mathematical enquiry. This child is the one who is valued, gains 'real' attainment, and is apparently 'free'. However, Boaler does not 'really theorise how subjects are produced – practices' (Walkerdine, 1997, p.59). She does not question what version of the child she is producing. Crucially she does not recognise that everyone is a product of discourses; even her 'free' students are part of a manufactured system, one that is controlled through surveillance and normalisation. What is most disquieting is that this surveillance masquerades under the facade of liberation. It supports the dream of the autonomous student and the autonomous classroom (Ball, 1994) which many educationalists strive towards; hence it is a very attractive fiction (Walkerdine, 1990). However, my concern is that we are only seeing/hearing what we want to see/hear.

My final point of contention is that Boaler fosters the romantic discourse of understanding by arguing that girls have a 'quest for understanding'. She contends that they cannot connect to mathematics in classrooms that are bound by transmission based pedagogies, and hence they remove themselves from them. She largely bases this on interviews stating that 'the girls were clear that their mathematical understanding would have been enhanced if they had been given more opportunity to work in an open way' (Boaler, 1997, pp.144–145). However, there are many reasons why they may have made such statements and it is too easy for Boaler to take their words literally and assume the meaning she was seeking. Indeed, having a quest or a desire for something is not straightforward; it 'involves a complex subjective investment in … "subject-positions"' (Walkerdine, 1990, p.30). In particular, the quest for understanding may be a quest for something else or it may be the correct response for the girls to give. In addition, the presence/absence of understanding may be a myth supported by gendered behaviour in the classroom. Hence boys may be more easily afforded the presence of understanding through social markers such as activity and rule-breaking (Walkerdine, 1998). Furthermore girls 'threaten the running of the child-centred classroom … [by] producing the wrong kind of development' (Walkerdine, 1998, p.33); femininity runs parallel to masculine rationality. This provides a sharp contrast to Boaler's findings, where child-centred pedagogies are viewed as girls' liberation.

Let's stop to consider what this means in relation to the maths classrooms. Why do people say the things they do and do they always literally mean what they say?

Write down a few things that have been said to you about mathematics, either by people in your maths classroom or by people in general. For example, do people say 'they're stuck', 'they hate maths' or that 'they are finding things too easy'? It may help to think of one or two specific students or people you have met.

Think of as many reasons as you can why they might say these things.

In summary I have argued that mathematics education research predominantly draws from a romantic discourse of understanding, where the correct version of the child is one who is autonomous and naturally curious. It is only from this that acceptable pedagogies are practised and 'real' understanding can arise. This romantic discourse of the child, of the classroom and of understanding perpetuates divisions in education and restricts discussion. Next I examine how this plays out in relation to policy, showing that policy constructs a functional discourse of understanding.

Understanding with/in policy

Before embarking on a deconstruction of current policy, it is important to be aware of the wider context in which this policy circulates (see also the chapter by Margaret Brown). We live in a neoliberal society which means that a particular model of selfhood as autonomous, psychological and entrepreneurial is normalised (Rose, 1999). However, this freedom is a myth as we are in fact governed through this notion of freedom; we are compelled to be free, to make our own choices and find our own way through life (Foucault, 1978; Rose, 1999). This neoliberal fiction is important to the production of understanding in educational policy, specifically as it is concerned with efficiency and the myth of autonomy.

With regards to government policy, in the first instance, the word 'understanding' is mainly absent. If it is mentioned it is not with romantic undertones but instead is functional. This is similar to other New Labour policy documents that talk of objectives being 'identifiable' and 'achievable'.

An example of this functional discourse of understanding is shared below. The statement, with its rare mention of understanding, comes from the 'Core position papers on literacy and numeracy' (DfES, 2006) which are the main policy document for primary mathematics in schools.

> Children need to understand when and why the decimal point can disappear and can move about in the [calculator] display. When £0.50 is entered, the number displayed is likely to be 0.5 as trailing zeros are not shown in decimal numbers.
>
> DfES (2006, p.59)

Above, understanding is aligned to a functional task (trailing zeros); it is not a romantic product of natural inquiry but instead is tied to a performative discourse that conforms to rules, routines and efficiency.

This functionality is found in other policy documents for example in the 'Making Good Progress' series of documents (from the government funded National Strategy for improvement in education). Here there is a more marked assertion that understanding mathematics is a 'good' thing.

> These [outstanding] schools place a great emphasis on children understanding the key concepts attached to each subject. They do not, however, shy away from teaching vital standard practices, for example, punctuation and grammar and mathematical algorithms. But the point here is that they make sure that children understand why these procedures are efficient and are fit for purpose.
>
> DfES (2007, p.21)

Here, successful schools are positioned as giving importance to understanding, however, if you read closely, you can again see that understanding is produced as functional, and specifically as an efficient and suitable method. This again contrasts to Boaler's romantic fantasy of liberation, but it is very much aligned to a neoliberal society and its need for a measurable and accountable education system.

This accountable and functional education system is supported by the replacement of the word understanding with skills, which is far more prevalent in policy documents. Skills seem to be more valued than both knowledge and understanding. For instance policy states that 'skills are methodically built up, practised and refined so that more challenging and complex work can be attempted' (DfES, 2007, p.21). This demonstrates how the praising of skills can simplistically lead to the praising of certain pedagogies. In addition, this emphasis on skills is representative of the wider marketisation of education; specifically 'the belief is that these skills combine contemporary relevance, future flexibility and hands-on experience' (Alexander, 2010, p.249).

I have argued that policy constructs understanding mathematics very differently to mathematics education research: as functional rather than romantic. However, both of these discourses are based upon the notion of a 'normal' cognitive child. As already discussed, in mathematics education research the child is presented as naturally inquisitive; however, in educational policy the functional child is more of an automaton, a product of an efficient production line. This is shown in the manner that understanding is presented as unproblematic. For instance, policy documents contain statements such as 'as children begin to understand the underlying ideas they … use particular methods' (DfES, 2006, p.40), suggesting that there is an expectation that understanding will occur in a straightforward manner, which positions those who do not follow this path as deviant. In addition the mention of 'underlying ideas' is both rational and prescriptive, suggesting a Platonic take on mathematical truths that is bound by certainty and the absolute (Ernest, 1991) rather than an idea of mathematical knowledge as a product of human activity (see the chapter by Leo Rogers).

In the next section I draw on interview data from one student teacher to provide an example of how the tension between these discourses (the romantic and the functional) can play out. In no way is this meant to be representative of the wider population but instead I use one person's story to give value and consequence to the situation. Specifically I argue that the tension between the romantic and functional discourses of understanding results in exclusion from mathematics for some.

What this means for Jane, a student teacher

'I didn't know what I was doing and I couldn't get it. Everyone else was understanding it and I wasn't'. On reading statements such as this one from Jane it can appear that she shares Boaler's girls' quest for understanding and perhaps Boaler's romantic take on understanding. However, as I discussed earlier, there are many reasons to desire understanding and/or to make such statements. For instance, in constructing her identity, Jane notably presents herself as different and as a non-mathematician, despite her higher than average grade B in mathematics GCSE (the current examination taken by most young people at age 16 in England and Wales, see the chapter by Ian Jones). In addition, she is keen to construct a narrative where 'not understanding' mathematics was not her fault:

> Because I always remember at school thinking every time we did anything in maths 'why are we doing this? I don't get it, why are we doing this? Why do we have to do it

this way? I don't understand'. And it was never explained so when I was doing my maths teaching I always made a point of saying 'we're doing it this way because it's easier'.

Moreover, the text above demonstrates how Jane's version of understanding is more concerned with efficiency and functionality rather than Boaler's natural curiosity. This is shown throughout her interviews, where understanding is functional – concerned with being able to do. Furthermore, not understanding is conflated with not being able to access the work:

> You never got taught anything, you just worked through a workbook and the workbook was supposed to explain how to do things but I quite often never understood what the workbook meant because there was not very often any example.

Jane constructs a powerful narrative, where understanding is the only way to achieve success in mathematics. This seems to be supported by her university lectures: 'that's why I really enjoyed the lectures about rote learning because it made sense to me that that's the way I'd learned'. Hence she is given a reason for her negative relationship with mathematics and can remove herself of personal blame. This narrative continues throughout her interviews:

> I just used to think, 'well surely if I had an embedded understanding it must have come back somehow', then I realised that in some areas I didn't have an embedded understanding, I just rote learned stuff and even though I did understand that I've realised in the past few months that even though I did a lot better in Year 10 and 11 [aged 14–16], I think it was still all rote learning ... I don't think there was any understanding towards it because you know I still don't understand things and sometimes I wonder how I got a B because in the things I got a B in I don't understand how to do it.

However, as I unpack below, this quest for understanding is perhaps fictional; a place that allows her to be separated from mathematics, yet to be normal. For instance in one interview I try to explain a mathematical concept to Jane, she rejects my attempt. This could be for many reasons; perhaps I am the 'maths person' and Jane is the other:

Jane: You have to put a three down and a one up so you add another one to the tens column, they said 'why?' and I was just, like, 'well just so you know where it's going' and they were like, 'why, why do you put it there? Why can't you just put it somewhere else?' 'Well that's just the way we do it'.

Anna: Where else did she want to put it?

Jane: Underneath.

Anna: Oh, right, ok. In the same column though because it's the column that's the important bit.

Jane: Yeah, I know that but it was still like, well, you know [laughter] I know, you're a maths person [laughter]. It was a question that just completely threw me because I never thought that.

Anna: Some people do put it underneath.

Jane: Do they?

Conversely to Boaler, I argue that Jane may prefer to not understand. Perhaps this is the place which offers the most comfort and self-protection from the romantic discourses, with their high status and the consequent failure. Hence she places understanding away from her, in a position she cannot access. According to Jane, understanding belongs to mathematicians, which in her classroom translates as the high achievers:

> If, like, the higher achievers find a different way of doing it then that's fine but just for the lower achievers to know that, you know, that first thing, it should circle the lowest number and then they need to find out how low it is and those were the key bits I wanted them to realise … But I think it's important for them to understand what they're doing and why they're doing it, you know, to know that they are finding the smallest number.

This position can result in value-laden pedagogies and certain types of teaching being reserved for some. Though yet again her version of understanding is concerned with being able to do; it is functional.

My interpretation is that throughout her interviews Jane is clear that teaching for understanding is the right thing to do, however, she struggles with this in relation to her emotions and experiences. For instance, she states, 'I think the main thing is to let children explore maths … But I think there will always be that ingrained thing with me that it's either right or wrong'. Hence she has rationalised expectations, but she also has her own 'irrational' emotions and investments. 'Teachers and their work calls for a massive investment of their "selves"' (Nias, 1989, p.2), though emotions tend to be absent from overtly rationalised policy and from most academic discussions of teaching for understanding. Similarly, Jane struggles with the tension between the complexity of the 'real' child she encounters and the simplicity of the rational child expected in both policy and academia (Llewellyn and Mendick, 2011). Hence Jane struggles to realise academic versions of understanding and is caught up in the measurable, functional world of policy. However, she cannot let the romance go completely, which can lead to her (and the children she teaches) feeling removed from mathematics.

What do you think of Jane's story? Do you agree with my interpretation?

How does it compare to how other people talk about understanding mathematics?

Do other people have 'excuses' for not doing maths?

Do they link understanding to functionality?

Do teachers restrict understanding to the more 'able' students?

Has your opinion of teaching for understanding altered at all?

Concluding remarks

In this chapter I question a commonsense truth that we often take for granted within mathematics education. This is part of a wider argument that stresses that nothing is intrinsically good or bad and no position is power or problem-free.

The pursuit of understanding seems to be one of those intangible debates that perpetually floats around mathematics education. I hope I have showed that placing something on a pedestal does not come without consequences; specifically for 'teaching for understanding', these unintentional forfeits can be inequity or dissolution. I am not arguing that understanding is bad or good for the classroom; instead I want to expose what it does and problematise its assumed goodness. As Foucault (2003, p.172) states:

> A critique does not consist in saying that things aren't good the way they are. It consists in seeing on just what type of assumptions, of familiar notions, of established and unexamined ways of thinking the accepted practices are based.

Instead of being caught in a romantic (re)presentation of the child, the classroom and of mathematics, I ask you to consider things more widely – and not just deeply – when you are in the classroom. Moreover mathematics education research does not exist in a vacuum but is part of the cultural context of the classroom and society which shapes and is shaped by it. So I am suggesting that all of us – teachers, student teachers and educational researchers – should take off the blinkers and think about how what we do affects everyone. Most importantly, we should always question the fiction that is presented as 'normal'.

Further reading

Alexander, R. (ed) (2010) *Children, their world, their education: Final report and recommendations of the Cambridge Primary Review*. Abingdon: Routledge. The report of the Cambridge Primary Review is a very comprehensive enquiry into English primary education. It provides an insightful alternative to government reports and policy.

Ball, S. J. (2008) *The education debate*. Bristol: The Policy Press. An excellent critique of neoliberal government education policies and politics. Stephen Ball takes a sociological approach to examining the changing face of education over the past twenty years.

Boaler, J. (1997) *Experiencing school mathematics: Teaching styles, sex and setting*. Buckingham: Open University Press. Described clearly in the chapter, Jo Boaler carries out a longitudinal study on two contrasting schools exploring 'traditional' and 'progressive' teaching methods. It is worth reading to form your own opinion of her highly respected study.

Llewellyn, A. and Mendick, H. (2011) 'Does every child count? Quality, equity and mathematics with/in Neoliberalism', in B. Atweh, M. Graven, W. Secada and P. Valero (eds), *Mapping equity and quality in mathematics education*. Dordrecht; New York: Springer. Here we unpack the notion of ability very similarly to how understanding is unpacked in this chapter. It offers a more developed debate that questions neoliberal values in education.

Walkerdine, V. (1990) *Schoolgirl fictions*. London: Verso. A brilliantly and imaginatively written collection of past articles and new thoughts that explore how masculinities and femininities are fictions lived as fact.

References

Alexander, R. (ed) (2010) *Children, their world, their education: Final report and recommendations of the Cambridge Primary Review*. Abingdon: Routledge.

Ball, S. J. (1994) *Education reform: a critical and post-structural approach*. Buckingham: Open University Press.

Barmby, P., Harries, T., Higgins, S. and Suggate, J. (2009) 'The array representation and primary children's understanding and reasoning in multiplication', *Educational Studies in Mathematics*, 70, 3, 217–241.

Bloom, B. (ed) (1956) *Taxonomy of educational objectives: handbook 1, cognitive domain/ by a commit tee of college and university examiners*. London: Longmans.

Boaler, J. (1997) *Experiencing school mathematics: teaching styles, sex and setting*. Buckingham: Open University Press.

Department for Education and Skills (DfES) (2006) *Primary framework for literacy and mathematics: Core position papers underpinning the renewal of guidance for teaching literacy and mathematics*. London: DfES.

Department for Education and Skills (DfES) (2007) *Making great progress: schools with outstanding rates of progression in key stage 2*. London: DfES.

Ernest, P. (1991) *The philosophy of mathematics education*. London: Falmer Press.

Foucault, M. (1978) *The history of sexuality (volume one): The will to knowledge*. London: Routledge.

Foucault, M. (2003) 'So is it important to think?', in P. Rabinow and N. Rose (eds), *The essential Foucault*. New York: The New Press.

Llewellyn, A., and Mendick, H. (2011) 'Does every child count? Quality, equity and mathematics with/in neoliberalism', in B. Atweh, M. Graven, W. Secada and P. Valero (eds), *Mapping equity and quality in mathematics education*. Dordrecht; New York: Springer.

Nias, J. (1989) *Primary teachers talking: a study of teaching as work*. London: Routledge.

Rose, N. (1999) *Governing the soul*. London: Free Association Books.

Skemp, R. (1976) 'Relational understanding and instrumental understanding', *Mathematics Teaching*, 77, 20–26.

Walkerdine, V. (1990) *Schoolgirl fictions*. London: Verso.

Walkerdine, V. (1997) 'Redefining the subject in situated cognition theory', in D. Kirshner and J. A. Whitson (eds), *Situated cognition: Social, semiotic, and psychological perspectives*. Mahwah, NJ: Lawrence Erlbaum.

Walkerdine, V. (1998) *Counting girls out: girls and mathematics (second edition)*. Abingdon: RoutledgeFalmer.

Chapter 12

A pedagogy for attainment for all

Hilary Povey

Introduction

Current practices in the teaching of mathematics in secondary schools in the UK do not promote attainment for all. Commenting on national public examination results, a recent report from the Joseph Rowntree Foundation finds that 'as so often, all seemed not too far from well at the top, but stubborn problems remained at the bottom' (Cassen and Kingdon, 2007, p.i). Despite the fact that attainment (as measured by public examinations) has risen in recent years, 'England ranks internationally among the countries with relatively high average educational achievement but also high inequality in achievement' (p.1). The report shows that low achievement correlates significantly with indicators of disadvantage and thus it is the case that 'underachievement is a social justice issue' (Watson, 2011, p.151).

The interplay between setting by previous attainment and 'ability thinking' is discussed elsewhere in this volume, notably, in the chapter I wrote with Mark Boylan and the chapter by Patricia George. There it is argued that setting practices and the 'ability thinking' on which such practices are based suppress the achievement of those whose current levels of attainment do not earn them a place in the top set, creating the notorious long tail of underachievement whilst not enhancing the attainment of those at the 'top'. Thus the most significant way to begin working towards high attainment for all is to tackle these two interconnected 'commonsense' notions: that ability is a given, fixed characteristic inhering in individuals and that grouping learners on the basis of previous attainment raises achievement. Re-organising mathematics classes into all attainment groups, however, is, firstly, not on its own enough (Hart *et al.*, 2004); and, secondly, is not within your gift as an individual teacher. In addition, many mathematics teachers in the UK who accept the desirability of all attainment teaching feel themselves ill prepared for the different pedagogical demands that they judge will be required. This is not surprising. As Susan Hart has noted, 'the search for pedagogical possibilities only *begins* once we have freed ourselves from deterministic notions about existing patterns and limits of human achievement' (Hart, 1998, p.160, original emphasis). Here, drawing on a substantial body of existing research, are set out some of those pedagogical possibilities which are designed to promote attainment for *all* learners of mathematics.

The notion of pedagogy employed here encompasses classroom practices; classroom relationships; philosophical understandings of the nature of mathematics; and ethical judgements about the purposes in teaching and learning mathematics. Pedagogical stances generate and are generated by the culture of the classroom, in itself dependent upon teachers' attitudes, conceptions, beliefs, views of the world and, perhaps most importantly, their values.

I begin by rehearsing briefly what is known about the ways in which current practices damage and alienate learners (including those in setted classes). From the work of Guy Claxton, I derive a framework for a pedagogy for attainment for all, drawing on four case studies from existing research to elaborate that framework. I conclude by considering the notion of 'transformability'.

WHAT DO WE CURRENTLY DO THAT DOESN'T WORK?

We know a great deal about what *doesn't* work – what doesn't work in terms of motivation and engagement and what doesn't work in terms of student learning, both damaging to attainment. In England, the Office for Standards in Education (Ofsted) recently reported that much – most – mathematics teaching is geared towards producing enhanced test scores and this leads to a high level of fragmentation in the mathematics presented with procedural approaches to the fore. It is known that such a pedagogy does not create learners who can think mathematically; it also leads to alienation, demotivation and disengagement (Nardi and Steward, 2003). In an extended case study, Jo Boaler describes teachers seeming to fracture mathematics to help their students get answers and she notes that 'it was the transmission of closed pieces of knowledge that formed the basis of the students' disaffection, misunderstandings and underachievement' (Boaler, 1997, p.145). Meaning-making is ignored and a sense of hopelessness is generated. And, ironically, such practices can undermine test scores.

In a rare case of an attempt to compare directly a traditional and an alternative approach to teaching and learning (Bell, 1994), two parallel classes in the same school with the same teacher were taught fractions using two very different methods; one involved carefully and gradually graded exercises including a large number of examples worked through individually and the other involved the students working in groups at fairly hard challenges involving the production mostly of their own examples. Although the groups performed comparably at the beginning with comparable improvement at the end of the nine lessons, when they were tested again after the summer holiday break the attainment of the graded exercise group had fallen off to a lower level than before the work began whereas the learning of the other group was well retained. The first class went from being highly motivated to bored and lethargic whereas the interest and involvement of the 'conflict and investigation' class increased.

Conventional approaches to mathematics teaching in the UK also produce fractured classroom relationships. When learners are working through 'bite-sized' exercises, they become separated from one another (Angier and Povey, 1999). Teacher-centred, test-dominated practices tend to encourage a competitive atmosphere which many learners find alienating: 'the students are unwilling to engage in this hierarchical game' (Nardi and Steward, 2003, p.359). Teacher–student dialogue comes to be framed as question–response–evaluation exchanges generating passivity and a fear of public and private shame (Boylan, Lawton and Povey, 2001).

Reflect on your own experiences of learning, in and out of school, and your observations of contemporary classrooms. Which aspects of your own and others' experiences have caused underachievement and alienation?

None of this analysis is new – we know what doesn't work. But we also know quite a lot about what does work – not enough attention is paid to this in current debates and this chapter is an attempt to redress that.

A PEDAGOGICAL FRAMEWORK FOR ATTAINMENT FOR ALL

Guy Claxton (2002) makes use of the notion of 'learning power' to help us understand how we can support young people to become effective learners. 'Learning power' refers to the personal traits, skills and habits of mind that enable a person to engage effectively with the challenge of learning – to be someone who knows what to do when they don't know what to do. Claxton (2002, p.67) highlights four key aspects of practice to which teachers need to pay attention if they are to succeed in enabling attainment for all:

1. How you talk to your students about the process of learning, the kinds of questions you encourage them to ask, the kinds of follow-up you expect and the visual images, prompts and records on the classroom walls;
2. The kinds of formal and informal comments and evaluations you make of students' work and how you respond when they are experiencing difficulty or confusion;
3. The kinds of activities and discussions which you initiate and what sense of purpose these engender in the learners;
4. And, perhaps above all, how you present yourself as a learner – what kind of model you offer, for instance, when things are not going according to plan or when a question arises that you have not anticipated.

> *Look at Claxton's list of specific things of which you need to become aware in order to develop learning power. All of these considerations are highly relevant to a mathematics pedagogy for attainment for all. For each, describe a practice that would support the development of learning power.*

I take these aspects as an organising structure for the rest of the chapter, with four specific case studies offering examples of alternative practice drawn from the research literature. I attempt to draw out some of the ways in which they exemplify engagement with these fundamental concerns.

Spenser: what is explicitly valued and shared with the whole class?

Spenser School, situated in an urban area of high deprivation, had a predominantly white working-class intake and a very low level of achievement. The department decided to undertake a radical change in the way that they taught mathematics: they knew that research evidence suggested that all attainment teaching would support their learners and, 'as a way of being able to address any issues of underachievement that were due to low expectations and inappropriate previous educational experience' (Watson and De Geest, nd), introduced it into the first two years of secondary school. Many of the ways they changed their thinking and their practice promoted the learning power which is vital to generating attainment for all; lessons can be learnt for all classrooms.

Right from the start, they knew they needed their students to develop a wide range of ways to work on mathematics to promote their thinking and engagement and to lay down habits for future work. They drew on a wide range of existing resources and evolved curriculum planning based on pairs of teachers preparing resources on a topic including a summary of the main activities, games, and ways to begin and end lessons; formative assessment activities and probing questions (see the chapter by Rachel Marks and Alice J. Onion); key words and mathematical ideas; and anticipated difficulties and misconceptions. Crucially, they then worked on the mathematics together and discussed the associated pedagogy. In addition, they expected to spend time together at the end of the day, being around and sharing ideas. They recognised that they had to 're-educate students to work together, to talk, to take risks, to "have a go", to discuss, and to do mathematics in other ways that were not worksheet or textbook exercises' (Watson and De Geest, nd).

Having decided to work in this way, Spenser became the subject of a research project focused on interventions with previously low attaining students (PLAS). Across the projects, the researchers reported:

> When videoing for research purposes, as well as when videoing for dissemination, we observed excitement, engagement and pleasure in mathematical activity in nearly all classes for some of the time. Teachers connected pleasure to understanding, citing instances where students had said 'I get it now'.
>
> (Watson and De Geest, nd)

Spenser had a dramatic rise in mathematics results in the high stakes national test at age 14, unmatched by similar increases elsewhere in the curriculum. As well as the move to all-attainment teaching, two replicable key factors relating to this rise in attainment were identified by the researchers. First, with the first-year students, there was to be a focus solely on mathematical methods of enquiry, returning only later to a programme of specific mathematical topics. Second, the teaching they observed was characterised by 'listening to learners, using their ideas, and developing reasoning' (Watson and De Geest, nd). Much of this teaching was by 'leading the collective thinking of a class through the orchestration of ideas' (Watson, 2011, p.149) and, as the project developed, a sense of zeal 'for their students to understand key mathematical ideas' (149). Anne Watson writes: 'I am convinced that many learners learnt mathematics during those whole-class episodes because of the methods of *knowledgeable mediation* used' (149, emphasis added).

There are two facets to the thinking and practice described here that link in with the first learning power focus: *what the teachers explicitly value and discuss with the whole class*. First, the teachers made direct and repeated reference to what kinds of mental activity were important and relevant to learning mathematics. This included some general effort and study skills but crucially also involved a wide range of specifically mathematical characteristics with which, it was made clear, everyone was expected to be able to engage.

Some of these specifically mathematical characteristics were:

- *Visualising without prompting.*
- *Being aware of difference and sameness.*
- *Volunteering conjectures.*
- *Creating examples to explore ideas.*
- *Asking good questions.*
- *Being aware some methods are more powerful than others.*
- *Asking why and why not.*
- *Providing answers that voluntarily include reasons.*
- *And taking time to understand mathematical ideas.*

Which of these mathematical characteristics do you want explicitly to share with learners in your classroom?

Choose one and explain why you value it. What might you do as a teacher to make it happen?

Second, the teachers were enabled to do this because they worked together themselves on the mathematical activities they were planning to use with their students. There was a focus throughout on the mathematics and 'planning was primarily about the best ways to give all students access to mathematical ideas' (Watson and De Geest, nd). This developed the depth of their own personal mathematical knowledge and thus their facility with responding to the mathematical thinking of their students as shared mathematical meanings were negotiated in their classrooms. It enabled them to give public praise for the sort of mathematical thinking they were wanting to encourage in their learners and to notice and reinforce such mental activity whenever it occurred; this in turn enabled all their students to become more effective learners.

Railside: talking to groups and individuals about their learning and achievements

Railside School, situated in the United States, had an ethnic and socially diverse intake and was on the 'wrong side of the tracks'. The mathematics department developed an effective approach to learning mathematics that promoted high achievement for all in absolute terms when compared to other schools and, most significantly, also reduced differences in achievement between learners (Boaler, 2008). Learners from all levels of prior attainment did well, substantially better than would be expected as the norm, but without opening up the gap between high and low attainers; no 'long tail' was produced, and systematic sites of disadvantage – gender, class and ethnicity – were overcome. The department was committed to all attainment teaching groups but, even outside that context, much can be learnt from studying their practices. Students' self-respect was developed as was their authority as learners and these qualities supported the growth of what Jo Boaler characterised as 'relational equity' (2008): students' respect and concern for their peers and for cultural and individual difference. Teacher behaviour which offers respect helps students to develop and enhance their self-image and their own expectations, which in turn enhance the students' academic achievement.

Central to the practices of the Railside teachers was a form of structured group work based on 'complex instruction'. They worked in class with mathematical problems having open and accessible starting points, ones which provided many opportunities for success: there were many more ways to be successful and many more students succeeded (Boaler, 2008). The key characteristics of their approach are summarised elsewhere (Boylan and Povey, 2009): they supported students to develop and carry out specific roles when working in groups; affirmed the competence of all and had high expectations of all; developed students' sense of their responsibility for each other's learning through classroom practices and forms of assessment including assessing collaborative outcomes; emphasised that success in mathematics was the product of effort rather than ability and all could succeed; and explicitly outlined the type of learning practices that would help students to learn.

Here I report on the practices of one of those teachers, Ms McClure who was successful in fostering collaborative interactions within groups that promoted the attainment of all. There is not room in this chapter to share all the useful things that can be learnt from Ms McClure's practices (Staples, 2008, 356–366); rather, here I attempt to draw out how in particular she built the students' learning power by *how she talked to groups and individuals about their learning and achievements*.

When students were working together in groups, Ms McClure expected any individual group member to be able to report the understandings of the group. If, when quizzed, it became clear that an individual did not fully understand the problem yet, she would leave the group explaining that she would come back, re-stating that she wanted everyone to 'have it'. She did not describe this initial response as 'incompetent or wrong, but rather as work in progress' and 'expected everyone in the group would understand'; she would comment 'not that it's wrong, it's just incomplete', prompting groups to continue their thinking and build on the work they had already done (p.360). The tasks she chose were 'group-worthy' and enabled a variety of approaches and solutions. Thus she was able to value each group's work and position each solution as 'evidence of competence and productive mathematical work' (p.361). She debriefed both on the mathematics and on the group processes, celebrating 'engagement, persistence, and good mathematical thinking' (p.357) always focusing on the whole group's achievement and the mutual responsibility for each other's learning that the groups had:

> Many of you are really thinking hard about how to approach the problem and coming up with great ideas. I'm a little concerned however that not everyone in the group is together always. Sometimes a group member is being left behind. Groups, be sure everyone understands what's going on. And everyone, be sure you ask questions!
>
> Staples (2008, pp.357–358)

Thus, we see throughout that Ms McClure's way of talking to the students about their learning and achievements reflected a commitment to the idea that all students are capable of engaging with mathematics and achieving more, especially those whose current attainment is lower. This enabled them to become powerful learners and produced results for all.

What do you want to be the key characteristics of how you talk to groups and individuals about their work? And what do you most want to avoid?

Phoenix Park: what activities are selected?

Phoenix Park was another school studied by Jo Boaler (1997) in which lower attainers benefited significantly and overall attainment at 16 outshone a socioeconomic comparator which used a traditional approach to teaching mathematics. Again, students at Phoenix Park worked in all attainment classes but some aspects of their teachers' practices contribute to building learner power in other contexts too. Here the focus is on the fact that the students worked on open-ended projects which they explored using their own ideas and mathematical knowledge.

> 'You're just set a task and then you go about it … you explore the different things, and they help you in doing that.'
>
> Boaler (1997, p.17)

Such projects involved problem posing and problem solving – this creates a classroom in which it is alright to take risks; where questioning, decision making and negotiation are the norm, where there is an expectation that all have a contribution to make and no-one is offered a restricted and diminished curriculum. The open curriculum (and their all attainment groupings) created 'can do' learners who could take their mathematics into their lives. They not only thought that they could use school mathematics in real-world mathematical situations; they also thought that school mathematics had equipped them to tackle real world problems that were not mathematical. When asked about the role of mathematics, a typical response was:

J: Solve the problems and think about other problems and solve them, problems that aren't connected with maths, think about them.
JB: You think the way you do maths helps you do that?
J: Yes.
JB: Things that aren't to do with maths?
J: It's more the thinking side to sort of look at everything you've got and think about how to solve it.

Jackie, Phoenix Park, Year 10 (p.100)

As noted in the chapter 'Ability thinking', the sense of self revealed by such responses had a long-term impact, spilling over into their understandings of their life chances and their possible trajectories (Boaler, 2005).

Because the students worked on large problems, activities that were mathematically rich, time and intellectual space were generated within which they could make links both within mathematics and between mathematics and other experiences (Angier and Povey, 1999). Mathematics then had the room to grow as an open and creative subject, not restricted to a rule-bound set of procedures, which allowed students the opportunity to change their view of themselves as learners. We know that students, especially working-class students, prefer informal relationships built on a basis of mutual respect (Povey and Boylan, 1998). In setted classrooms these are typically offered only to top-set students and, more generally, less to working-class students. At Phoenix Park there is a strong sense that these were offered to all, *growing out of the nature of the mathematical activities taking place.*

In both these ways, *the activities that the teachers selected* played a key role in building learning power: those activities could be approached in a variety of ways with a wide range of appropriate tools thus providing opportunities for learners to see themselves as active, as choosing, deciding, producing arguments for and against, assessing validity and generating questions and ideas. This sense of self was instrumental in generating productive relationships between teachers and learners and between learners and achievement. (Readers may be interested to compare this with the critical account of Boaler's work in the previous chapter by Anna Llewellyn).

Choose five such mathematical activities. For each, list what might be gained from using the activity in your classroom and what difficulties you think you might encounter.

A spacious classroom: how learning is modelled

The last case study involves a spacious classroom in which learning power was built by the way in which *learning was modelled by the teacher.* When describing how she worked with her students, Corinne Angier explained, 'I was thinking about the students as being apprenticed as learners of maths and of me being a model learner not a teacher'. She regarded it as key that, at least part of the time, the teacher and the students were engaged in the *same* activity: that is, learning to be mathematicians (Leo Rogers, in his chapter, offers some ways of doing this). This has a powerful effect on how learners think about themselves and of what they think they are capable.

> If one enters the educational enterprise with arrogance one's own views of knowledge quickly overpower the insights of the children. When the classroom norms are developed in such a way as to promote the exchange of student methods with mutual tolerance and respect, the children themselves become increasingly confident of their contributions and the system becomes self-reinforcing. In both peer relations and in adult–child interactions, *the roles of expert, teacher, learner, and novice, are flexibly drawn.*
>
> Confrey (1995, p.41, emphasis added)

When the teacher is, at times, a co-learner, the expected source of mathematical authority – the teacher, the textbook and the answer book making up a united authority which needs no specification or justification (Alro and Skovsmose, 1996, p.4) – is unsettled. In Corinne's classroom, there was room for the students to have insights she did not already have as they learnt together:

> 'She treats you as though you are like … not just a kid. If you say look this is wrong she'll listen to you. If you challenge her she will try and see it your way.' (Donna)

'She doesn't regard herself as higher.' (Neil)

'She's not bothered about being proven wrong. Most teachers hate being wrong … being proven wrong by students.' (Neil)

'It's more like a discussion … you can give answers and say what you think.' (Frances)

Angier and Povey (1999, p.157)

And all the students interviewed knew that Corinne found passionate enjoyment in the subject they were studying together:

'She loves doing triangles!' (Dan)

'She loves it … she's right interested in it.' (Frances)

Angier and Povey (1999, p.151)

Although they smiled and found this strange, they knew it was a key element in their own learning. By modelling her engagement with the subject as one worthy of study, effort, application and the strive for understanding, she offered both the learners and the subject respect: and showed her students what it was to learn.

> *What difficulties would you experience in teaching a lesson where you did not expect to know all the outcomes in advance? What are the mathematical benefits and problems of unexpectedness?*

Working on mathematics alone or with departmental colleagues also supports us in enhancing attainment. By doing so, we gain a deep understanding of mathematical activity which in turn helps us understand how learners are thinking (Watson, 2006).

Conclusion

I have taken from four case studies specific characteristics related to the framework for attainment for all. Each of the studies gives a much richer account of pedagogical possibilities than has been able to elaborate here. However, what they all have in common is a notion of 'transformability' defined as:

> a firm and unswerving conviction that there is the potential for change in current patterns of achievement and response, that things can change and be changed for the better, sometimes even dramatically, as a result of what happens and what people do in the present.
>
> Hart *et al.* (2004, p.166)

As Watson (2006) notes, it is the belief that learners *can* change which seems to make the difference. The transformability perspective echoes the concept of 'learning how to learn' based on the development of learners' resilience, resourcefulness, reflectiveness and reciprocity (Claxton, 2002). It finds support in the work of Carol Dweck (2006) written about in the chapter 'Ability thinking' about fixed and malleable mindsets which offers an alternative, evidence-based view of human capacity which has been found to improve motivation and attainment.

This pedagogic approach has three interrelated sets of purposes that can guide us in our practice:

- Intellectual purposes which include ensuring everybody has access to the curriculum that it is relevant and meaningful and that thinking and reasoning are enhanced.
- Social purposes which include a focus on the inclusion of everybody and promoting a sense of belonging and community.
- Affective or emotional purposes which include developing learners' confidence, security and control over their own learning.

We need our classrooms to be places where learners set up productive relationships with themselves as learners and with the processes of coming to know mathematics. Studying closely accounts of what teachers who have achieved this have done is both an inspiration and an effective way for us to learn, helping us to understand what more innovative pedagogical practices are available to us. Crucially, however, they also help us call into question currently dominant ideas about how to support attainment – setting, testing, targeting, differentiated expectations and so on – thus making a vital contribution to debates about how to enhance long term attainment by creating learners who both believe in their own capacity to learn and deem it to be worthwhile engaging in doing so.

Further reading

As noted above, each of the four case studies referred to in the chapter would repay exploring further. Each of them is accompanied by relevant references and I can think of no better further reading than engaging more deeply with these sites of practice.

Also recommended is *Inclusive Mathematics* by Mike Ollerton and Anne Watson (2001), London: Continuum. It is written by two highly experienced teachers both of whom are deeply committed to attainment for all and is based on the principle that all learners are capable of sophisticated mathematical thought. It presents the tools with which we can work to reach all students of mathematics.

Acknowledgements

I am very grateful to Mark Boylan for his helpful comments on earlier drafts of this chapter.

References

Alro, H., and Skovsmose, O. (1996) 'On the right track', *For the Learning of Mathematics*, 16, 1, 2–40.
Angier, C. and Povey, H. (1999) 'One teacher and a class of school students: their perception of the culture of their mathematics classroom and its construction', *Educational Review*, 51, 2, 147–160.
Bell, A. (1994) 'Teaching for the test', in M. Selinger (ed), *Teaching mathematics*. London: Routledge.
Boaler, J. (1997) *Experiencing school mathematics: teaching styles, sex and setting*. Buckingham: Open University Press.
Boaler, J. (2005) 'The "psychological prisons" from which they never escaped: The role of ability grouping in reproducing social class inequalities', *Forum*, 47, 2 and 3, 125–134.
Boaler, J. (2008) 'Promoting "relational equity" and high mathematics achievement through an innovative mixed-ability approach', *British Educational Research Journal*, 34, 2, 167–194.

Boylan, M., Lawton, P. and Povey, H. (2001) '"I'd be more likely to talk in class if …": some students' ideas about strategies to increase mathematical participation in whole class interactions', *Proceedings of 25th Psychology of Mathematics Education (PME) Conference*, Utrecht, Holland, July.

Boylan, M. and Povey, H. (2009) 'Mathematics', in Cole, M. (ed), *Equality in the secondary school: promoting good practice across the curriculum.* London: Continuum.

Cassen, R. and Kingdon, G. (2007) *Tackling low educational achievement.* York: Joseph Rowntree Foundation. Available at: http://www.jrf.org.uk/publications/tackling-low-educational-achievement (accessed 5 February 2012).

Claxton, G. (2002) *Building learning power: helping young people become better learners.* Bristol: TLO.

Confrey, J. (1995) 'A theory of intellectual development: part III', *For the Learning of Mathematics*, 15, 2, 36–45.

Dweck. S. (2006) *Mindset.* New York: Random House.

Hart, S. (1998) 'A sorry tail: ability, pedagogy and educational reform', *British Journal of Educational Studies*, 46, 2, 153–168.

Hart, S., Dixon, A., Drummond, M. and McIntyre, D. (2004) *Learning without limits.* Maidenhead: Open University Press.

Nardi, E. and Steward, S. (2003) 'Is mathematics T.I.R.E.D.? A profile of quiet disaffection in the secondary mathematics classroom', *British Education Research Journal*, 29, 3, 345–367.

Povey, H. and Boylan, M. (1998) 'Working class students and the culture of mathematics classrooms in the UK', *Proceedings of 22nd Psychology of Mathematics Education (PME) Conference*, Stellenbosch, South Africa, July.

Staples, M. (2008) 'Promoting student collaboration in a detracked, heterogeneous secondary mathematics classroom', *Journal of Mathematics Teacher Education*, 11, 5, 349–371.

Watson, A. (2011) 'Mathematics and comprehensive ideals', *Forum*, 53, 1, 145–151.

Watson, A., and De Geest, E. (nd) 'Changes in mathematics teaching project'. Available at: www.cmtp.co.uk (accessed 6 February 2012).

Part III

Debates in mathematics curriculum and assessment

Introduction to *Debates in mathematics curriculum and assessment*

The structure of this book starts wide, looking to mathematics education within the social and the political; then it narrows, in the middle section, to focus on teaching and learning within individual classrooms. In this final section we look at the processes around curriculum and assessment that have so much power over what individual teachers and students feel able to do. In working on this book, we have been haunted by our former teacher-selves. Although she works closely with student teachers, Dawn's research is in physics and, whilst Heather has done research in mathematics education before, she's worked on nothing so focused on teaching as this book. So, in our final introduction, Heather has included a few memories of being a maths teacher into our discussion of the five chapters in this section.

The section opens with Margaret Brown's survey of debates around the mathematics curriculum in England. In tracking the history of what's in and what's out of the curriculum (from long division to circle theorems) she shows clearly that these decisions are driven by values and ideologies, not objectivity, and so reminds us of the messages from Richard Barwell's chapter that politics is mathematical and mathematics is political. Margaret also notes the impossibility of exploring what is taught separately from how it is measured. The way that assessment drives teaching recurs through the chapters in this section and at no time has this relationship been more apparent in England than now; teachers and schools (and students, of course) find themselves judged by the results they get, with funding tied to this. As David Gillborn and Deborah Youdell (2000) have argued, this leads to educational triage, where some children become the educational equivalent of swing states in the US presidential election; those on the border between success and failure that consequently attract disproportionate resources.

Margaret reminds us of the failure of mathematics education, with children, despite having an hour a day of mathematics teaching for seven years, often leaving primary school unable to accomplish the 'basics' of calculation, fractions, etc. However, she complicates this account by drawing on research which shows that many children, who can perform calculations fluently outside school, fail at these same tasks when tested on them inside the classroom. This again raises questions, which resonate through the book, about what mathematics we're teaching and why.

These questions are taken up in the next chapter by Hamsa Venkat. Hamsa writes from the South African experience of introducing a programme of mathematical literacy alongside a more traditional mathematics curriculum. For us, her work challenges the division between mathematics and its context, one which, regrettably, we now realise we have reproduced in the structure of this book. Hamsa looks in detail at an example of how we measure social inequality which is, like Richard Barwell's example of climate change, difficult despite using what we have come to think of as 'elementary' maths (cumulative frequency, percentages, summation of differences and measures of the size and spread of a distribution). This challenges our ideas of what mathematics is and what makes a mathematical task easy or difficult, and in so doing, 'the walls that traditionally make mathematics an enterprise that is restricted to mathematics classrooms start to be chipped at'. As a teacher it is challenging to follow Hamsa and 'take a critical advocacy position for mathematical literacy that calls for the "literate learning of mathematics" as well as "mathematical literacy" as a life-related competence'.

The next, and final, three chapters of the book look at various aspects of assessment: Assessment for Learning (AfL) and the English and Welsh examinations at 16+ (GCSEs) and 18+ (A-levels). Rachel Marks and Alice J. Onion begin with AfL, an approach which emphasises the relationship between assessment and teaching and looks to shift the balance from summative to formative assessment practices – ones that aim to feed into future teaching and learning rather than simply to provide a terminal grading. Their chapter raises questions about how policies such as AfL are implemented – a process which, as Stephen Ball (1994) shows, is never predictable being shot through with contingency and contradiction, as teachers take up some parts and reject or subvert others. In particular, Rachel and Alice highlight how traffic lights, intended for use formatively to get a sense of how far students feel they understand an issue, are often used summatively.

In Rachel and Alice's chapter, as in Margaret's, we can see the loss of pedagogies that develop mathematical processes, for: 'processes cannot be assessed on a screening for errors basis; they cannot be marked as right or wrong. It is necessary instead to make judgements on the quality of work and students' thinking'. As a maths teacher, Heather marked work most school nights. Many times since leaving teaching she has wondered how useful this was. Perhaps had she had access to the ideas in this chapter while she was a teacher this would have enabled her to question, or even change, this practice. Or would the expectations of her students as well as her own image of what 'good mathematics teaching' should look like have proved too strong? As all the chapters in this section suggest, mathematics carries expectations from students, teachers, parents, politicians and society in general – so enacting any practice that jars with these expectations is difficult.

The political nature of examinations is apparent in the chapters by Ian Jones and Cathy Smith: these look at terminal examinations, which feel like the complete opposite of the assessment cycle with students at its heart that motivates Rachel and Alice's writing. Mathematics and English, above all other subjects, are embroiled in ideas of 'standards' and 'quality' (Atweh *et al.*, 2011). Indeed the summer of 2012 brought a scandal in England and Wales, as students who had been confidently predicted a critical C grade in their English GCSE, instead secured 'failing' D grades (Vasagar, 2012). In the aftermath it emerged that higher marks were expected to secure a C in these summer exams than in those taken the previous January, a shift that was later revealed to have been related to political pressure exerted by the Education Minister Michael Gove.

Ian gives us a rare insider view of the workings of the Awarding Bodies that design GCSE examinations. In this way we can see the restrictions within which they currently operate and how this results in questions that require only short reasoning chains and so cannot assess processes. Like Margaret, Ian asks us to reflect on why we teach mathematics, foregrounding pleasure, wonder and creativity, things that are not facilitated by fragmentary examinations. His table of alternative ways of assessing mathematical skills reminds us that it doesn't have to be this way. Towards the end of Heather's time as a school student there were mathematics GCSEs that were 100% coursework, based on the endearingly named SMILE course. As a teacher she enthusiastically taught the SMP A-levels that included both investigations and mathematical comprehension within their assessments.

Finally, Cathy Smith closes the book by comparing and contrasting three advanced mathematics qualifications. Her work again draws attention to the dominant way of thinking about mathematics as a hierarchical subject and one embedded in broader hierarchies of knowledge, highlighting tensions between this and processes that map the equivalence of different qualifications. As in all the previous chapters, her analysis of mathematics examination questions shows that these limit how students and teachers come to view mathematics, as they: 'use a structure and wording that restrict opportunities for students to select strategies, to move back and forth between representations and to organise responses. They signal a very clear procedure for candidates and mark-schemes to follow'.

Cathy is interested in how opting into or out of the different mathematics courses available to young people allow them to work on themselves, that is, to express who they are and who they want to be. We will end our introduction by using this idea to reflect on one commonly held belief about maths: that it is 'hard'. The idea that mathematics should be hard is part of what Margaret refers to as the 'mental hygiene' purpose of maths. This leads to courses that are more accessible and have higher pass rates being viewed not as successes – for opening up maths to more people – but as failures in making maths too easy. Easiness becomes something bad that must be avoided (and perhaps left to other subjects like media studies and sociology that Heather has given up mathematics to pursue). Heather recalls that at one college where she worked, she and the other maths teachers decided to teach the part of the statistics curriculum that students found most difficult first, lest students get the impression that maths is easy. Whilst the 'hardness' of mathematics is often given as a reason for dropping the subject, Cathy shows how it can also appeal to students allowing them to prove their intelligence. This leads us to reflect on our own reasons for choosing mathematical courses of study – how are we invested in maintaining the idea that maths is hard and so that we are special for having achieved some success at it? How can teachers get away from the need to reproduce mathematics as accessible to the few rather than the many?

References

Atweh, B., Graven, M., Secada, W. and Valero, P. (eds) (2011) *Mapping equity and quality in mathematics education*. Dordrecht: Springer.

Ball, S. J. (1994) *Education reform: a critical and post-structural approach*. Buckingham: Open University Press.

Gillborn, D. and Youdell, D. (2000) *Rationing education: policy, practice, reform, and equity*. Buckingham: Open University Press.

Vasagar, J. (2012) 'GCSE row: pupils, schools and councils launch legal action'. Available at: http://www.guardian.co.uk/education/2012/oct/26/gcse-english-grade-legal-action (accessed 7 January 2013).

Chapter 13

Debates in mathematics curriculum and assessment

Margaret Brown

LIMITATIONS

The word 'curriculum' has many meanings; it can at one extreme be interpreted as incorporating all the experiences that students have in school both in and out of the classroom and, at the other extreme, as a dry two-page statement of a prescribed national curriculum.

A helpful distinction in this broad spectrum, often used in international comparison contexts, separates out three different aspects of the curriculum:

- The 'intended' curriculum: the 'official' agreed specifications that teachers are expected to work to, whether these originate at national, regional or school level.
- The 'implemented' curriculum: what students actually experience in the classroom.
- The 'attained' curriculum: what students really learn as a result of the teaching they experience.

I will focus this chapter around debates concerned mainly with the 'intended' curriculum, and more specifically to the national curriculum in England, past and present. Although country-specific, the debates which arise are universal and likely to affect all mathematics curricula at any level.

What is perhaps more particular to the English context is that the implemented curriculum that students experience in classrooms is likely to be greatly influenced by the nature of the examinations for which they are being prepared. This is because of a strong emphasis in England on national examination results at ages 11 and 16 in mathematics and English as an evaluation of schools, and not just of individual learners. It is therefore impossible to discuss curriculum sensibly without any reference to the form of the associated high stakes external assessment regime in place.

As with curriculum, assessment can have many meanings within education, but the only debates concerning assessment I will describe here are those concerned with the types of external assessment which have a strong effect on the implemented curriculum. (See the chapter by Rachel Marks and Alice J. Onion for a contrasting focus on formative assessment).

The chapter is structured by questions which indicate the areas of dispute and debate. I have given particular attention to debates which are current, at the time of writing, in relation to the long-expected first draft of a new national curriculum for mathematics in England in spring 2012 (finally issued in February 2013).

WHAT IS THE PROBLEM WITH SPECIFYING A MATHS CURRICULUM?

Most people outside education believe that the mathematics curriculum in schools and colleges is pretty uncontroversial. Education Ministers in the past (Keith Joseph and Kenneth Baker in England in the 1980s) chose to start their curriculum reforms with mathematics in the expectation that it would be easy to reach agreement, and it would be free of the emotional battles which hover around English (phonics versus real books, creative writing versus grammar and spelling, and so on).

There even seems to be a quite short list of what is important. At primary school, most people would probably include counting, learning addition and subtraction facts and multiplication tables, doing written 'sums' in the four operations, and using simple fractions and decimals. In fact ministers find it difficult to understand why primary teachers seem to have problems instilling this apparently limited body of knowledge into all children when they have an hour a day for seven years to do it. It almost seems reasonable to conclude that if children cannot get a reasonable score in the national tests at 11, then teachers must be incompetent.

At secondary level, admittedly, things become a bit more complicated. It might well be a common view that to do well at GCSE (the General Certificate of Secondary Education, taken at or before age 16), you need to be able to shift letters around to solve simultaneous and quadratic equations, to know names and properties of various types of angles, triangles and quadrilaterals, to use trigonometry to work out the sides and angles of triangles, and to be able to do written calculations with decimals, percentages and fractions. Why all this is important knowledge may be a bit obscure to the average person or even a philosopher of education (White and Bramall, 2000), but there is an acceptance that it is there because it is important as a preparation for studying mathematics in the 16–18 phase, and A-level content is itself determined by the requirements of university departments in mathematics, physics and engineering (see the chapter by Cathy Smith). Most people understand that a good maths GCSE is helpful in getting a well-paid job, even if the knowledge and skills you acquire don't always seem of much practical use.

Some holes were blown in this perception of the appropriateness of traditional mathematics content by researchers who started to talk to children and adults about how they went about solving problems. For many years before English translations became widely available in the 1950s, Jean Piaget in Geneva had been discovering all sorts of interesting things about children's thinking. For example:

- Children might be able to count two sets of objects perfectly in order to check there are the same number of objects in both sets, but might still believe that the line that is more spread out contains more objects.
- Children might have learned rules at school for working out ratios but very few seemed to be able to use this knowledge to solve scientific problems.

Many other researchers joined in during the 1970s and 1980s (e.g. Hart, 1981) and found, for example, that:

- Children who can accurately recite number names in the correct order can still often obtain the wrong answers to counting problems.

- Many children have problems remembering mathematical facts and procedures for written sums like subtraction of three-digit numbers, and can only reconstruct the steps they have forgotten if they have sufficient understanding of the ideas underpinning the process.
- Children who found the rules for doing written calculations difficult to remember at school could sometimes perfectly well perform the same calculations in everyday life using their own mental methods.
- When doing written calculations, many children and adults choose to use methods different to those they were taught at school.
- Children may be expert at written routines for multiplication and division, but faced with a real-life problem they do not always recognise which operation is needed or which number to subtract from or divide by.
- Children may come up with crazy answers without noticing, because they have no idea what sort of number they are expecting as an answer.
- Very few students have sufficient understanding of secondary mathematics to be able to solve problems other than those they have been trained to solve, and many find difficult even those they have been trained to solve.

Suddenly there was a large body of research which suggested that it was not effective for many students to be taught mathematics as mainly facts and procedures, since they find them hard to remember and apply. This did not mean that some students could not manage to work out for themselves the meanings and connections lying behind the facts and procedures, depending on the complexity of the operations involved. But clearly most students, most of the time, struggled with remembering and applying the procedures more than a few weeks after they had been taught them. As Gwen Ineson and Sunita Babbar discuss in their chapter, to use procedures flexibly, students also needed teaching which helped them to understand, at least to some degree, the concepts which lay behind the procedures, and to practice in applying them in non-routine problems, both purely mathematical and in realistic contexts.

> *Can you think back to when you were at school and were taught a particular rule or procedure where you felt you had little idea why it worked? How did it make you feel? Did you have problems remembering the steps? What sort of understandings would have helped?*

WHAT TYPES OF KNOWLEDGE SHOULD A CURRICULUM INCLUDE?

The research referred to in the previous section was published just in time to strongly affect a major report on mathematics teaching, the Cockcroft Report (DES/WO 1982). This in turn influenced both a 1985 report on the mathematics curriculum from the national inspectorate and then, in 1989, the first national curriculum in England to be imposed for more than 80 years. There was also by this time a new awareness of broad curriculum objectives based on an innovative American report on assessment by Benjamin Bloom. This analysed test items into types designed to assess different types of knowledge and had a strong effect also on curriculum design. The 1985 HMI report reflected Bloom's work in suggesting that the mathematics curriculum should not just be a string of facts and procedures but be described as a set of objectives under the headings of Facts, Skills, Concepts, Strategies and Attitudes. Here 'skills' were used to describe procedures like solving linear equations, and 'strategies' to describe broad processes like 'being systematic' and 'proving'.

During the formulation of the 1989 national curriculum it became clear that there was a chasm in understanding between, on one side, the politicians and civil servants and some employers, who took a 'traditional' view of the mathematics curriculum, and, on the other side, the mathematics education specialists in schools, local authorities, universities and national bodies, who were strongly affected by the new research and hence felt a much wider curriculum specification was necessary, including material under all the headings used in the HMI report.

The battles over this first formulation of a mathematics national curriculum were reported and analysed by two researchers, Stephen Ball (1990) and Paul Ernest (1991). They each used an analytical framework provided by Raymond Williams to describe the differing orientations to education among different actors in the negotiation.

These authors characterise as 'industrial trainers' those we have already described who expect the mathematics curriculum to contain a narrow set of traditional facts and skills, focusing at primary level on written procedures (or algorithms) for the four arithmetical operations. In the 1980s one such was the then Prime Minister, Margaret Thatcher (1993, p.593), who told us in her memoirs that she was only interested in 'key subjects' and had envisaged a 'basic syllabus' and 'simple tests' in calculation skills at the end of primary schools (and the equivalent in English), rather than the much more detailed curriculum and assessment which emerged. When Labour came to power in 1997, their first Secretary of State for Education, David Blunkett, also issued populist press releases which echoed this 'industrial trainer' view, demonstrating that it is by no means the preserve of a single part of the political spectrum. His aims seemed to be restricted to the ability to 'know their tables, can do basic sums' (Brown *et al.*, 2000).

Indeed the first Conservative junior minister with responsibility from 2010–2012 for drafting a new curriculum, Nick Gibb, also espoused the view that facts, tables and written procedures (algorithms) are all that is needed to specify the primary curriculum. When concerns were expressed to him about the omission of understanding and problem-solving processes from the curriculum drafts, they were brushed aside, first as something that students will automatically acquire later (which the research quoted earlier demonstrates rarely to happen) or as related to pedagogy rather than curriculum.

Michael Gove (2010), the Conservative Secretary of State as I write this, appears to take a less harsh view over concepts but not over processes/strategies, which he described as 'vague generic statements of little value'.

This debate about what forms of knowledge should be specified in a curriculum is thus ongoing and critical.

> *To illustrate each in turn of the following categories, think of one objective (other than those already used as examples) which would usefully appear in a mathematics curriculum under that heading: a) Facts, b) Skills, c) Concepts, d) Strategies and e) Attitudes?*

WHAT STYLE OF EXTERNAL EXAMS?

Returning to the Thatcher view, it is interesting that a reference is made to simple tests. The belief that the facts and procedures which are thought to constitute the mathematics curriculum can be readily assessed by short questions, which test recall of facts and procedures, is part of the industrial trainer orientation as described by Ernest (1991). Again this is a cause of debate with educationalists who argue not only that concepts and strategies/processes are essential aspects of mathematics learning, but that these require longer and more complex items for their assessment. Indeed some strategies, like systematic planning, may only be adequately assessed in classwork or extended coursework, for example, planning food for a party or investigating number patterns. Further, if these extended items are not included in high stakes tests, then the broader aspects of maths will not be adequately taught. For example the English inspection agency, Ofsted (2008), suggest that high stakes tests with routine short questions are driving the curriculum to focus on fragmented procedures, since teachers are expected to 'teach to the tests'.

To avoid this situation, the first sets of national curriculum assessments in the early 1990s were designed as linked tasks of different lengths (known as Standard Assessment Tasks). These were to assess the ability to understand and to use and apply mathematics as well as the ability to recall facts and procedures. At age seven the tasks were administered to all children in small groups by their teachers. They included a task in which children had to take it in turn to add the scores on two dice, then to play a board game using addition and subtraction, and finally to design a game of their own.

At age 14 where the tasks only got as far as the pilot stage, short and long tasks were designed using a common theme and were integrated into a 2–3 week teaching programme (one set of tasks related to investigations with, and properties of, sets of octagonal beer mats). In spite of the fact that these were shown to be reliable and valid assessments and were popular with teachers and students, they were abandoned when a new Conservative Education Minister (Kenneth Clarke) dismissed them as 'elaborate nonsense' and required them all to be replaced by straightforward written tests (Daugherty, 1995).

Under the same government, the coursework element of mathematics GCSE was limited to 25% of the marks, and gradually under different administrations this has been reduced until it has been removed from maths GCSE entirely. This was partly for practical reasons in that the way coursework was assessed had led to abuse of the system, but instead of trying to improve the methods used to assess coursework so as to achieve the original aims of assessing a wider range of understanding and strategies, it was simply abandoned. When examinations and tests are high stakes, there is pressure from teachers, government and awarding bodies to reduce tests to those features which are regarded as routine and easily coachable. (The chapter by Ian Jones looks at these issues in detail in the context of GCSE examinations).

The key adviser to the curriculum review at the time of writing, Tim Oates, suggests that he understands these issues:

> If the specifications do not identify those elements of 'deep learning' essential to understanding in subjects (and focus only on a narrow range of surface elements of subjects) and do not identify those elements essential to progression … then tests are likely to be narrow in scope, and lead to narrow 'teaching to the test'.
>
> (Oates, 2010, p.8)

Nevertheless, at primary level ministers are currently (Autumn 2012) suggesting that the only specified mathematics curriculum will be a core set of number facts and skills, which are expected to be assessed by routine recall items and written sums.

Using the specific examples of objectives you thought of which could be classified under concept, strategy and attitude in the previous task, can you design a way of assessing each of them?

WHAT ARE THE JUSTIFICATIONS FOR SELECTION OF CONTENT?

So far, the debate has been described as between those politicians who take an 'industrial trainer' stance favouring facts and procedures and educationists who believe that even for efficient recall and use of procedures, a wider curriculum definition is necessary which includes both understanding of the mathematical ideas which underpin the procedures, and more general problem-solving processes.

However there is a broader debate about which facts and procedures, and indeed which understanding and processes, it is important for students to learn.

Conservative Education Ministers in the Coalition government which came into power in May 2010 lost little time in announcing that there would be a new national curriculum. The rationale for changing the curriculum was entirely phrased in terms of declining standards in the international PISA (Programme for International Student Assessment) surveys. (Whether and to what extent such a decline has taken place is not in fact as clear as is claimed (Brown, 2011), but that will not be pursued here).

It followed from this that the government's intention was to use as a basis for the new curriculum the knowledge that was included in curricula in high-attaining administrations. This strategy has many problems in terms of validity (Askew *et al.*, 2010), but additionally it results in ministers needing to give no reason for including specific curriculum content other than that some high-attaining country does so. Even this strategy for a cut-and-paste curriculum ran into problems as the draft curriculum promised for September 2011 did not appear even informally until July 2012; thus the national implementation has had to be delayed until 2014.

The failure to consider justifications other than borrowing from a range of 'successful' countries means that it will be very difficult to arrive at a consistent and coherent curriculum which is demonstrably relevant for English students in the future.

It has long been a shortcoming of the national curriculum in England that it has not been devised on the basis of a clear set of aims, but is normally a result of haggling by committee. This means that faced with the question, for example, of whether long multiplication and long division should be taught to Year 6 children, it is not clear in an English context what would count as a strong justification, for or against. This is not simply a hypothetical question as these methods of efficiently calculating multi-digit multiplication and division, commonly taught up until the 1950s, are in the current draft of the new primary curriculum, although they had not been included in the national curriculum since it began in 1989. The reason these and other algorithms may occur in curricula of some high-attaining administrations such as Singapore and Hong Kong is probably that they were exported from England in earlier days of the Empire.

However, in considering whether such procedures should be included in the 1989 national curriculum the working group with responsibility for drafting the curriculum, of which I was a member, agreed that people no longer needed highly efficient methods of written calculation in an era where anyone who was required to carry out such calculations regularly would, and should, use a calculator. Nevertheless the group felt it was important for students to understand enough about addition and the number system to have some way of carrying out such a calculation, so we agreed to include multiplication and division of a three-digit by a two-digit number, while leaving open what method might be used (Brown, 1996: 20).

These arguments about present-day utility do not only affect calculation but also significant areas of the secondary curriculum, which look archaic in an era of mobile phones and iPads (see the discussion of technologies in the chapter by Kenneth Ruthven).

But clearly utility is not the only reason for deciding whether or not to include a specific bit of content. Geoffrey Matthews, as early as 1970, gave what I regard as still the best list of criteria:

- Pleasure: is it likely to engage and intrigue students?
- Profit: is it likely to be useful in everyday life, employment or further study?
- Purity: is it a rigorous and important aspect of mathematics?
- Polyvalence: does it connect with other mathematical ideas to increase the range of application and the coherence of the curriculum?

Long division, and, to a lesser extent, long multiplication, do not do very well on any of these criteria. There is undoubtedly some pleasure, or at least satisfaction, to be gained by mastering an algorithm and getting lots of ticks by applying it correctly on repeated occasions. However there is also ample evidence that many adults have found these particular procedures are up there with addition of mixed fractions in having given them strongly negative feelings about mathematics; they have found it difficult to understand the basis for them and hence hard to remember the algorithmic steps in the longer term.

Nor are they in themselves significant pieces of mathematics, although they could be used as examples of algorithms, an idea which is central to mathematics and coding for computers. But even this would not require mastery and practice of these algorithms, but rather analysis and critique.

As noted earlier, they have no obvious use in an age where everyone will have a calculator to hand on their mobile phone. Finally they do not especially connect with other ideas.

So why does long division remain an icon among politicians of the 'industrial trainer' persuasion? Could it merely be a warm nostalgia for their own schooling, or some notion of ideal education civilising the lower classes with teachers demonstrating a procedure to attentive children sitting in rows who then dutifully practise it? Could this be a type of Victorian moral-discipline view of maths, as a sort of mental hygiene – a necessary drill to train the mind working in parallel to physical education acting as training for the body?

WHAT AIMS SHOULD UNDERPIN THE MATHEMATICS CURRICULUM?

Ideally all content in a national mathematics curriculum should be subject to the sort of criteria proposed by Matthews described in the previous section. But a good curriculum should derive these criteria from its publicly agreed and openly stated aims, which has never been the case for the English national curriculum (White, 2007).

White also suggests that the four general aims for education are that it should enhance students':

- Personal fulfilment.
- Social and civic involvement.
- Contribution to the economy.
- Practical wisdom.

This list marks out a position which Ernest (1991) would characterise as that of a 'public educator'; indeed John White did act as an adviser on the 2007 curriculum under the Labour government.

These aims are in contrast with the culture-based position taken by Conservative politicians like Kenneth Baker in the 1980s and Michael Gove, the current Secretary of State. (It may be of significance that both were Oxbridge English graduates from relatively modest backgrounds). The remit for the national curriculum review seems to reflect Gove's view in suggesting that the new curriculum:

> should embody our cultural and scientific inheritance, the best that our past and present generations have to pass onto the next.
>
> DfE (2011a, para.10)

There is of course the important question of which part of society will make these value-judgements about culture, but we will sidestep that here as there is no space to do it justice. Gove's position would have been characterised by Ball (1990) as that of an 'old humanist' and by Ernest as that of a 'cultural restorationist'. However pejorative these titles, it is difficult to deny that White's list seems to be lacking an important cultural component, which is key to the aims of society, if less central from the point of view of an individual student. So to maintain balance I would propose adding to White's list a fifth aim:

- Knowledge and understanding of culture.

These or a similar set of generic aims should then be used to derive a set of aims for teaching mathematics. There are many alternative formulations of such aims given by educationalists (e.g. Ernest, 1991) or by national curricula from different countries, but there is not space to debate the ideal set here, and most relate to the aims given by White, generally with the cultural supplement. The aims can then be translated into a set of content criteria such as those given by Matthews (1970). Indeed the pithy Matthews set can be related directly to White's aims as in Table 13.1.

The debate of course resides less in the agreement of aims and criteria than in the comparative weighting given to them. This is an important point which is rarely discussed.

The case of long division which seemed to have little to offer on any of Matthews' criteria was easy to decide. But what if we take an example like the circle theorems in Euclidean geometry? This could be argued on grounds of teachers' experience:

- To give real *pleasure* to a few, but boredom and frustration to many.
- To have some *profit*/utility for intending undergraduate mathematicians (about 1% of the population), but almost none for the remaining 99%.
- To have a high value in *purity* and *polyvalence* by illustrating the idea of proof, which is central to mathematics, and also additional purity value as a demonstration of Euclidean geometry, a key area of the historical development of mathematics and an aspect of classical culture.

Circle theorems have been in and out of the curriculum since the 1950s, and this evaluation suggests why this is a matter of debate. It depends crucially on the weighting of utilitarian social criteria valued by 'public educators' against those valued by 'cultural restorationists'/ 'old humanists'. So the betting has to be that circle theorems will remain in the GCSE curriculum with a Conservative Secretary of State!

Table 13.1 Relation between content criteria and educational aims

Matthews' criteria	White's supplemented aims
Pleasure	Personal fulfilment
Profit	Social and civic involvement
	Contribution to the economy
	Practical wisdom
Purity Polyvalence	Knowledge and understanding of culture

HOW MUCH DIFFERENTIATION SHOULD THERE BE IN CURRICULUM AND EXTERNAL ASSESSMENT?

Take two other topics which might be included in a mathematics curriculum and compare them using Matthews' four criteria above. Which has the best claim to be part of the new curriculum?

Finally, even having decided on mathematical content, there is a further debate about differentiation and sequencing, affecting both curriculum and assessment structures.

There is considerable evidence about the wide range in mathematical understanding, from Year 1 or earlier (Brown *et al.*, 2008), which broadens out further at the secondary stage and has increased rather than reduced over time (Hart, 1981; Hodgen *et al.*, 2010). The current national curriculum is only specified by key stage (periods of two to four years) and is not very precise about depth of content coverage. This allows teachers considerable freedom in sequencing the curriculum, dividing it between year groups, and in the degree of differentiation. Thus they can either provide the same curriculum for all children in the year group or can differentiate it within or between classes. There is some tension here between satisfying opposing equity aims, either exposing all children as a matter of right to the same curriculum, or in offering each child a curriculum designed to best meet their perceived needs and to provide the best chance of individual progression. The current situation allows teachers to come to their own point of resolution of this tension. Differentiation has been provided by an assessment structure divided into statutory levels, with non-statutory but much used sub-levels, all independent of age. The internal use of externally provided tests and of teacher assessment based on key objectives to continually assess which sub-level children have reached has probably led to increased curricular differentiation, especially at the lower end of the attainment scale.

However the new proposals, now fleshed out by a report of an expert committee (DfE, 2011b), suggest a rather different structure. For primary mathematics there will be a year-by-year set of tightly specified attainment targets for all children. Each target will be tested separately by teachers at the end of each year, and externally at ages 11 and 16. Children will be judged either to be ready to progress or not, depending on the outcome.

Questions as to what happens to children judged not able to progress have been avoided by the claim that schools will put in additional resources to make sure no children are in this position. This will allow no differentiation, except possibly in any aspects of the mathematics curriculum taught but not specified or tested. External tests and league tables will remain at Year 6, but will presumably change in the detail of reporting.

At secondary level, mathematics seems likely to have targets only at the end of each two- or three-year key stage.

There is clearly an interesting debate to be had here. The research cited at the start of this section suggests that not all children may be able to succeed with a demanding uniform mathematics curriculum focusing on knowledge and skills, at least unless they are given significant additional resources of extra learning time and teacher support. For example, although in high-attaining East Asian countries there is such a uniform curriculum, this is maintained by children receiving considerable additional support in the evenings from cramming schools, private tutors and parents. It remains to be seen whether this uniform system can do justice to children at both ends of the attainment range.

Final word

> *What are the advantages and disadvantages of having a uniform curriculum for all students?*

There are clearly many important debates around the mathematics curriculum and its assessment, which are equally likely to occur in all countries. These include the aims, structure and content of the curriculum, the form of assessment to be used, and the degree of differentiation in the implemented curriculum which is either possible or encouraged.

The current changes proposed in England are the greatest since the national curriculum was first introduced in 1989, and have revived the national discussion of these issues. It can only help if all parties are informed by the research and arguments underpinning the debate.

Further reading

Askew, M., Hodgen, J., Hossein, S. and Bretscher, N. (2010) *Values and Variables: Mathematics education in high-performing countries*. London: The Nuffield Foundation. A review of literature and discussion about the factors which may or may not contribute to national attainment by examining differences between England and those countries which score well in international mathematics surveys.

Ball, S. J. (1990) *Politics and Policy-making in Education*. London: Routledge. An account of the politics and policy-making of the 1989 national curriculum from a sociological standpoint, with partial focus on the evolution of and arguments about the mathematics curriculum, including interview evidence with some of the main actors.

Brown, M. (2011) 'Going back or going forward? Tensions in the formulation of a new National Curriculum in mathematics', *The Curriculum Journal*, 22, 2, 151–165. A fully referenced review of the sources of likely tension in the early stages of the Coalition review of the national curriculum.

Department for Education and Science/The Welsh Office (DES/WO) (1982) *Committee of Inquiry into the Teaching of Mathematics in Schools. Mathematics Counts ('The Cockcroft Report')*. London: HMSO. A major, comprehensive report on mathematics education in England and Wales which has had considerable influence in the UK and overseas and in particular informed many aspects of the first mathematics national curriculum in 1989.

Ernest, P. (1991) *The Philosophy of Mathematics Education*. Basingstoke: Falmer Press. An authoritative and comprehensive account which examines the nature of mathematics, the aims for teaching mathematics, and an account of the different philosophical positions of the major players in the introduction of the 1989 curriculum.

Hart, K. (ed) (1981) *Children's Understanding of Mathematics: 11–16*. London: John Murray. Results from a large-scale study of secondary school students' understanding of many different areas of mathematics, incorporating qualitative data describing student strategies and proposing learning hierarchies of concepts within topics. Also demonstrates the wide attainment range among students in relation to the progress from year to year.

Hodgen, J., Küchemann, D., Brown, M. and Coe, R. (2010) 'Multiplicative reasoning, ratio and decimals: A 30-year comparison of lower secondary students' understandings', *Proceedings of the 34th Psychology of Mathematics Education (PME) Conference*, Belo Horizonte, Brazil, July. Early results of a large-scale survey using the same instruments as in Hart (1981) demonstrating that there has been little change in the areas of multiplicative reasoning, ratio and decimals over more than 30 years, but with more students towards the lower end of a broad range of attainment.

White, J. and Bramall, S. (2000) *Why Learn Maths?* London: London Institute of Education (Bedford Way papers). A series of challenges to the mathematics education community as to why mathematics should be a key or even a compulsory subject in secondary schools.

References

Askew, M., Hodgen, J., Hossein, S. and Bretscher, N. (2010) *Values and variables: mathematics education in high-performing countries*. London: The Nuffield Foundation.

Ball, S. J. (1990) *Politics and policy-making in education*. London: Routledge.

Brown, M. (1996) 'The context of the research – the evolution of the national curriculum for mathematics', in D. C. Johnson and A. Millett (eds), *Implementing the mathematics National Curriculum: policy, politics and practice*. London: Paul Chapman.

Brown, M. (2011) 'Going back or going forward? Tensions in the formulation of a new National Curriculum in mathematics', *The Curriculum Journal*, 22, 2, 151–165.

Brown, M., Askew, M., Hodgen, J., Rhodes, V., Millett, A., Denvir, H. and Wiliam, D. (2008) 'Progression in numeracy ages 5–11: results from the Leverhulme longitudinal study', in A. Dowker (ed), *Mathematical difficulties: psychology and intervention*. San Diego: Academic Press/Elsevier.

Brown, M., Millett, A., Bibby, T. and Johnson, D. C. (2000) 'Turning our attention from the what to the how: the National Numeracy Strategy', *British Educational Research Journal*, 26, 4, 457–471.

Daugherty, R. (1995) *National Curriculum assessment: a review of policy 1987–94*. Abingdon: RoutledgeFalmer.

Department for Education (DfE) (2011a) *Review of the National Curriculum in England: remit*. Available at: http://www.education.gov.uk/schools/teachingandlearning (accessed 10 December 2011).

Department for Education (DfE) (2011b) *The framework for the National Curriculum: a report by the expert panel for the National Curriculum review*. London: DfE.

Department for Education and Science/The Welsh Office (DES/WO) (1982) *Committee of inquiry into the teaching of mathematics in schools. Mathematics Counts ('The Cockcroft Report')*. London: HMSO.

Ernest, P. (1991) *The philosophy of mathematics education*. Basingstoke: Falmer Press.

Gove, M. (2010) Foreword, in T. Oates (2010) *Could do better: using international comparisons to refine the National Curriculum in England*. Cambridge: Cambridge Assessment.

Hart, K. (ed) (1981) *Children's understanding of mathematics: 11–16*. London: John Murray.

Hodgen, J., Küchemann, D., Brown, M. and Coe, R. (2010) 'Multiplicative reasoning, ratio and decimals: A 30-year comparison of lower secondary students' understandings', *Proceedings of the 34th Psychology of Mathematics Education (PME) Conference*, Belo Horizonte, Brazil, July.

Matthews, G. (1970) *Hailstones and folkweave: an inaugural lecture*. London: Chelsea College of Science and Technology.

Oates, T. (2010) *Could do better: using international comparisons to refine the National Curriculum in England*. Cambridge: Cambridge Assessment. (Reprinted in 2011 in *The Curriculum Journal*, 22, 2, 121–150).

Office for Standards in Education (Ofsted) (2008) *Mathematics: understanding the score: Messages from inspection evidence*. London: Ofsted.

Thatcher, M. (1993) *The Downing Street Years*. London: HarperCollins.

White, J. (2007) *What schools are for and why (No. 14 in a series of policy discussions)*. London: Philosophy of Education Society of Great Britain.

White, J. and Bramall, S. (2000) *Why learn maths?* London: London Institute of Education (Bedford Way papers).

Chapter 14

Mathematical literacy

What is it? And is it important?

Hamsa Venkat

Introduction

The debate at the heart of this chapter is centred on what we teach mathematics for. One reason given for teaching mathematics is to lay the ground for the future learning of mathematics – for A-level Mathematics in England, and post-compulsory/tertiary mathematics more generally in many parts of the world. Another argument for teaching mathematics is that it provides experiences of the skills and reasoning needed to function productively in a world that brims with quantitative data – data that needs to be made sense of for effective participation in everyday life. People with these latter competences are sometimes described as 'mathematically literate'. I will also explore the tensions between these two positions.

At the centre of this chapter is a contextualised task based on a newspaper article drawn from the weekly South African broadsheet *The Mail and Guardian*. Penned by journalist Keith Levenstein (Levenstein, 2010), the article – entitled 'Let the Gini out of the bottle' – describes ongoing inequality in South Africa. In the middle of the article, this sentence appears:

> In any country some people are wealthier than others. This is represented by the income distribution curve. Recent reports … show that South Africa's Gini coefficient, which represents income inequality, is the worst in the world.

To me, being mathematically literate means being, or becoming, willing and able to engage with such claims. As a mathematics teacher, it means providing opportunities for learners to become mathematically literate as well – and that means looking for ways to turn issues drawn from everyday life into tasks to work with in mathematics classrooms.

In this chapter I share the ways in which I have used this newspaper article to learn about and use the 'Gini coefficient' – a widely used, but contested, measure of inequality, in a PGCE course for secondary mathematics teachers. Students' work on the task provides a basis for discussing the idea of mathematical literacy. I describe how the task has been presented, including examples of questions asked that allow a range of agendas – some more mathematical and some more life-competence focused – to emerge.

Arguments for why it is important to work across the range of goals associated with mathematical literacy in mathematics classrooms (rather than limiting oneself to traditional mathematical goals) are discussed at the end of this chapter. I take a critical advocacy position for mathematical literacy that calls for the 'literate learning of mathematics' as well as 'mathematical literacy' as a life-related competence.

MATHEMATICAL LITERACY: HOW IS IT DESCRIBED?

The term 'mathematical literacy' is associated with a range of descriptions. Eva Jablonka points out that in some descriptions of mathematical literacy, the need to understand the situation, or to solve a problem in context, drives mathematical selections, whilst in other descriptions the situations are just 'vehicles' on which specific mathematical content/ processes are carried (Jablonka, 2003). Dealing with a range of situations that require mathematical thinking is a life-related competence, so the trajectory here is into adult lives and citizenship. On the other side, where contexts are selected to 'surface' particular mathematical ideas, the trajectory is into further mathematical learning.

In England, Mike Tomlinson's report (Tomlinson, 2004) called for education in the 14–19 age range to prepare students for 'participation in a full adult life' whilst also providing openings for specialised discipline-based trajectories matched to individual 'interests, aptitudes and ambitions' (p.4). The 'core' component included the need for 'Functional Mathematics', which was aimed at supporting students to 'succeed and progress in learning, HE, employment and adult life' (p.29). Here, both Jablonka's orientations are explicitly noted.

In the United States, Lyn Arthur Steen (2001) supports what he terms 'quantitative literacy' – summarising the ways in which it differs from traditional school mathematics:

> Whereas the mathematics curriculum has historically focused on school-based knowledge, quantitative literacy involves mathematics acting in the world. Typical numeracy challenges involve real data and uncertain procedures but require primarily elementary mathematics. In contrast, typical school mathematics problems involve simplified numbers and straightforward procedures but require sophisticated abstract concepts. The test of numeracy, as of any literacy, is whether a person naturally uses appropriate skills in many different contexts.
>
> Steen (2001, p.6)

Steen argues that in an era where data and technology abound, quantitative literacy, involving a 'uniquely modern blend of arithmetic with complex reasoning', is required by all citizens for full participation in society (Steen, 2004, p.3). In this view, mathematical working is conducted in service of the situation under consideration rather than for its own sake. Behind his advocacy is evidence from many countries that traditional mathematics courses may not provide the experiences needed to manage the quantitative demands of life. In England, a Skills for Life survey found over 1 in 5 adults had 'poor' or 'very poor' numeracy skills (DfES, 2003).

Bernard Madison points to school mathematics' presentation of highly restricted problem types – 'very sanitized template exercises' (Madison and Steen, 2009, p.5). The routine nature of traditional mathematical problems is criticised as figuring within students' lack of experience in working with the complex and emphatically non-routine nature of problems in real-life situations.

Whilst the English and US terrain have seen small-scale attempts to incorporate mathematical literacy with one or other, or both orientations, a large-scale implementation occurred in South Africa with the national introduction of a subject called Mathematical Literacy into the post-compulsory phase curriculum in 2006, as an alternative option to 'Mathematics'. (I use the capitalised 'Mathematical Literacy' to refer to the South African subject and the small 'mathematical literacy' to refer to the general concept described in different ways in the international literature). Mathematical Literacy in the recently revised South African Curriculum and Assessment Policy Statement (DBE, 2011) is described thus:

> The competencies developed through Mathematical Literacy allow individuals to make sense of, participate in and contribute to the twenty-first century world – a world characterised by numbers, numerically based arguments and data represented and mis-represented in a number of different ways. Such competencies include the ability to reason, make decisions, solve problems, manage resources, interpret information, schedule events and use and apply technology. Learners must be exposed to both mathematical content and real-life contexts to develop these competencies. Mathematical content is needed to make sense of real-life contexts; on the other hand, contexts determine the content that is needed.
>
> DBE (2011, p.8)

Here, the rhetoric points to mathematics as a tool with which to understand real-world situations and solve problems. Progression across the three grades (Grades 10–12, learner minimum age range 15–18) occurs in terms of mathematical content and processes, and contextual complexity. Like the Tomlinson report, the South African Mathematical Literacy curriculum requires teachers to incorporate mathematical development alongside competence in real-world related problem solving.

Some writers question whether 'juggling' between mathematical and situational problem-solving goals is (a) desirable and (b) feasible. Essentially, this juggling can be reduced to asking: should life-related mathematical literacy figure within the goals of the mathematics curriculum? Proponents argue that the confidence and competence to deal with the multitude of ways in which quantitative data and mathematical models 'format' our lives (see Skovsmose and Yasukawa, 2009, for a detailed discussion, and the earlier chapter by Richard Barwell) is imperative for constructive and critical citizenship. Detractors point to mathematical goals being disrupted if the need for 'relevance' predominates within mathematics curricula (e.g. Gardiner, 2008).

A feature that unites more mathematical and more life situational orientations to mathematical literacy is the incorporation of contextual tasks. For advocates of more mathematical orientations, contexts are springboards for 'mathematising' activity – moving from contexts to their mathematical descriptions (Freudenthal, 1983). The contexts selected within this framework are chosen for their potential to 'surface' particular mathematical content and processes – and contexts can be contrived for this purpose. In contrast, within the life-situation orientations to mathematical literacy, contexts matter in their own right, even though they may be 'trimmed' in the earlier stages of learning. The nature of the context selected (or at least, the degree to which it is trimmed from real life) often provides clues about the orientation being followed. Subsequently, the extent to which the context remains within the frame of problem-solving is also a key indicator of the orientation.

In South Africa, empirical studies have led to the development of frameworks for thinking about teaching that promotes mathematical development *and* real-life-related problem-solving using mathematics as a tool.

Drawing from our studies of Mathematical Literacy teaching, Mellony Graven and I (2007) proposed a 'spectrum of agendas' that we saw at work in classrooms. This spectrum explores differences in the nature of links between content and context, within, and across, the teaching we observed. The 'spectrum of agendas', with some terminology adapted, is summarised below:

Table 14.1 A 'spectrum of agendas' of the nature of interlink between content and context (with some terminology adapted), drawn from Graven & Venkat, 2007

Driving agenda	1. Context driven: by learner needs	2. Context and context dialectic driven	3. Mainly mathematical content driven	4. Mathematical content driven
Description	To explore contexts that learners need to interact and engage with in their lives (current everyday, future work & everyday, and for critical citizenship) and to use maths to achieve this.	To explore a context so as to deepen maths understanding and to learn maths to deepen understanding of that context.	To learn maths and then to apply it in some contexts.	To give learners a second chance to learn basic maths.

In the first two agendas, the context retains importance in its own right – in the first agenda, from a life-relevance/citizenship perspective, and in the second agenda, in a dialectical perspective, where the need for mathematical development is retained alongside the need for contextual understanding. I think it is sometimes necessary and useful to work in Agendas 3 and 4, whilst maintaining an overall emphasis on the first two agendas.

> *Think about a 'best buy' problem relating to buying a cellphone. What questions could you ask related to the four agendas above?*

I now share the ways in which I have used the article on socioeconomic inequality in South Africa to promote discussion and understanding of mathematical literacy. In this work, some episodes indicate more mathematical orientations (Agendas 3 and 4) and some push towards the need to understand the situation that is described (Agendas 1 and 2). I show that the two orientations can be linked, and then present an argument for why this linking might be useful to incorporate more often within mathematics teaching.

WORKING WITH THE GINI COEFFICIENT NEWSPAPER ARTICLE

The task drawn from the newspaper article (which has been used several times now with PGCE student groups), deals with a topic of recurring interest in South Africa – the ongoing presence, and indeed, exacerbation of socioeconomic inequality in the post-apartheid terrain. Some figures about South Africa's economic situation provide background for this discussion:

- Population (mid-year 2011 estimate): 50.6 million.
- Official unemployment rate (1st quarter 2012): 25%.
- Mean monthly earnings (Nov 2011 figure): R6970.

These opening questions kick off the process of engagement:

> Have you seen this article? [Some nod]. Have you seen other articles like this? [Many more nod]. Do you think South Africa does have the worst income inequality in the world? [Some nod their heads, some shrug their shoulders, some mention that Brazil and India also have many poor people]. And have you heard of this Gini coefficient before? [Most shake their heads. In some years, one or two say they heard about it in Economics courses as undergraduates]. But most of you said you have read articles like this before. And I know that many of these articles do mention the Gini coefficient like this one does. Did you just ignore those words? [Some laugh, many nod, some say that this is how most people read newspapers – that you often come across things you don't know about, and you just read "over" them].

I note that this reading 'over' makes it quite hard to come to an informed decision about whether the claim in the article is true, so I then ask:

> Might it be possible to find out about the Gini coefficient? [Most nod vaguely, some say: "Yes, Google it"].

So this is what we do, noting that being a mathematically literate citizen involves the inclination and the ability to understand the indices we read about. In some years, I say at this stage that I have already done this, and share some pages of explanation about how the Gini coefficient is defined, and how it is calculated – drawn from internet pages. There are variations, but centrally, all definitions rest on two hypothetical scenarios – 'perfect equality' and 'perfect inequality' in a society. One example, drawn from the web, describes the Gini coefficient is shown in Figure 14.1.

We talk about this graph to see if we can understand the three lines/curves that are named. X represents the cumulative population percentage. Y represents the cumulative income percentage arranged in order from highest income to lowest income. Students start to see that 'perfect equality' is based on a situation in which 10% of the population (10% on the X axis) take home 10% of the total income (10% on the Y axis), and cumulatively,

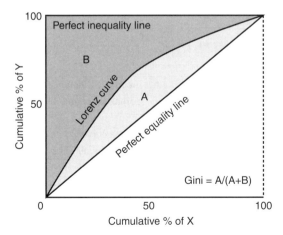

Figure 14.1 Graph showing the components of the Gini coefficient calculation.
(Source: http://people.hofstra.edu/geotrans/eng/ch4en/meth4en/ch4m1en.html)

20% of the population take home 20% of the total income, and so on. In this situation, there is no 'poorer' or 'richer' – everyone takes an equal share of the total income, and that is why it is called 'perfect equality'. This means that the 'perfect equality' scenario can be represented as a straight line graph that connects (0,0) to (100, 100).

In contrast, 'perfect inequality' is a hypothetical situation in which the highest earner (1st earner on the X axis) takes the total income (100% on the Y axis), and everyone else takes home nothing. In cumulative terms, this can be represented as a straight line that connects (0,100) to (100, 100).

The actual situation in any population sits somewhere between these two scenarios. In real populations, the richest 10% might, for example, take home 25% of the total income of that population – so we plot (10, 25). If the next 10% takes home 18% of the total income of that population, then cumulatively, this would mean that the richest 20% of the population takes home 43% of the income, so we plot (20, 43). Continuing like this produces the 'Lorenz curve' – a graph representing the actual cumulative income of the population. This graph always lies somewhere between perfect equality and perfect inequality.

The Gini coefficient value compares the total of the differences between the Lorenz curve and the perfect equality scenario, and the total possible inequality (represented by summing the differences between the equality and inequality lines). Summing can be done in a number of ways: integration can be used, but we can also just measure and total the differences – between the equality value at a range of points and the Lorenz curve value at the same points – and between the inequality and equality lines. The measuring method involves the 'elementary mathematics' that Steen describes as a feature of the mathematical literacy needed for an informed citizenry. An example using this measuring method is given on the same webpage with an explanation, reproduced in Figure 14.2.

This example considers 10 trucking companies and their market share. If each company had the same market share, the plot of their cumulative number (X) and cumulative traffic (Y) would be the perfect equality line. In this case, there is an unequal distribution of traffic with the three largest companies accounting for 60% of the market. The largest company

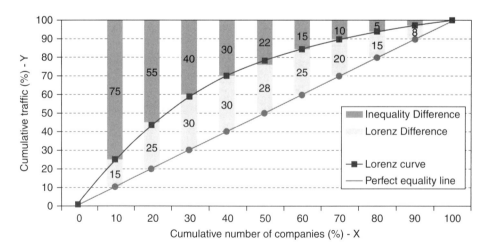

Figure 14.2 Graph showing the figures involved in an example of the Gini calculation.
(Source: http://people.hofstra.edu/geotrans/eng/ch4en/meth4en/ch4m1en.html)

accounts for 25% of the market and thus has a Lorenz difference of 15% (25%–10%) and an inequality difference of 75% (100%–25%). The Gini coefficient (G) would be calculated by dividing the summation of Lorenz differences by the summation of Lorenz differences added to the summation of inequality differences. G = 196 / (196+254) = 0.435.

In this graph, adding together the Lorenz differences gives us a measure of how 'far' from equality the actual situation is. Adding together all the Lorenz and inequality differences tells us the total amount of inequality that is possible. Comparing these two totals in a fraction gives us the Gini coefficient value, and is usually stated in decimal form.

Over the years I have found that it usually takes at least a couple of reads to make sense of the mathematical models and calculations. After some reading, I ask the following questions to check student understanding – you can use them to check your own understanding at this stage too.

So how is total equality viewed within the Gini coefficient calculation? And total inequality?

Can you follow how they got the answer given in the scenario above?

I then present the class with a precursor task. Each student in the group is given an 'occupation' – one that occurs in the context of the city we live in (Johannesburg, in our case): shop assistant, domestic help, television producer, newly qualified teacher, financial executive, etc. Students are asked to find out typical annual gross and monthly net salaries – by speaking to people in these jobs, or by looking up available data sources. With this data in, we have a discussion about whether annual gross or monthly net figures should be used to calculate inequality in this population. Most agree that monthly net salaries are better to use for comparison in the context of a significant informal and temporary work sector. We also discuss the extent to which our group – based on 30–40 occupations – is typical of the national population. A point commonly made is that the unemployed do not figure in our population. In some years, a decision is taken to include some unemployed people in the group, with data gathered on monthly social benefit income for different people in this group; in other years, students acknowledge that an inequality figure based on a working population is likely to underestimate actual inequality in the national population.

The dataset typically looks something like Table 14.2.

Are you persuaded that we have an authentic dataset here?

Do you have any comments on the figures? Are you surprised at some of the figures, and some of the differentials – or lack of differential – between professions?

So if we wanted to look at inequality in this dataset, how might we describe it? What kind of statistical tools can we use here?

And can we use the reading we did to calculate the Gini coefficient for this dataset – there is data available on Gini coefficients across many countries that we can compare with?

What agendas from my research with Mellony Graven do each of these questions fall into?

Table 14.2 List of Johannesburg occupations developed for the task

Occupation: Location	Monthly net salary (Rands)
1 Street hawker: Berea	1 900
2 Domestic worker: Sandton	4 200
3 Domestic worker: Mondeor	3 100
4 Casual labourer, 8 days employment/month: Johannesburg	2 600
5 Shop assistant, department store: Cresta	6 200
6 Building site foreman: Johannesburg	11 900
7 Mining engineer, large mining house: Johannesburg	31 300
8 Journalist – Sowetan	21 800
9 Car mechanic – Alex	10 700
10 Newly qualified school teacher – Soweto	13 400
11 Nurse – public hospital	9 400
12 Hardware store manager – Glenvista	18 800
13 Security guard: CBD	7 700
14 Junior lecturer – University	19 600
15 Power company executive	94 500
16 Homeless magazine seller	900
17 Dancer: Independent theatre group	9 000
18 Administrative assistant – university	8 400
19 Executive PA: Mining company	21 200
20 Junior accounts clerk	16 900
21 Waiter: Rosebank restaurant	9 100
22 Architect: Johannesburg	35 600
23 NGO fieldworker: Diepsloot	11 200
24 Junior doctor: Johannesburg General Hospital	18 200
25 Government department worker	11 400
26 IT support desk worker – engineering company	16 700
27 Airport security personnel	12 900
28 Factory packaging worker	7 700
29 Parking attendant	6 900
30 Mining executive	88 600
31 Partner – accounting firm	68 800
32 Electrician's assistant	8 600

In answering the questions in the text box above (which move from Agenda 1 to Agenda 3), students note that we could calculate the range or the interquartile range; others say we can express the highest salary as a multiple of the lowest salary, or variations on this idea – we can calculate the mean of the lowest quintile or decile, and compare this to the mean of the highest quintile/decile. They suggest calculating the values derived from similar lists from other countries/parts of South Africa and representing the inequality with mean and standard deviation values, or in a box and whisker plot. Student groups proceed in a range of ways, some using pen/paper and calculators, and others working on Excel, entering formulas based on the Gini calculation (Agenda 4). Entered on Excel, working based on each of the 32 data points can be used to produce an associated Gini graph (see Figure 14.3).

Each group presents their Gini coefficient result and calculation processes. Some argue that the formula has not been applied 'correctly' in the above instance as 32 differences have been added up rather than working at 10% intervals as in the earlier example. Others argue that dividing the population into 32 groups (there were 32 values in the dataset) uses the same idea, and is therefore okay. Apart from errors, most groups end up with Gini values just over 0.5, but methodological/rounding differences produce different answers in this

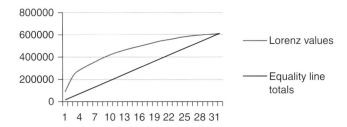

Figure 14.3 Gini graphs of the Johannesburg dataset

region (Agendas 2, 3 and 4 figure here, but the overall frame is Agenda 2). This figure can be compared with the international Gini coefficient figures available through a range of sources online (e.g. en.wikipedia.org/wiki/List_of_countries_by_income_inequality).

This working, whilst constrained by my questions, is clearly more open, more non-routine, and 'messier' than many of us have seen and experienced in more traditional mathematics lessons. It starts to address Madison and Steen's criticism that the 'routineness' of much mathematical problem-solving works against flexible problem-solving from a citizenship perspective.

In Table 14.3, I note the understandings – life-related, dialectical and mathematical – that have been incorporated into the working.

Concluding comments: why do this?

A range of objectives are achieved in working through a contextual task drawn from real life in this way. Conversations across race/class are configured into the task structure. Messy data requiring decisions on what statistics to include in ways that are sensitive to the situation, rather than imitative calculations, is incorporated. Mathematical sense-making/critiquing of existing models of situations is encouraged, alongside openings for seeing basic mathematics in new ways – e.g. a straight line graph as a cumulative frequency graph in a situation of complete equality. Mathematical content from a range of curriculum areas are integrated within the need to understand the dataset – number work, graphs and data handling. Flexible and efficiently integrated application of mathematics is often described as a hallmark of 'mathematical proficiency' (Kilpatrick, Swafford *et al.*, 2001) and is viewed as central to developing problem-solving competence – the 'predilection to quantify and model' in Alan Schoenfeld's (1992) terms. Additionally, the certainties commonly associated with more traditional mathematics are disrupted here – models of inequality are 'created' and existing models are adapted and critiqued. Mathematical tools gain 'breadth' in this working – useful beyond the 'chapters' in textbooks where they usually surface. Above all, the walls that traditionally make mathematics an enterprise that is restricted to mathematics classrooms start to be chipped at. Evidence suggests that such experiences help to create a disposition to bring mathematical sense-making to bear on mathematical and extra-mathematical situations, replacing the 'reading over' acknowledged by my students and the more serious avoidance/phobia that have been widely documented.

Note, we are not economic experts at the end of this activity; we are using public information, not all of which may be accurate. Some argue that this makes the activity spurious.

Table 14.3 Life-related, dialectical and mathematical understandings that have been incorporated into the working

Life-related competences/ understandings	Dialectical competences/ understandings	Mathematical competences/ understandings
Learning about net salaries across a range of professions – in a context of significant inequality; considering the consequences of this for lifestyle choices.	Decision making around what constitutes 'appropriate' data to use; understanding the implications of these decisions.	Working through a given formula, looking at the calculation structure and sequence. 'Applying' the given formula to a new dataset.
Encouraging conversations with people 'different' to ourselves.	Ways of measuring inequality – developing understanding of creating mathematical formulas and processes that can be put to use in the social world; critiquing these models – is the Gini model appropriate? What about the simpler ratio-based model? And rather than using 'total equality' as the baseline for comparison, could we use a different baseline model – a normal distribution for example? How might we do this?	Discussing 'unusual' cumulative frequency graphs – the equality line in the Gini calculation is actually a cumulative frequency curve, produced with unit increases. Linking the mathematical structure of the equality line with the $y = x$ equation. Summations leading into integration.
		Representing data distributions. Creating measures of dataset distribution.

The dangers are there, but I would argue from a citizenship perspective that such activity starts to enable us to become more informed consumers of information, and in this lays the ground for more active citizenship. At school level, we have evidence of such work providing openings for participation in social conversations and practices that students were previously locked out of by lack of awareness and understanding (Venkat and Graven, 2008). Thus, such work marks possibilities for greater participation, and for demanding more information and explanation from the 'experts' whose models format significant aspects of all of our lives.

Further reading

DBE (2011) *Curriculum and Assessment Policy Statement: Grades 10–12, Mathematical Literacy.* Available at: http://www.thutong.doe.gov.za/Default.aspx?alias=www.thutong.doe.gov.za/ mathematicaliteracy. It is worth glancing into this curriculum specification document to see how mathematical literacy has been configured into a curriculum. It is also worth noting that the Mathematical Literacy curriculum specification and assessments have been criticised as well. From a mathematical perspective, critics focus on the level of the mathematics being dealt with. From a life-related perspective, critics argue that contexts are artificial and that students' working is too heavily scaffolded to support the development of real-life competence.

National Numeracy.org.uk: http://www.nationalnumeracy.org.uk/home/index.html. This organisation takes a strongly life-oriented view of numeracy. The website provides detail on the organisation's aims, some links to research findings on numeracy levels amongst the adult population, and some reports on the associations between 'innumeracy' and economic consequences for individuals. It is quite interesting to look at their claims and the ways in which they present their data, given the organisation's position on numeracy.

Skovsmose, O. and Yasukawa, K. (2009) 'Formatting power of "mathematics in a package": A challenge for social theorising?', in P. Ernest, B. Greer and B. Sriram (eds), *Critical Issues in Mathematics Education*. Charlotte, NC: Information Age Publishing. This chapter notes the multitude of ways in which mathematics 'formats' our everyday lives – at home, in the workplace, and in society. It tells the story of a particular case of mathematical formatting – encryption software systems, briefly detailing the mathematics underlying these systems. It also details the commercial and political ramifications of Phil Zimmerman's creation and free distribution of a particular software encryption package, in a context where 'packaging' of mathematics into commercial products can be highly lucrative. With mathematical models permeating so much of society, the authors call for mathematically literate investigations to interrogate not just the mathematics within packages, but to ask further: 'What is in the package?', 'Whose package is it?' and 'What technical effects does the package have?'.

Venkat, H., and Graven, M. (2008) 'Opening up spaces for learning: Learners' perceptions of Mathematical Literacy in Grade 10', *Education as Change*, 12, 1, 29–44. In this paper, the experiences of Mathematical Literacy students in one school are discussed. In a situation where the majority of these learners had come into Mathematical Literacy with mathematical histories populated with failure, central findings related to the ways in which working with everyday problems supported both their ability to make sense of problems and solve them, and in turn, supported their participation in social conversations and practices related to the post-school environment.

References

DBE (2011) *Curriculum and assessment policy statement: grades 10–12, Mathematical Literacy*. Pretoria: Department of Basic Education.

Department for Education and Skills (DfES) (2003) *The skills for life survey. A national needs and impact survey of literacy, numeracy and ICT skills*. London: DfES.

Freudenthal, H. (1983) *Didactical phenomenology of mathematical structures*. Dordrecht: Reidel.

Gardiner, A. (2008) 'What is mathematical literacy?', *Proceedings of the 11th International Congress on Mathematical Education (ICME)*, Monterrey, Mexico, July.

Graven, M. and Venkat, H. (2007) 'Emerging pedagogic agendas in the teaching of mathematical literacy', *African Journal of Research in Mathematics, Science and Technology Education*, 11, 2, 67–86.

Jablonka, E. (2003) 'Mathematical literacy', in A. J. Bishop, M. A. Clements, C. Keitel, J. Kilpatrick and F. K. S. Leung (eds), *Second international handbook of mathematics education*. Dordrecht: Kluwer Academic Publishers.

Kilpatrick, J., Swafford, J. and Findell, B. (2001) *Adding it up: helping children learn mathematics*. Washington, D.C., National Academy Press.

Levenstein, K. (2010) 'Let the Gini out of the bottle', *Mail and Guardian*. Available at: http://mg.co.za/article/2010-02-04-let-the-gini-out-bottle (accessed 7 January 2013).

Madison, B. L. and Steen, L. A. (2009) 'Confronting challenges, overcoming obstacles: a conversation about quantitative literacy', *Numeracy*, 2, 1, 1–25.

Schoenfeld, A. H. (1992) 'Learning to think mathematically: problem solving, metacognition, and sense-making in mathematics', in D. Grouws (ed), *Handbook for research on mathematics teaching and learning*. New York: Macmillan.

Skovsmose, O. and Yasukawa, K. (2009) 'Formatting power of "mathematics in a package": a challenge for social theorising?', in P. Ernest, B. Greer and B. Sriram (eds), *Critical issues in mathematics education*. Charlotte, NC: Information Age Publishing.

Steen, L. A. (2001) 'The case for quantitative literacy', in National Council on Education and the Disciplines and L. A. Steen (eds), *Mathematics and democracy*. Washington D.C.: The Mathematical Association of America.

Steen, L. A. (2004) *Achieving quantitative literacy: an urgent challenge for higher education*. Washington, D.C.: The Mathematical Association of America.

Tomlinson, M. (2004) *14–19 curriculum and qualifications reform: final report of the Working Group on 14–19 Reform*. Annesley: DfES.

Venkat, H. and Graven, M. (2008) 'Opening up spaces for learning: learners' perceptions of Mathematical Literacy in Grade 10', *Education as Change*, 12, 1, 29–44.

Chapter 15

Assessment in mathematics education

Key debates

Rachel Marks and Alice J. Onion

Introduction

The intention of assessment is to tell us something about a learner's attainment and is at the heart of learning. We can model learning in many ways. One way we find useful is to view an episode of learning as a gap to be bridged between what was not known and what is now understood. Teaching, in supporting learning, is about crossing this bridge. To effectively support students in crossing this bridge, the teacher must know where the bridge starts. This is where assessment begins. Assessment is then used in a continuous process to ensure the bridge is successfully crossed and the endpoint reached, before informing the start of the next 'bridge'. This process forms an assessment cycle (Figure 15.1).

Broadly, assessment is categorised as summative – including examinations and the traditional marking or testing at the end of a piece/unit of work – or formative – activities that provide feedback into developing the next stages of teaching and learning. However, assessment is more nuanced, and both forms may be used together for different needs; virtually all assessment activities, even terminal examinations, have both a summative and a formative element. Mathematics tends to have more formal, and often summative, approaches to assessment. This may, in part, be a result of a long-held view of mathematics as a set of hierarchical procedures with one correct answer. But views of mathematics have and are changing; as such assessment approaches are also changing. Teachers do use assessment to support learning but do not always see their activities as assessment, particularly if they are not 'formal'.

In this chapter we explore the background to, and current debates within, Assessment for Learning (AfL) – the processes involved in implementing formative assessment – and the broader system of personalised assessment which involves giving individualised feedback and targets to learners. We examine how AfL fits within different views of what mathematics is, and views on how it should be taught and assessed. This includes current emphases on feedback, discussion, and self and peer assessment. We illustrate the issues raised through examining AfL materials and their relationship to teachers' practice. Our proposal is that we need to explicitly include students within the assessment cycle. As such we set out our adaptation of this cycle, which we name Assessment *as* Learning.

FORMATIVE ASSESSMENT: THE EVIDENCE AND IMPACTS

Formative assessment, as understood in classrooms today, developed during the 1960s. It is perhaps surprising, given this timeframe, that the term is still applied fairly loosely without

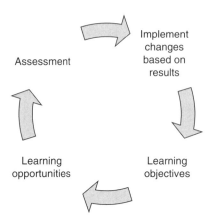

Figure 15.1 The Assessment Cycle

a widely accepted definition. One reason may be that formative assessment is not so much a thing in itself, but a way of talking about how assessment information is used to inform future teaching and learning.

Whilst now over ten years old, the most influential work on formative assessment is *Inside the Black Box* (Black and Wiliam, 1998). This text, which provides an excellent summary of the research evidence, has been followed up with several publications in the Black Box series, including: *Beyond the Black Box, Working inside the Black Box* and *Mathematics inside the Black Box*. In this chapter we draw on a number of key ideas presented in these documents, including the findings that:

- Effective formative assessment raises standards of attainment.
- Feedback is important: but different types of feedback lead to different outcomes.
- High-quality discussion and questioning are essential in formative assessment but, particularly in mathematics, can be difficult to implement.
- Self assessment is difficult for students: they need to be taught *how* to do this.

These insights suggest the importance of extending the use of AfL within mathematics classrooms. However, AfL in practice in England is embedded in the current competitive and consumerist culture of education and so it is important to be aware of this.

Personalised learning and assessment

Personalised learning, in the words of the government who introduced it, is the: 'high expectation of every child, given practical form by high-quality teaching based on a sound knowledge and understanding of each child's needs' (Milliband, 2004). AfL, as one component of Personalised Learning, focuses on setting personal targets and individualised feedback. This seems unproblematic. However, personalisation is not without its debates.

The concept of personalisation has many different and contested meanings. It is not unique to education but is part of wider thinking in developments to public services (this is the neoliberal thinking discussed by Anna Llewellyn in her chapter). Hospitals, schools and other public services are now required to consider the people who use their services in a different way. Personalisation is a move away from the one-size-fits-all approach towards an understanding that individuals have different wants and needs that must be foregrounded in the provision of everything from prescription drugs to university degrees. Whilst this seems positive, and may be within some public sector services, it positions the learner as a consumer. While appearing democratic, this has been shown to result in unequal access dependent, for instance, on social and parental resources and on people's perceptions of different learners' needs (see the chapter by Patricia George).

Forms of attempted personalisation have been around in education – in different guises – for some time. Schools try to match learning tasks to students' levels of need through practices such as ability grouping (setting and streaming). However, far from personalisation of learning, one of many concerns with this practice is that it leads to teachers teaching an imaginary middle student in the group and treating all learners as the same. Ability grouping results in a lack of personalisation and may make the use of personalised approaches difficult (it also has other problems as Mark Boylan and Hilary Povey discuss in their chapter). Outside of grouping practices, personalised assessment approaches can still be problematic. These approaches should support students in developing their learning, but in England, as in many countries, they are used in schools where there is an almost universal preoccupation with target-setting and movement between sub-levels. A target-setting culture and personalised learning are unlikely to be compatible and are difficult to challenge when assessment is so high stakes, being used to judge both students and their teachers and to compile public performance tables of school results.

Formative and summative assessment: can they work together?

We suggested that mathematics may be more inclined towards the use of summative assessment. If this is the case, it is possible in the educational climate of accountability that the use of summative assessment in mathematics may be more intense. Summative assessment has been suggested as problematic because it emphasises competition and beliefs about fixed ability, and only tells the student what they can or cannot do, not what they need to do to improve.

However, the issue is broader than saying summative assessment is problematic and should be replaced with formative assessment. Due in part to the influence of national testing and target-setting, even informal assessments may stray into the use of levels originally designed for summative assessment. In essence, *both* summative and formative assessment have become target-driven with the result that various forms of assessment exist in our classrooms in a state of confusion and tension. This makes it harder for any form of assessment to work as intended. For instance, some AfL practices may be implemented in a way that is only superficially formative, or possibly even summative. Evidence gathered through students' 'traffic light' responses – a practice where students use green/amber/red cards to indicate their understanding and designed to inform teachers' subsequent interactions – may not be being used by teachers to inform future learning directions, but instead to record summative levels of understanding. Similarly, teacher questioning is central to effective formative assessment. However, where questions are closed, they not only reinforce the view of mathematics as having one correct answer, but tend to lead to summative judgements about students.

Even if used as intended, it would still be wrong to say that one form of assessment is 'better' than all alternatives. We need to consider how we are using assessment and for what purpose. It is the inappropriate use of assessment methods that is problematic. Each system is very sensitive, with, for instance, the potential for summative assessments to undermine the potential benefits of other forms of assessment. The difficulties that come with assessment are illustrated by the huge amount of material, including Government programmes, available to support assessment. One such programme is Assessing Pupil Progress (APP). APP was developed under the Labour Government in 2008 to support schools in England and Wales in applying AfL across the national curriculum. This is an interesting programme in relation to the debates in this chapter. Although APP has an AfL focus it also links assessment foci (of which there are 208 in mathematics) to Levels 1–8 of the national curriculum. The linkage of AfL and national curriculum levels illustrates how different forms of assessment may conflict with or undermine each other.

Mathematics is possibly more complex in terms of assessment than many other subjects. Traditional views of mathematics lead to an overuse of summative assessment, but also neglect to assess a whole area of mathematics learning: processes. Mathematical processes include, but are not limited to: the choice and efficiency of methods, thinking and assumptions; and the communication of solutions. These are all parts of the problem-solving process which is gradually developing in the secondary mathematics classroom. By their very nature, processes cannot be assessed on a screening-for-errors basis; they cannot be marked as right or wrong. It is necessary instead to make judgements on the quality of work and students' thinking. Certain approaches to teaching, learning and assessing lend themselves better to mathematical processes and to AfL. We examine these in the following sections, looking at the features of effective formative assessment in practice. Before that, we would like you to consider this:

Formative or summative?...

Identify an assessment activity you have used or seen recently such as an examination question or a question asked to check understanding. List the summative and formative outcomes. How might you make the activity more formative? Revisit your ideas after reading the next section.

FORMATIVE ASSESSMENT IN PRACTICE

We noted that effective formative assessment raises attainment. The important term here is *effective*. There may be multiple barriers to the implementation of effective formative assessment in practice. In this section we take some of the key features of formative assessment and examine how they can be used effectively in the mathematics classroom.

The importance of feedback

One of the significant findings from the Black Box series is the importance of feedback and the differing impacts of different types of feedback. Feedback to students is a normal consequence of assessment. For example, the screening for errors that occurs when marking a textbook exercise is a form of feedback when the marked work is returned to the student.

Students are often given feedback in the form of grades or levels. Sometimes they are also given qualitative feedback, either in writing on their work or verbally as the teacher circulates the room.

The Black Box research focuses specifically on feedback within formative assessment. This finds that, rather than the quantity, it is the nature of the feedback given that is critical to the success of formative assessment. Feedback can only be considered formative if it guides the students in the next stages of their work. In practice, this means that the feedback given – written or verbal – should not only highlight where the student has been successful, but also explicitly identify what the student needs to do next. It may also be beneficial to plan specific assessment time into lessons in which the formative assessment can be acted upon and a dialogue set up between the student and teacher.

The key issue in providing feedback is in its interaction with other types of assessment. We discussed earlier how different forms of assessment may conflict with each other. Feedback is a key area where this can be seen and it is a particular issue within mathematics where giving marks and grades is commonplace. Giving students marks only tells them their achievement on a particular task; it does not tell them very much about what they need to do to improve their work. It would be a reasonable assumption that giving a written comment in addition to the mark would fill this gap, telling the students how well they have done and also what they need to do next. However, the Black Box research identified that where both marks and written feedback are given, students tend to ignore the written feedback in favour of the mark. 'Where the classroom culture focuses on rewards, "gold stars", grades or place-in-the-class ranking, then students look for ways to obtain the best marks rather than at the needs of their learning which these marks ought to reflect' (Black and Wiliam, 1998, pp.8–9). Other research confirms this. Angelo Kluger and Avraham DeNisi (1996) looked across a large number of studies into assessment and found that giving students grades can lower attainment, whilst comments collected within the Bowland Maths Project show how students may reject feedback in favour of marks:

> If you've got something like A, ten out of ten, if you have got a little comment on what you could improve on you kind of think, "well I don't need to look because I'm doing fine", whereas if it's just a comment and it's written in like a question form, it makes you like think about it more and question your work and the way you're doing it and it gets you like more thinking and so it helps a lot more.
>
> Bowland (2010a)

What does this mean in the mathematics classroom? This research suggests that to give effective feedback, teachers should only tell the student, in words, what they have done well and highlight the next step(s) to take. Grades and marks should not be given. The Black Box research gives two possible approaches. First, teachers can record marks but provide only written feedback to students; second, they can give students their marks *after* they have responded to the written feedback. This is a huge shift from traditional practices in mathematics classrooms and may conflict with school policies.

Discussion, questioning and classroom talk

In order to support students in their learning the teacher needs to know what the student knows. This is not straightforward, particularly with mathematical processes. Using AfL, the teacher needs to find a way to access what the student knows and assess the nature of their thinking, as well as guiding the student in the next steps of their learning. Doing this requires the teacher to use personalised assessment. One strategy that may be useful in supporting this is carefully planned discussion, teacher questioning and classroom talk. This approach requires setting up a classroom environment where interaction is the norm and students are actively engaged in lessons.

Unfortunately, such an environment is far from the experiences of many students. In most classroom questioning, particularly in mathematics, the teacher already knows the answer. The students, if they choose to take part in the game, try to guess what is in the teacher's head. Questioning, in such classrooms, is often about control and maintaining learner attention. John Mason (2010) argues that genuine questioning may be particularly difficult within the culture of the mathematics classroom where students are expecting to play a guessing game and may take on quite a defensive stance. However, it is worth pursuing. The Black Box research shows that well planned questions, which lead into follow-up activities, can extend students' engagement and allow teachers to conduct effective formative assessment. These questions do not need to be elaborate; simply asking students 'why do you think...?' may be enough.

However effective the questioning, the teacher is only one part of what happens in the classroom. It is important in developing an AfL classroom that space is given to teacher and student dialogue. Dialogue must be planned in order to be effective. Traditional 'guess what's in my head' questioning tends to close down classroom talk; strategies need to be implemented to open this up. These include: asking probing questions and being interested in the response, setting up longer wait-times (the period between asking a question and accepting an answer) to allow more students to respond with extended answers, and asking students to discuss their answers before responding – or to try and come up with multiple responses.

Self and peer assessment

Self and peer assessment are integral to AfL and are also considered important in education more generally. Since 1998, publications in England have provided guidance on self and peer assessment to teachers, for example from the Qualifications and Curriculum Authority (QCA, 2003) and the National Strategy for School Improvement (Department for Education and Skills, 2004). However, both can be difficult to effectively implement; this is acknowledged in the Black Box research. Often assessments made by students focus on extrinsic aspects of the work such as presentation or have a tendency towards being over-critical. Neither helps the student in identifying the next steps to take. Students need to be taught *how* to self and peer assess with appropriate responses modelled by the teacher. They need to understand what the intention of the assessment is and what is expected from them. Students need to understand what to do with the assessment in the same way as they need to know what to do with feedback from the teacher.

Further, students need to be clear about the criteria against which they are carrying out assessments. These expected learning achievements must be made transparent to students. Without knowing what they are supposed to have achieved or where they are going with a particular task, it is very difficult to make informed judgements of their own, or others', performance. Particular strategies that may support self and peer assessment include: writing up expected learning achievements in transparent language; extending students'

'Traffic Lights' responses by asking them to justify them to their peers; and using progression descriptions to support dialogue and provide a structure to peer assessment.

Imagine you're working with a class without giving grades and a parent complains that their child's work has not been marked. How would you respond?

Using an AfL approach can be difficult and parents are just one group to be convinced. Can you think of other possible barriers to AfL implementation and think about how they might be overcome?

TEACHERS' USE OF AFL: AN ILLUSTRATED EXAMPLE

We have looked theoretically at some factors to be considered in using formative assessment effectively but what would these look like in a mathematics classroom? We are aware that classrooms are dynamic environments. There is always much more going on and much more for teachers to consider in addition to implementing AfL. In this section we explore some teachers' implementation of AfL and look at some assessment materials.

Our discussion of classroom practices is taken from the Bowland Maths professional development materials. Two secondary mathematics teachers, Shane and Elnaz, worked together to explore how assessment materials could be effectively implemented in the mathematics classroom. We are particularly interested in what the teachers did during their lessons and how their practices illustrate the concepts of AfL, and personalised assessment and the issues raised in this chapter.

What did the teachers do during lessons?

When a task was introduced to students, the teachers made sure the students understood the context the problem was set in. Importantly, the teachers did not introduce any of the mathematical content that might be needed at this stage. The students drew on what they already knew in the first instance. The teachers collected in the students' work and wrote comments and questions to help students progress. In a subsequent lesson, students were given the opportunity to reflect on formative comments and to polish their work.

For the self and peer assessment stage Shane and Elnaz used 'progression charts' to show students what to look for when making assessments of mathematical processes. Progression charts are included in the assessment materials we look at later. They are written for teachers and show how students might demonstrate their skills with mathematical processes. Although progression charts are very useful to teachers, they are quite wordy and the language can be inaccessible to students. Drawing on the Black Box recommendation that learning achievements need to be transparent for students to be effective in self and peer assessment, Shane and Elnaz produced more student-friendly versions.

What did the students do during lessons?

Initially students had difficulty engaging with self and peer assessment. There was a tendency to focus on the quality of presentation and other superficial features. Students were also self-critical and needed encouragement to look for what was positive in their work. Over time, this improved. Here are some of the comments that Elnaz's students wrote on one anothers' work:

> "The way you explained it is clear and it's really easy to understand"
> "You could add more assumptions / more work explained."
> "The titles are fine. The layout is fine. The border is random. I can't really understand how you worked it out."
> "There's good pictures to show what's going on."
>
> Onion and Javaheri (2011, p.30)

Students in Shane and Elnaz's classes successfully identified, often on the basis of peer feedback, what their next steps should be. This links to personalisation; each student, or group of students, is working on something directly identified as within their own learning needs.

NUFFIELD AMP AND BOWLAND MATHS INITIATIVES

Classroom materials have been developed that draw on the latest research in AfL. Since it is easier to assess content areas of mathematics, recent developments have focused more on the assessment of mathematical processes as that is where teachers need more support. The materials that Shane and Elnaz used came from Nuffield AMP (Applying Mathematical Processes) and Bowland Maths. These are two of a number of initiatives that provide materials to support teachers in implementing AfL in their mathematics classrooms. We look at these as examples of how mathematical processes can be assessed and how materials can be used to address the key issues related to AfL. We also draw on these materials in the next activity. A key feature of Nuffield AMP activities is that they link and address both content and process skills, something we noted earlier to be a potential difficulty and hence important in mathematics education today. In the Bowland self-contained assessment tasks, teachers are carefully guided in developing students' process skills through teachers' notes that focus on: representing a situation mathematically, analysing, interpreting and evaluating, and communicating and reflecting. These correspond with the progression chart we mentioned earlier. Further, both Nuffield AMP and Bowland Maths materials strongly support formative assessment. The materials draw on the Black Box recommendations for the effective implementation of formative assessment we discussed previously. Each set of teacher notes (Nuffield, 2012; Bowland Maths, 2010b) provides examples of feedback that could be given to students, such as:

> Encourage pupils to draw together their various observations and conjectures and to present them clearly and coherently. Stress the importance of explaining their choices and their reasoning.

The notes (ibid.) also provide possible probing questions to develop discussion and classroom talk, such as:

- What are you trying to find out?
- Have you found all the different ways? How can you be certain?

- What are the maximum or minimum areas for each number of tiles?
- You've made a prediction. How will you decide if you are correct?

Finally, as discussed in looking at Shane and Elnaz's work, the materials, through their progression tables, can be used to support self and peer assessment.

Here are two examples of these classroom activities:

1. 'Lottery' from Bowland Maths involves a simplified version of the National Lottery where players choose a pair of numbers from six options. Two balls are drawn at random to select the winning numbers. Pupils decide whether or not this lottery will be a good way to raise money – See more at: http://www.bowland.org.uk/assessment/tasks/pdf/lottery_v3_1.pdf
2. 'Sending Texts' from Nuffield AMP involves establishing the number of text messages sent if four people send texts to each other, and then extending this to different numbers of people – See more at: http://www.nuffieldfoundation.org/applying-mathematical-processes/sending-texts#

Choose one of the classroom assessment activities above.

Based on the discussion in the previous sections, what could you do to ensure the assessment activity is used as formatively as possible in a classroom?

Each activity comes with progression tables (via the urls). Write out the criteria for evaluating learning achievements in language that is explicit and accessible to students.

What questions or discussion points could you use to: Help students make progress with the task? Assess students' progress through the task?

INTEGRATING THE LEARNER: ASSESSMENT *AS* LEARNING?

In this chapter we examined some key debates in mathematics education, specifically those related to the nature of mathematics and how it should be taught and assessed, relating to AfL and personalised assessment. Through the key literature – particularly the Black Box series – we identified some barriers to, and strategies to implement, effective formative assessment.

Recognising the role of students as central to effective formative assessment, we finish this chapter by presenting an updated assessment cycle. This is offered as a thinking point which we hope will stimulate discussion. Earlier notions of formative assessment were very much to do with the teacher finding out about students' understandings in order to plan future learning appropriately, taking into account students' learning needs. The students themselves were not directly involved in the assessment process except as objects of observation. It was with the Black Box research that we saw a change in this emphasis. The student became important, involved in all stages of the assessment process. This is no more evident than in the focus on self and peer assessment. Students are required to become reflective, active learners with responsibility, in collaboration with the teacher, for all stages of the learning, and hence assessment, process (Figure 15.2). With such an active role, assessment processes form part of the learning process. Hence, assessment *as* learning.

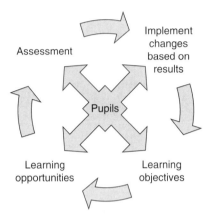

Figure 15.2 The Assessment as Learning Cycle

Further reading

Black, P. and Wiliam, D. (1998) *Inside the black box: raising standards through classroom assessment*. London: GL Assessment. This booklet offers a summary of the extensive research literature into formative assessment. It shows that there is clear evidence that improving formative assessment improves results, and offers evidence showing how formative assessment may be improved.

Black, P., Harrison, C., Lee, C., Marshall, B. and Wiliam, D. (2003) *Assessment for learning: putting it into practice*. Buckingham: Open University Press. This book gives a fuller account of the earlier booklets: *Inside the black box* and *Working inside the black box*. It discusses four types of action: questioning, feedback by marking, peer- and self assessment and the formative use of summative tests.

Bowland Maths: http://www.bowland.org.uk/assessment/tasks.htm. Currently the following materials can be found on the Bowland Maths website: 18 'case studies' – these are substantial secondary mathematics, classroom-rich projects that take about a week's worth of lessons to complete; seven professional development modules – each includes classroom video material and stimulating activities for teachers; and, 35 stand-alone assessment tasks.

Earl, L. (2003) *Assessment as learning: using classroom assessment to maximise student learning*. Thousand Oaks, California: Corwin Press. This book uses mini-cases to illustrate assessment as learning. It deals with motivation, making connections, reflection and self-monitoring. Chapter 6 includes a mathematical mini-case.

Hodgen, J. and Wiliam, D. (2006) *Mathematics inside the black box*. London: Granada Learning. This booklet applies the findings in the earlier Assessment Reform Group publications to mathematics. It considers some principles for mathematics learning, activities that promote challenge and dialogue, questioning and listening, peer discussion, feedback and marking, and self and peer assessment.

Nuffield AMP: http://www.nuffieldfoundation.org/applying-mathematical-processes. This website contains classroom trialled activities to support the teaching and assessment of mathematics processes. The teacher support material is similar to that for Bowland assessment tasks.

Onion, A. J. and Javaheri, E. (2011) Self and peer assessment of mathematical processes. *Mathematics Teaching*, 224, 30–32. This short and easy-to-read article extends our discussion of Elnaz's work with her Year 8 (age 12 to 13) mathematics set. They are Set 4 out of 6 where set 1 contains the highest attaining students. She explains how she uses self assessment.

References

Black, P., Harrison, C., Lee, C., Marshall, B. and Wiliam, D. (2002) *Working inside the black box: assessment for learning in the classroom.* London: nferNelson.

Black, P. and Wiliam, D. (1998) *Inside the black box: raising standards through classroom assessment.* London: GL Assessment.

Black, P. and Wiliam, D. (1999) *Assessment for learning: beyond the black box.* Cambridge: Assessment Reform Group, University of Cambridge.

Black, P. J., Harrison, C., Lee, C., Marshall, B. and Wiliam, D. (2003) *Assessment for learning: putting it into practice.* Maidenhead: Open University Press.

Bowland Maths (2010a) 'Bowland Maths professional development, module 6, activity 2, video clip: Pupils discuss assessment feedback.' Available at: http://www.bowlandmaths.org.uk/ (accessed 3 October 2012).

Bowland Maths (2010b) 'Bowland Maths assessment tasks.' Available at: http://www.bowland.org.uk/assessment/tasks.htm (accessed 3 October 2012).

Earl, L. (2003) *Assessment as learning: using classroom assessment to maximise student learning.* Thousand Oaks, California: Corwin Press.

Hodgen, J. and Wiliam, D. (2006) *Mathematics inside the black box.* London: Granada Learning.

Kluger, A. N. and DeNisi, A. (1996) 'The effects of feedback interventions on performance: a historical review, a meta-analysis, and a preliminary feedback intervention theory', *Psychological Bulletin*, 119, 2, 254–284.

Mason, J. (2010) 'Effective questioning and responding in the mathematics classroom' reworked and updated from: Mason, J. 2002, 'Minding Your Qs and Rs: effective questioning and responding in the mathematics classroom', in Haggerty, L. (ed), *Aspects of teaching secondary mathematics: perspectives on practice.* London: RoutledgeFalmer.

Milliband, D. (2004) *Personalised learning: building a new relationship with schools.* Speech given to the North of England Education Conference, Belfast, 8 January 2004.

Nuffield (2012) *Nuffield AMP Investigations.* London: The Nuffield Foundation. Available at: http://www.nuffieldfoundation.org/applying-mathematical-processes/nuffield-amp-investigations (accessed 20 September 2012).

Onion, A. J. and Javaheri, E. (2011) 'Self and peer assessment of mathematical processes' *Mathematics Teaching*, 224, 30–32.

Chapter 16

The fitness and impact of GCSE mathematics examinations

Ian Jones

The General Certificate of Secondary Education (GCSE) in Mathematics is a course that is assessed by written examination at the end of compulsory schooling in England, Wales and Northern Ireland. As Margaret Brown elaborates in her chapter, the exam papers and the grades awarded are the subject of ongoing debates in the media and among people interested in secondary mathematics education. In this chapter we will explore two central themes of these debates. The first is the contention that the exam papers sat by children are not fit for purpose because they lack 'rigour' and are getting 'easier' over time. This is a widely held belief commonly propagated by some politicians and by elements of the media. The key evidence for this contention is the year on year increase in the number of students getting higher grades. The second debate theme we will consider is that GCSE exams present mathematics as a fragmented discipline made up of isolated ideas, rather than as a coherent body of connected ideas. This is a belief common among teachers, researchers and other professionals who are concerned this fragmentary presentation has a detrimental impact on how maths is perceived, taught and learned in many secondary classrooms.

I begin the chapter by providing a brief summary of the history and purpose of GCSE maths exams, before describing how they are designed, administered and marked. We will then consider the debates around fitness for purpose and fragmentation in some detail. Finally we will reflect on the promise and potential drawbacks of alternative approaches to the current ways of doing things.

BACKGROUND

In England, Wales and Northern Ireland, GCSE courses were introduced in 1986 as a replacement for the previous 'two-tier' system in which children considered academic high achievers were entered for 'Ordinary level' exams intended as preparation for post-compulsory education towards 'Advanced level' exams. Children considered academic low achievers were instead entered for 'Certificate of Secondary Education' (CSE) exams intended as preparation for the world of work. The tiered system was intended to cope with the wide diversity of student achievement at age 16 but was increasingly considered unfair due to the perception of CSEs as second-rate.

A key GCSE development across many subjects was the introduction of coursework to complement exams. Since then mathematics assessment has often been somewhat out of step with other GCSE subjects. For example, in 2009 coursework was dropped from mathematics, but no other subject, due to overwhelmingly negative responses from mathematics teachers (QCA, 2006). Their main concerns were that it was difficult to know if the work was wholly the students', and some coursework tasks assumed a high level of literacy.

Unlike most other subjects, mathematics was offered at three tiers of difficulty until 2006 when it changed to two tiers in line with other GCSEs. Mathematics differed from the two other 'core' subjects, namely English and Science, by only offering a single qualification rather than two or three, despite requiring a similar amount of effort (Smith, 2004). For example, many students are entered for two qualifications in English for language and literature. More recently, the linked pair pilot GCSE, offering two qualifications in 'Methods in Mathematics' and 'Applications of Mathematics', was intended to address this perceived imbalance (Vorderman *et al.*, 2011).

What mathematical knowledge and skills should we expect of school leavers? Should GCSE exams assess pure mathematics as preparation for further study, or applied mathematics as preparation for work and life?

HOW EXAMS GET MADE

Unlike national Key Stage tests, commonly called SATs, terminal school exams have traditionally been produced by several independent organisations known as exam boards or 'awarding bodies' (ABs). Originally the ABs were regional but over time they have merged, resulting in a handful of competing ABs in England, Wales and Northern Ireland. At the time of writing, five ABs produce GCSE mathematics exams although there are calls to replace them with a single national body (e.g. Stewart, 2011).

The ABs work to tight government requirements setting out the percentage of each exam paper that must test content knowledge and problem-solving skills, and the percentage of questions that must be set in 'real-world' contexts. Each AB produces detailed specifications of the mathematics students are expected to learn, and these are submitted to the government regulator for accreditation.

A given exam paper and its mark scheme are usually drafted by an individual examiner. Examiners tend to be practising or retired teachers who draw on their knowledge of students and previous exams when producing new papers. They work to very tight deadlines and often recycle old questions, tweaking the contexts and examples used. In order to ensure the paper conforms to government regulations the exam writer completes a tick list known as an 'assessment grid'. The assessment grid contains columns referencing the required content (statistics, algebra and so on), processes (knowledge recall, problem solving and so on) and difficulty (questions spanning all grades from A* to G) that the exam paper must cover. For every question part the writer completes a row of the assessment grid to create an at-a-glance picture of the overall balance across the paper.

Once a paper has been drafted the writer sends it to other examiners for feedback and then revises it accordingly. The paper is further reviewed and modified at a meeting of a Question Paper Evaluation Committee (QPEC). A QPEC meeting usually lasts a day or two, during which time several papers by different writers are tabled. QPECs are chaired by a Chief Examiner and attended by up to a dozen examiners, including the writers of the tabled papers. QPEC meetings can be intensive events in which papers are picked apart and writers have to decide when to concede and when to defend their work. The committee works through each paper one question at a time, checking everything from punctuation and formatting to mathematical content and coherence.

In addition the QPEC will consider the accessibility of questions to all candidates from a wide spectrum of economic, social and cultural backgrounds. I observed one meeting in which the phrase 'elderflower cordial' was changed to 'orange squash' as it was felt this would make the question more accessible to a broader range of candidates, particularly those from working-class backgrounds. However, ensuring that all candidates are equally well-served by the phrasing and situating of questions is an all but impossible task, and research shows that working-class students are systematically disadvantaged by the contexts used (see Cooper and Dunne, 2000 and the chapter by Peter Gates and Andy Noyes).

This question proofing is demanding work and takes up the bulk of time and energy in QPEC meetings. The assessment grid is continually referenced and often amended for each question, and then checked again once the paper is complete. Sometimes a paper is signed off for publication at the end of a meeting, other times the writer has to undertake revisions and present it to the committee again at a later date. Interestingly, and perhaps worryingly, GCSE exam papers are never trialled with students before publication.

A given exam paper might be sat by any number of students, from a few dozen up to tens of thousands. Once complete, the scripts are collected and scanned and a sample analysed in order to amend the mark scheme. Marking procedures vary across ABs. Some contract teachers to mark entire scripts, others contract clerics, undergraduates and teachers to mark individual questions. The work is usually done electronically to avoid the costs and inefficiencies of transferring thousands of paper scripts around the country. Examiners moderate the marking, checking the quality and remarking a sample to ensure consistency. Statistical analyses are conducted to check the performance of the exam, and an examiners' report is produced describing how students responded to the questions.

Once every script has been allocated a mark a great deal of effort goes into assigning grade boundaries. Much of this work is undertaken by awarding meeting panels made up of examiners using statistical data and samples of scripts. Examiners tend to be conscientious people who go to great lengths to ensure that students are treated fairly and given the benefit of any doubt. Nevertheless, the panel is under great pressure to ensure the grade boundaries are consistent with other exam papers, other ABs and previous years (see Robinson, 2007 for detailed descriptions of the processes involved).

The final outcome is that every script is assigned a grade. Where a school is concerned that a student may not have received the correct grade, an enquiry can be made. The AB investigates to check for errors, and corrects the grade where necessary. If the school is still not satisfied it can appeal against the grade. This is a more serious process that only results in a handful of grade changes every year across all GCSE subjects (Ofqual, 2011).

FIT FOR PURPOSE?

GCSE results are published every August to great media fanfare and, almost inevitably, frenzied concerns about the standards of education compared to previous years. This often leads to claims that GCSE exams are not fit for the purpose of assessing school leavers' mathematical achievement. This is partly because recent decades have seen increasing numbers of students obtaining higher grades year on year.

For example, in 2001 the number of students achieving a grade C or higher was 50.1%, by 2011 it had crept up to 58.8%. This could be interpreted as implying children's mathematical achievement is increasing in some objective manner. Perhaps students really are improving due to better teaching, or higher aspirations and expectations. However, the improvements in GCSE grades over time are not matched by international measures (e.g. OECD, 2010) or independent research (e.g. Coe, 2007).

A common perception is that exam papers are getting easier over time (e.g. Clark *et al.*, 2010). ABs have been accused of making exam papers predictable, producing textbooks that focus narrowly on tested content (e.g. Paton, 2012) and advising teachers how to gameplay exams (e.g. Newell and Watt, 2011). Others claim that an increased performativity culture is putting greater pressure on students and teachers to ensure high grades (Science and Learning Expert Group, 2010). This is said to have led over time to more cramming and exam training in classrooms, as well as schools directing a disproportionate amount of resources towards borderline students and, up until their abolishment in 2012, an over reliance on re-sits. Further reasons offered for recent 'grade inflation' are that markers are overly generous (e.g. Cooper, 2012), and awarding meeting panels tend to give borderline students the benefit of the doubt (Cresswell, 1986). More generally, the number of qualifications has increased as students are offered more 'pathways' through learning mathematics (see the chapter by Cathy Smith), stretching the capacity of the national assessment system. Some researchers (e.g. Coe, 2010) have questioned the very notion of maintaining a fixed standard from the past, arguing it is undermined by the updating of content to ensure qualifications remain relevant, and by ongoing changes to government regulations such as the introduction and subsequent dropping of modular courses.

Despite the controversies and differences of opinion about standards over time, there does exist some consensus among educators, researchers and other interested parties that the content of GCSE mathematics exams is inadequate. For example, researchers scrutinised 100 Grade-A students' scripts and concluded that the exam papers did not adequately assess algebra (Noyes *et al.*, 2011). Some students had got full marks on supposedly algebraic questions by using purely arithmetical trial-and-improvement techniques. Others had obtained their grade A despite avoiding algebra questions altogether.

Is it meaningful to have a single measure or grade for everything that is encompassed by the term 'mathematics'? What would be the pros and cons of measuring and grading different components of mathematics separately?

THE FRAGMENTATION OF GCSE MATHEMATICS

Another widely expressed concern is that GCSE mathematics exams contain too many short questions that test rote learning, and not enough long questions that test sustained reasoning (Vorderman *et al.*, 2011). In a typical exam paper each question part is worth less than three marks on average, and most question parts are worth just one or two marks. Taking a mark per minute as a rough guide this suggests that the average length of reasoning chains expected of students is less than three minutes, including the time required to read the questions. This fragmented nature of mathematics exams stands in contrast to many other GCSEs, and this remains the case despite attempts by government regulators to encourage more substantial questions.

The combination of pressure to achieve high grades and the fragmentary nature of exam papers is reported to have a detrimental impact on the teaching and learning of mathematics in secondary classrooms (DfE, 2011). The short questions that make up the bulk of GCSE exams test the recall and application of memorised facts, and so this is where many teachers focus their mathematics lessons to help students achieve high grades. The Office for Standards in Education (Ofsted, 2008) reported that:

> higher order skills underpin what it means to behave mathematically. It is of serious concern, therefore, that national tests do not require students to use and apply mathematics in substantial tasks through which they are able to decide what approaches to adopt, use a range of mathematical techniques in exploring the problem, find solutions, generalise and communicate their reasoning. The importance of these skills is highlighted in the new National Curriculum's key processes and they underpin the recently published standards for functional mathematics. However, unless external assessments reflect these important processes, they are unlikely to influence a significant shift in teaching and learning mathematics.
>
> Ofsted (2008, p.35)

As such, even those students who obtain high grades are sometimes unable to use or apply their mathematics outside of the narrow constraints of GCSE exam papers. Higher education institutions and employers report that school leavers lack the necessary mathematical knowledge and skills for further study and the workplace (Science and Learning Expert Group, 2010). It is now common for employers and higher education institutions to offer in-house mathematics training and support to compensate for this (Hoyles *et al.*, 2010). Moreover, many 16-year-olds are turned off by the thought of studying mathematics beyond compulsory schooling. Less than 20% go on to study any further mathematics at all, far fewer than most comparable countries (Hodgen *et al.*, 2010).

THE CAUSES OF FRAGMENTATION

Why are the questions in GCSE mathematics exams so fragmented? There are several contributing mechanisms (Jones, 2010). As described above, ABs must ensure their exams conform to precise government regulations. The most direct way to achieve this is to use many short questions, each of which corresponds to a specific requirement that can be ticked off in the assessment grid.

Market forces are also considered to be a fragmentary pressure on exam papers. ABs are in financial competition with one another to sell their assessment services to schools, and teachers are in a performativity culture that incentivises them to choose those exams papers they consider the most predictable and passable. It is easier to train students to pass exams containing many short questions that test recall than fewer long questions that test sustained reasoning.

Another fragmentary pressure is the need for exams to achieve acceptably high marking reliability. Marking reliability can be thought of as 'marking repeatability'; the extent to which each student would have obtained the same grade if his or her exam script had been marked by a different examiner. Marking reliability can be increased by making the exam up from many short questions that have a limited range of 'right' answers. For example, multiple choice tests have perfect marking reliability because there is no ambiguity as to whether each question has been answered correctly or not.

In light of these contributing factors, and the often high-octane reporting of exam standards in the media, it is helpful to reflect on the intended purpose of GCSE mathematics. This is set out succinctly in the national curriculum as a 'Statement of importance' for Key Stage 4 mathematics. It runs as follows:

> Mathematics can stimulate moments of pleasure and wonder for all students when they solve a problem for the first time, discover a more elegant solution, or notice hidden connections. Students who are functional in mathematics and financially capable are able to think independently in applied and abstract ways, and can reason, solve problems and assess risk.
>
> Mathematics is a creative discipline. The language of mathematics is international. The subject transcends cultural boundaries and its importance is universally recognised. Mathematics has developed over time as a means of solving problems and also for its own sake.

These intentions for Key Stage 4 mathematics are widely debated in mathematics education, in particular, many have questioned the assumed universality of mathematical language (e.g. Ernest, 1991). However there is little debate among mathematics educators that stimulating mathematical pleasure, wonder and creativity are at odds with training students to pass fragmented exam papers. In the next section we will consider ways in which this mismatch might be addressed.

ALTERNATIVE FORMS OF *ASSESSMENT*

Are there alternative ways to assess students that might better match the stated intentions for Key Stage 4 mathematics? We don't have to look too far for ideas. As noted above, mathematics is one of the few GCSE subjects to be assessed entirely by written exams. Until recently, most other GCSE subjects at least included a 'controlled assessment' component, which typically involved practical work completed under exam-like conditions. Inspiration can also be found around the world. For example, summative mathematics assessment in Sweden includes an oral component.

Many experts agree that summative assessments should be based on a diverse set of evidence including written exams, project work, practical investigations and oral exams. This can help overcome problems that undermine the appropriateness of more traditional assessments. It can also address the detrimental aspects of 'teaching to the test' by providing 'tests worth teaching to'. A broad base of evidence might better assess the intentions of Key Stage 4 mathematics reproduced above, and could include the components shown in Table 16.1.

> *What do you think might be the benefits and drawbacks of each type of assessment listed below? What other types of evidence not listed could be used to assess students' mathematical achievements?*

Table 16.1 Possible components of a broader approach to assessing Key Stage 4 mathematics

Content-based	Recall and application of content assessed using short, structured questions requiring short answers, which might include well-designed multiple-choice questions.
Problem-based	Deep understanding of mathematics assessed through problem-solving questions. Examples of such questions designed for use in the United States can be seen on the website of the Mathematics Assessment Project (see Further Reading).
Practical	Mathematical proficiency assessed using a variety of mathematical tools to complete a given task. These might be manual, using protractors, compasses and so on, or digital, using, for example, spreadsheets, simulations or graphical calculators. Evidence collected could include the finished artefact as well as multimedia files (photographs, movies, audiorecordings).
Choice	Students choose from a range of questions within a paper. The nature of choice offered would need to be carefully designed. For example, all questions might require similar mathematical knowledge and understanding but focus on applying it to different contexts.
Oral	Students attend a face-to-face interview in which they are asked about the mathematics they have learnt.
Comprehension	A mathematical text is presented followed by a set of questions to test understanding, analogous to a comprehension test in language subjects. Following the example of Nuffield A level Physics (Black, 2008) the text might be about a topic not explicitly taught during the course.
Essay	Students produce a creative piece of mathematical work in response to a short, open prompt. Such a prompt might be "Write everything you know about prime numbers", or a carefully chosen photograph and the statement "Describe all the mathematics shown in the picture."
Portfolio	Samples of work are collated over the two-year duration of a GCSE course and compiled to produce a portfolio of evidence of mathematical learning for each student.

ALTERNATIVE FORMS OF *ASSESSING*

As discussed above, awarding bodies outsource marking to clerics, undergraduates and teachers who undertake extra work in their holidays. Students and their teachers are not involved in assessing their own work, and some argue that they should be. This might enable learners to feel more engaged with assessment, and teachers to use it diagnostically to help with further learning (see the discussion of Assessment for Learning in the previous chapter by Rachel Marks and Alice J. Onion).

There are understandable concerns about placing the assessment process in the hands of students and their teachers. The system is open to abuse and indeed this was one of the concerns that led to the abandonment of coursework for GCSE mathematics in the late noughties, and any shift must be approached cautiously. However, quality can be checked by independently reassessing a sample of students' work. Moreover, research suggests that peers tend to be fair and are often more consistent than their teachers when assessing one another (Topping, 2003). In addition, teacher assessment is used for summative assessment in some countries around the world, demonstrating that it is possible to do (Askew *et al.*, 2010).

Another concern about involving students and their teachers in summative assessment is that it implies a shift away from using standardised mark schemes and towards relying on peer and expert judgement. This is problematic because judgement is based on subjective opinion whereas mark schemes attempt to set out what should be credited in an objective manner (Laming, 2004). Using judgement for assessment has been shown to be consistently less reliable than using standardised mark schemes. Low reliability is not merely a technical inconvenience; in practice it has been shown to introduce bias into the assessment system, to the detriment of students from ethnic minority backgrounds (Gillborn, 2008).

Until recently this was perhaps an insurmountable challenge. However, recent technological developments mean that it is now possible to produce rank orders of students in terms of mathematical achievement that are based on human judgement and yet are as reliable as rank orders produced by marking. This is achieved by presenting judges with pairs of students' work and asking them to decide which of the two has demonstrated the greater mathematical achievement. The outcomes from many such pairings can be used to construct a robust rank order (Pollitt, 2012). Objections to placing peer and expert judgement at the heart of assessment may therefore weaken over coming years.

Concluding comments

How might an aspiring mathematics teacher respond to the burdens, opportunities and debates around GCSE exams? For many teachers the existing regime is undesirable but real. The only fair thing to do is to train students to obtain the best grades they can, thereby improving their life chances. For others the exam system is a challenge, but not a barrier to teaching mathematics in an engaging and conceptually satisfying manner. Some argue that, despite all the problems and debates, the best way to prepare students for GCSE exams (as well as further study, the world of work and life in the modern world) is to teach as well as possible, and in the style most suited to you and your students.

Further reading

Cambridge Assessment (2010) *Exam Standards: The Big Debate*. Cambridge: Cambridge Assessment. In April 2010 Cambridge Assessment held a high-profile event exploring many aspects of high-stakes assessment. You can download the report and listen to podcasts of key speakers at the event from http://www.cambridgeassessment.org.uk/ca/Viewpoints/Viewpoint?id=132622.

Commons Education Select Committee (2012) *Education Committee: Publications*. London: UK Parliament. What do politicians, regulators, awarding bodies and others in positions of power really think about GCSE exams? The Commons Education Select Committee publish a wealth of candid and revealing minutes and reports that can be downloaded for free from http://www.parliament.uk/business/committees/committees-a-z/commons-select/education-committee/publications/. It takes a little perseverance to dig through, but for those interested in high-level politics it is well worth the effort.

Lesh, R., and Lamon, S. (1992) *Assessment of Authentic Performance in School Mathematics. AAAS Press Series on Assessment and Evaluation*. Washington D.C.: American Association for the Advancement of Science. Due to space restrictions I have only hinted at alternative ways of assessing school mathematics. This edited book explores other possibilities, many of which have been tried and tested in the past and in other countries. It can be downloaded for free from http://www.eric.ed.gov/ERICWebPortal/detail?accno=ED352262.

Mansell, W. (2007) *Education by Numbers: The Tyranny of Testing*. London: Politicos Publishing Ltd. Warwick Mansell is a well-known education journalist with a particular interest in the effects of testing on teaching and learning. His book and blog (http://www.naht.org.uk/welcome/comment/blogs/warwick-mansells-blog/) offer a highly readable and somewhat alarming overview of issues and debates surrounding high-stakes assessment across all school subjects including mathematics.

Mathematics Assessment Resource Service (2012) Mathematics Assessment Project. The mathematics education group at the University of Nottingham are well known internationally for producing high-quality assessment materials. Sample prototype materials from the 'Mathematics Assessment Project' can be downloaded for free from http://map.mathshell.org/materials/index.php.

Newton, P., Baird, J.-A., Goldstein, H., Patrick, H., and Tymms, P. (eds) (2007) *Techniques for Monitoring the Comparability of Examination Standards*. London: QCA. This edited book offers an authoritative and detailed overview of how exam standards are monitored and maintained and provides thoughtful discussions of the debates and limitations of different methods. It can be downloaded for free from: http://www.ofqual.gov.uk/how-we-regulate/134-comparability/265-techniques-for-monitoring-the-comparability-of-examination-standards.

Swan, M. (2006) 'Learning GCSE mathematics through discussion: what are the effects on students?', *Journal of Further and Higher Education*, 30, 3, 229–241: Malcolm Swan challenges the widespread assumption that teaching to the test is the most efficient way to improve students' grades. Swan demonstrates this for the case of students retaking GCSE mathematics after compulsory schooling. These students are often particularly disheartened and demotivated.

WJEC (2012) *Mathematics GCSE Examiners' Reports*, Cardiff: WJEC. Awarding bodies publish specifications, past papers, mark schemes and examiner reports on their websites. These are well worth looking through when thinking about approaches to teaching GCSE mathematics. This – URL – http://www.wjec.co.uk/index.php?subject=90andlevel=7andlist=docsanddocCatID=82 – is for GCSE mathematics examiner reports from WJEC, which mainly serves schools in Wales. It is recommended you also search for specifications, papers, mark schemes and examiner reports on other awarding bodies' website in order to make comparisons.

References

Askew, M., Hodgen, J., Hossain, S. and Bretscher, N. (2010) *Values and variables: mathematics education in high-performing countries*. London: Nuffield Foundation.

Black, P. (2008) 'Strategic decisions: Ambitions, feasibility and context', *Educational Designer*, 1, 1, 1–26.

Clark, L., Harris, S. and Walton, M. (2010) 'GCSE results 2010: record number pass a year early including a 5-year-old', *Mail Online*. Available at: www.dailymail.co.uk/news/article-1305902/GCSE-RESULTS-2010-Record-number-pass-year-early-including-5-year-old.html (accessed 27 January 2012).

Coe, R. (2007) *Changes in standards at GCSE and A-level: evidence from ALIS and YELLIS*. Durham: Durham University.

Coe, R. (2010) 'Understanding comparability of examination standards', *Research Papers in Education*, 25, 3, 271–284.

Cooper, R. (2012) 'Generous examiners to blame for inflated A-level and GCSE grades', *Mail Online*. Available at: www.dailymail.co.uk/news/article-2088717/Generous-examiners-blame-inflated-A-level-GCSE-grades.html (accessed 27 January 2012).

Cooper, B. and Dunne, M. (2000) *Assessing children's mathematical knowledge: social class, sex and problem-solving*. Buckingham: Open University Press.

Cresswell, M. J. (1986) 'A review of borderline reviewing', *Educational Studies*, 12, 2, 175–190.

Department for Education (DfE) (2011) *The Independent Evaluation of the Pilot of the Linked Pair of GCSEs in mathematics – First Interim Report*. London: DfE.

Ernest, P. (1991) *The philosophy of mathematics education*. Basingstoke: Falmer.

Gillborn, D. (2008) *Racism and education: coincidence or conspiracy?* London: Routledge.

Hodgen, J., Pepper, D., Sturman, L. and Ruddock, G. (2010) *Is the UK an outlier? An international comparison of upper secondary mathematics education*, London: Nuffield Foundation.

Hoyles, C., Noss, R. and Kent, P. (2010) *Improving mathematics at work: the need for techno-mathematical literacies*. Abingdon: Taylor and Francis.

Jones, I. (2010) 'Why do GCSE examination papers look like they do?' *Informal Proceedings of the British Society for Research into Learning Mathematics (BSRLM)*, 30, 3, 61–66.

Laming, D. (2004) 'Marking university examinations: some lessons from psychophysics', *Psychology Learning and Teaching*, 3, 2, 89–96.

Newell, C. and Watt, H. (2011) 'Exam boards: "We're cheating, we're telling you the question cycle"' *The Telegraph*. Available at: www.telegraph.co.uk/education/secondaryeducation/8940799/ Exam-boards-Were-cheating-were-telling-you-the-question-cycle.html (accessed 27 January 2012).

Noyes, A. Drake, P., Wake, G. and Murphy, R. (2011) *Evaluating mathematics pathways: final report*. London: Department for Education.

Office for Standards in Education (Ofsted) (2008) *Mathematics: understanding the score*. London: Ofsted.

Ofqual (2011) *Appeals against results for GCSE and GCE: Summer 2010 Examinations Series*. Coventry: Office of Qualifications and Examinations Regulation.

Paton, G. (2012) 'Head attacks "aggressive commercialisation" of exams' *The Telegraph*. Available at: www.telegraph.co.uk/education/educationnews/9003153/Head-attacks-aggressive-commercialisation-of-exams.html (accessed 27 January 2012).

Pollitt, A. (2012) 'Comparative judgement for assessment', *International Journal of Technology and Design Education*, 22, 2, 157–170.

Organisation for Economic Cooperation and Development (OECD) (2010) *PISA 2009 Results: what students know and can do – student performance in reading, mathematics and science (volume 1)*. Paris: OECD.

Qualifications and Curriculum Authority (QCA) (2006) *QCA's review of standards: description of the programme*. London: QCA.

Robinson, C. (2007) 'Awarding examination grades: Current progresses and their evolution', in P. Newton, J.-A. Baird, H. Goldstein, H. Patrick and P. Tymms (eds), *Techniques for monitoring the comparability of examination standards*. London: Qualifications and Curriculum Authority.

Smith, A. (2004) *Making mathematics count*. London: The Stationery Office.

Stewart, W. (2011) 'MPs to ponder the virtues of a single exam board' *Times Educational Supplement*. Available at: www.tes.co.uk/article.aspx?storycode=6138985 (accessed 27 January 2012).

Topping, K. (2003) 'Self and peer assessment in school and university: reliability, validity and utility', in M. Segers, F. Dochy, and E. Cascallar (eds), *Optimising new modes of assessment: in search of qualities and standards (volume 1)*. Dordrecht: Kluwer Academic Publishers.

Vorderman, C., Porkess, R., Budd, C., Dunne, R., Rahman-Hart, P., Colmez, C. and Lee, S. (2011) *A world-class mathematics education for all our young people*. London: The Conservative Party.

Science and Learning Expert Group (2010) *Science and mathematics secondary education for the 21st century: report of the science and learning expert group*. London: Department for Business, Industry and Skills.

Chapter 17

Choosing the future

A-level mathematics

Cathy Smith

In this chapter I look at two questions that concern policy and research in post-compulsory mathematics. The questions are:

- How can we understand and compare different mathematical courses of study?
- How can we understand students' choices to study mathematics?

As in most long-lasting education debates, the answers are not simple: they depend on how you approach – and theorise – education, what you think is convincing evidence, and whether you are setting out to understand mathematics in schools or to change it. I discuss these ideas in the context of A-levels: the standard university preparation in England and Wales where 16-year-olds choose typically only three or four subjects to study over two years. In doing so I introduce some of my own research; notably my perspective that the way we understand and try to change school mathematics are not just about mathematics but also about how we view adolescence and progress.

The first occasion when UK students make a choice about studying mathematics is at age 16. And when they do get that choice, they use it. Research into students' experiences of learning mathematics suggests that many are profoundly disengaged from their mathematics lessons, at all levels of achievement, and simply do not want to continue. As one oft-quoted student puts it, 'I would rather die!' (Brown, Brown, and Bibby, 2008), while another less dramatically comments 'You have done it every year and it just gets kind of tiring' (Murray, 2011, 278).

These findings of stable and widespread disengagement suggest a downturn in A-level mathematics. In fact, examination board data over the last fifteen years has shown a dramatic fall, but then rise in the number of candidates (Figure 17.1). It is clear that students' choices do not depend just on past experiences but also involve their future aspirations and society's expectations. Families, schools and governments understand choosing mathematics as a way to brighten individuals' life prospects and the whole country's economic future. One of the roles of mathematics education research is to examine how the curriculum could (or should) meet these economic and political goals in the light of our knowledge about students' learning.

Think of an adult colleague who chose to stop studying mathematics at 16. What arguments might convince him or her that mathematics should have remained compulsory?

How would you argue differently to convince a current 16-year-old?

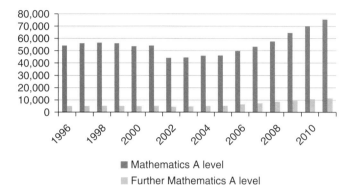

Figure 17.1 Number of Mathematics A-level candidates (16–18 year olds entering A2 in English schools and colleges)

Since 2008 there have been three mathematics A-levels, although (capital-M) Mathematics is by far the most common, with 70,000 students completing in 2011. Representing 9% of all A-levels taken, this was the highest proportion since 1996. It is notoriously hard to match examination data over time, but this is probably below 1980s numbers. The second A-level, Further Mathematics, is a traditional option for students who want to extend their mathematics. It has also been viewed as an elite option available only in a minority of schools, mostly large or private ones (Matthews and Pepper, 2007). Recently numbers have risen (Figure 17.1) after government-funded promotion by the Further Mathematics Support Programme (FMSP). Further Mathematics is of particular interest because of its gateway function for high-status STEM fields of science, technology and engineering and mathematics. This gives it a prominent role in the processes of including and excluding students through mathematics (Smith, 2010).

In contrast, Use of Mathematics (UoM), the third A-level I consider here, has existed only as a restricted pilot from 2008–12, with fewer than 1500 candidates. UoM is designed as an alternative to Mathematics. Its core syllabus includes algebra, functions and calculus topics recognisable from the AS-level Mathematics syllabus. However, teaching focuses on skills of mathematical modelling and communication across context-related problems rather than fluency in the techniques needed for STEM applications. It is the least common A-level, but worth discussing as it is often mentioned as a basis for a compulsory post-GCSE pathway for students who do not intend to follow STEM courses (ACME, 2010).

Potentially then, current A-levels could provide three parallel courses for pre-university study: 'parallel' in their timing but pitched at different conceptions of mathematics and its uses. These particular examples are specific to A-levels, but we find similar stratifications and purposes in other western education pre-university systems, for example Australia, or the European and International Baccalaureates. Of course, in most Baccalaureate systems mathematics is compulsory, while in the UK (and Australia) students enjoy more autonomy. However, this self-determination comes with the responsibility to make – and be seen to make – successful choices and to achieve the grades that prove them. It is a combination of freedom and self-scrutiny that follows the contemporary western model of neoliberal governance, through which individuals will to act is acknowledged and utilised to reinforce institutional practices (Rose, 1999, see also the chapter by Anna Llewellyn).

THE QUESTION OF EQUIVALENCE

We are used to thinking of mathematics as a hierarchical subject, where each topic relies on knowledge lower down in the hierarchy. When we do recognise strands, we talk of organising them in a spiral curriculum, with topics building on each other and increasing in complexity and abstraction. So in describing the three courses above, it made sense to acknowledge their different starting and end points: Further Mathematics extends Mathematics, and UoM overlaps with it. Implicitly, then, we think of mathematics courses as lying along a single dimension. Unidimensionality makes them easy to compare and hard to claim as equivalent.

However, we are also used to thinking that summative assessments should be equivalent between subjects and over time. If we want to understand different routes within mathematics A-levels we have to consider how to reconcile the evident hierarchy within mathematics with the social aim that assessments are worth the same over time and between subjects (Coe *et al.*, 2008).

First, why do we think of A-levels as equivalent? One reason is because many of the institutional structures of schools suggest it. We can see this in how the curriculum is organised into timetable slots, in the spread of eclectic mix-and-match subject combinations, in how schools and students compare module results, and universities ask for 'ABB or equivalent'. On top of this we have examples in other subjects. French, Spanish and German are equivalent modern languages; it is no better to be 'Late' than 'Early' when it comes to parallel Modern History A-levels. The wider practices of the A-level curriculum emphasise equivalence and ensure that students and schools are not unduly restricted (and academic disciplines do not lose out) when options narrow to only three or four subjects.

Against these institutional assumptions, we have the hierarchy of disciplines and the social judgements of employers and universities. In 2011 the elite Russell group of universities published a list of 'facilitating' A-levels. These included Mathematics and Further Mathematics and excluded newer A-levels such as Law. The existence of elite preferences is not surprising; it is part of the 'grapevine' knowledge that sustains middle-class educational privilege (Ball, Maguire, and Macrae, 2000). However it re-opened arguments that A-level subjects do have different intrinsic values, and specifically that mathematics needs more recognition and must be defended from innovation. The pilot A-level UoM was a particular focus of criticism. Educators for Reform (2009) suggested that 'poorly-informed students – in particular those at the weaker schools' would be distracted by the implied equivalence, choose the wrong AS-level and end up excluded from further STEM study.

These same concerns both for and against equivalence are repeated *within* Mathematics A-level. The full A-level has four compulsory pure modules plus two applied options chosen from lists in Mechanics, Statistics and Decision Mathematics. This pair can be combined to give breadth (Mechanics 1 and Statistics 1) or depth (Statistics 1 and 2) or to reflect teacher expertise. Many schools allocate students in relation to other subjects so that physicists study mechanics and geographers study statistics. Universities have supported this diversity because it allows the range of applications to flourish – particularly mechanics, which is difficult without physics. However a government review of A-level (Matthews and Pepper, 2007) reports diversity as a problem, citing evidence that teachers and students treated Decision Mathematics as an easier option. They were particularly concerned that universities may penalise students for choosing an easier option, when it is the school that did so.

We can see here how the temptingly mathematical notion of equivalence becomes enmeshed with political significance. Arguments for and against equivalence call on ideas of equity and of protecting students from unexpected consequences. For some, the problem lies in subject choice itself, and these arguments support a baccalaureate system and/or compulsory mathematics. For others individual choice is not inherently problematic but requires managing so that students are responsible only for their own decisions, not other people's. This individualisation feels appealing, but we have seen in Peter Gates and Andy Noyes' earlier chapter how social class inequalities are reinforced by treating students only in terms of school-based identities.

We can also see equivalence being used as a defence when students choose 'easier' but not 'harder' mathematics, so that UoM is criticised while Further Mathematics is promoted. In the next section I look at another way of unpicking the unidimensionality perspective by comparing examination questions.

COMPARING A-LEVEL QUESTIONS

Work through the two AS-level questions below, and consider:

What are their different conceptual demands: how many algebraic variables are involved? What kind of operations? Are variables introduced one at a time or together? What numbers and number operations are involved? Do students need to move between different representations of mathematics? (You might find it helpful to draw on the approach to thinking about examples elaborated by Tim Rowland in his chapter.)

What are their different reading demands: how much text? Is all the information you need in the text? How closely linked are the question and the information? Do students need to organise how they give their responses?

Do students need to devise their own strategy for answering a question? Do they need to confirm its appropriateness?

I selected these two questions because they have a similar structure. Both ask the student to complete a table of values with pre-labelled columns for relevant algebraic variables, and both provide a set of labelled axes for plotting a graph. As well as these similarities, you will have identified a range of differences between them. Let's discuss those that are characteristic.

Question A is from Further Mathematics, and this is evident in the abstraction of the mathematical components and the links between them. Here the variables a, b, x and y are all introduced together and operated on together. In two sub-questions the students need to devise a strategy: part (a) algebraic manipulation to show $Y = aX + b$, and part (ciii) reading off graphs to estimate gradient and intercept. Each of these requires technical comprehension. Apart from these parts, the necessary information is linked closely to the question, and responses need little organisation.

Question B is from UoM. This is evident from the foregrounding of the finance context, and the way that variables are connected through calculation rather than algebraic substitution.

4 The variables x and y are related by an equation of the form

$$y = ax + \frac{b}{x+2}$$

where a and b are constants.

(a) The variables X and Y are defined by $X = x(x+2)$, $Y = y(x+2)$.

Show that $Y = aX + b$.   (2 *marks*)

(b) The following approximate values of x and y have been found:

x	1	2	3	4
y	0.40	1.43	2.40	3.35

    (i)   Complete the table in **Figure 1**, showing values of X and Y.   (2 *marks*)

    (ii)   Draw on **Figure 2** a linear graph relating X and Y.   (2 *marks*)

    (iii) Estimate the values of a and b.   (3 *marks*)

Figure 17.2 Question A (redrawn from AQA 2008a)

---

3   Maria has completed a university course and has a student loan of £10 000 to repay. Each year Maria has to pay back 9% of anything she earns over £15 000 during that year.

Throughout this question, you may assume that interest is not charged on a student loan.

Maria earns £25 000 in the first year and gets an increase in her earnings of £2000 per year in each subsequent year.

The following recurrence relations are used to model this situation until the loan is repaid:

- $E_n = E_{n-1} + 2000$ gives Maria's earnings each year ($E_1 = 25\ 000$);

- $R_n = 0.09(E_n - 15\ 000)$ gives the amount Maria repays each year;

- $L_n = L_{n-1} - R_n$ gives the amount of Maria's loan that remains at the end of each year ($L_0 = 10\ 000$).

(a) Given that $E_1 = 25\ 000$ and $L_0 = 10\ 000$, show that:

    (i) $R_1 = 900$;

    (ii) $L_1 = 9100$.   (4 *marks*)

(b) Use the recurrence relations to complete the table on the answer sheet.   (6 *marks*)

(c) How long will it take Maria to pay back her student loan?   (1 *mark*)

(d) Complete the graph of loan remaining, L_n, plotted against year, n, on the grid on the answer sheet.   (2 *marks*)

(e) Explain why the points on your graph do not lie on a straight line.   (2 *marks*)

Figure 17.3 Question B (redrawn from AQA 2008b)

Initially, after introducing E_n, variables are defined one at a time. In (b) they require evaluating in a different order, by year, and rounding off. Students also need to devise a strategy in part (c) to move from table to context, and in (e), to comment on the graph. The suggested answer is 'Maria does not pay off equal amounts each year', which requires some technical comprehension of gradient, and organising a response. Information is given early in the text, distant from where it is needed, but is often repeated close by.

Comparing these two questions shows that they do have distinctive features that reflect the courses' purposes and different classroom practices. There is a hierarchy of complexity: Further Mathematics is concerned with abstract relationships and algebraic manipulation, while UoM focuses on producing and interpreting numerical and graphical representations. But there is also evidence here to challenge a unidimensional model: UoM has weaker links between the question and the information needed to answer it. It demands that students read and write about mathematics in a way that is absent in the pure questions of Further Mathematics or indeed in Mathematics.

In the end, what strikes me most about analysing these questions is how similar they are despite their different purposes. Both use a structure and wording that restrict opportunities for students to select strategies, to move back and forth between representations and to organise responses. They signal a very clear procedure for candidates and mark schemes to follow. That is not to say that candidates would find the questions easy: many would not. However, this perception that examinations systematically reduce variation lies behind calls for mathematics curricula to move away from a hierarchy of technical fluency and towards problems that prepare students to think mathematically (London Mathematical Society, 2010, see the chapters by Margaret Brown and Ian Jones for further discussions of these debates).

The analytic framework I introduced here is drawn from studies that compare the demands of examination questions through their structure (Hughes, Pollitt, and Ahmed, 1998), their mathematical steps, complexity and familiarity (Kathotia, 2012) and grammatical complexity (Morgan, Tang, and Sfard, 2011). You might wonder why recent research does not try the intuitive experiment of assessing demand by comparing the performance of similar groups of students. A little thought shows us that it is not so easy. Firstly, we meet problems in defining the ways in which the groups should be similar. Secondly, these are not questions that can be accessed without teaching. Although it would be politically popular, it is impossible to design an experiment that can distinguish whether differences in performance are due to easier examinations or the fact that students have better learning experiences (Coe *et al.*, 2008).

STUDYING MATHEMATICS

Research into student experiences gives another perspective through which to understand different mathematics courses. Studies agree that the students most likely to study A-level Mathematics are students who have already achieved well at GCSE, and are thus more likely to have higher socioeconomic status. Exploring the interactions of gender, ethnicity, class and prior attainment leads to intriguing variations, with one being that students from certain ethnic groups (Chinese, African, Indian and Pakistani) are more likely to choose mathematics regardless of attainment (Noyes, 2009; Reiss *et al.*, 2011).

This gives us a background for the Transmaths project (Wake, Williams, and Drake, 2011), which tracked non-traditional participants in AS-level mathematics, i.e. students with B or C grades at GCSE mathematics. They found UoM students were quite different from the students who studied Mathematics: unlikely to choose STEM careers and more diverse in ethnicity, class and prior attainment. Those with the lowest GCSE grades made more progress than similar Mathematics students, and were less likely to drop out or get an ungraded result. We are back to unpicking whether UoM is easier or more engaging.

Transmaths points to the impact of lesson activities preparing for UoM coursework tasks. Students found it refreshing to research what mathematics to use, to make and connect meanings for themselves, and to explain mathematics to others. They talked about the challenge but also how these lessons increased their understanding. From this research we get another response to the criticisms above: different mathematics courses should not be viewed as competing for students. UoM has proved engaging for a particular group of learners and successfully made it easier for them. There are issues in generalising from these experiences to a wider school population, not least because coursework has finished. Nevertheless there are many students with Bs or Cs in GCSE mathematics who currently do not continue mathematics studies, and UoM may prove an instructive model in how to engage them.

Comparing Further Mathematics and Mathematics has been much less controversial. STEM employers, universities and schools largely agree that further mathematics should be similar to mathematics just more extreme: deeper in its abstraction, broader in its applications and sharper in its eventual function of selection. Further mathematics is even more closely linked with the 'clever core' of high-attaining students, and is popular amongst students from professional backgrounds and Asian ethnicities (Matthews and Pepper, 2007). My own research has followed the promotion of Further Mathematics in state schools, investigating the accounts of non-traditional students who took up Further Mathematics as a twilight-hours course. Unlike the research above, I take a poststructural approach that considers what identities are offered and formed in these experiences. Students' accounts of doing mathematics have to make sense of the practices they engage in and also the fact that they chose/choose to participate, and because of this reflexivity I consider experience and choice together.

> *Think back to when you chose to continue mathematics, perhaps to A-level or degree standard. What kind of decision was this? Who influenced you?*
>
> *Would you describe your choice as rational – weighing up the costs and benefits? Or as expressive – reflecting who you are, setting out who you want to be?*

WHY CHOOSE AN A-LEVEL IN MATHEMATICS OR FURTHER MATHEMATICS?

Students who describe their reasons for choosing Mathematics A-level usually give one or more of the following:

- Mathematics leads to good careers.
- Mathematics is useful.

- I have always been good at maths.
- I enjoy mathematics.
- Mathematics is hard.

> *Which of these reasons entered into your decisions?*

Calling these 'reasons' suggests that choosing is a practice of weighing up contributory factors; some concerned with mathematics, some with the social world, and some with the individual chooser. In this approach to theorising choice, the next step is to identify such factors and to investigate how changing the image of mathematics, the practices of society and students' self-perceptions would make a difference to choice 'calculations'. Debate in this area is often quasi-statistical in tone, centred on identifying which factors are significant and how they interact. For example, the political think-tank Reform has suggested that mathematics should have more university-entry points than other subjects so students understand its higher value (Kounine, Marks and Truss, 2008). This would change social practices (university entrance procedures) in order to affect the image of mathematics; it is a 'policy lever' that influences people without constraining them. Another example is often suggested in response to girls' continued lower participation in A-level Mathematics (stuck around 40% since 2001): adopting classroom teaching methods that promote confidence and enjoyment for girls would encourage them to stay on (Brown, Brown, and Bibby, 2008, see also the discussion in the chapter by Mark McCormack).

Nevertheless it seems likely that choice is more complex, because sociological research tells us that choices are both rational *and* expressive (Rose, 1999). Choosing articulates what we think is important, and that gives a message about who we are. In the list above, the first two reasons – 'mathematics leads to good careers' and 'mathematics is useful' – are about the role of mathematics in a western technological society. When students choose mathematics for these reasons they align themselves with high-status, powerful positions in society and with modernist views of progress and utility. We can see here how easily the qualities of mathematics in society can be read onto the choosing student as showing a self-entrepreneurial spirit.

What about the next two reasons in the list? 'I have always been good at mathematics' and 'I enjoy mathematics' are both qualities of the student. Using knowledge about yourself is a widely accepted rationale for making life-choices. Still, for these to be valid factors in choosing mathematics, we need to understand them as stable characteristics, unlikely to change or to become irrelevant as learning shifts to A-level. The first in particular suggests that mathematical ability resides in a person, and makes that person apt for any formulation of school mathematics. The earlier chapter by Patricia George interrogates this fixed conception of mathematics ability, whereas sociocultural research such as Solomon (2007) examines what teachers and students do to give value to some mathematical efforts and not others, *constructing* rather than uncovering ability.

The 'personal enjoyment' rationale also suggests taken-for-granted understandings about there being kinds of people who like 'mathematics', rather than perhaps enjoying solving equations but not sketching asymptotic graphs. It can come as a surprise to students that A-level topics such as statistics and mechanics have very different feels. Although enjoyment may feel quite a trivial reason to continue or discontinue mathematics, it is intricately bound up in how we present ourselves as successful in making choices and in managing the work we need to do. I take an example drawn from an interview project considering how students account for themselves as studying mathematics and simultaneously on themselves as becoming mature, autonomous, disciplined adults (Smith, 2010).

Hayley and Esther have just explained that they chose AS-level because they enjoyed mathematics. Esther contrasts it with biology where she once cried because she couldn't understand her homework:

Cathy: And you wouldn't see maths making you cry?

Esther: Oh it probably could! Stats probably could make me cry.

Hayley: Frustration. I don't cry like with things like that but ... but frustration could make me like, ugh! I can't work it out, I can't work it out. I don't know how she has done it!

Esther: Oh, I get like that when I don't understand something. But I still enjoy the subject.

Hayley: Yes. I love numbers.

Esther: I will still come back and try to learn more.

Hayley: I love the fact that if I can't do it I will just do more and more to see how I can get to the answer. Like try different methods and you always know that there is a way that you can do it. And if you haven't done it then you need to work out what it is.

Both girls emphatically describe unhappy feelings in mathematics but still claim to 'enjoy the subject'. They make sense of this tension by separating Statistics and things they don't understand from their relationship with mathematics as a whole, which Hayley describes as loving 'numbers'. By returning to primary school mathematics (and emotions), she carries the successes of the past into the present, and positions enjoyment as an expression of an 'authentic' identity. Such repositioning that looks both backwards towards childhood and forward towards accomplishment is part of the self-work of contemporary adolescence (Lesko, 2001). Hayley's last sentences repeat her love of mathematics as something established through practice and over time, giving her knowledge about mathematics and about herself-in-mathematics. She reworks frustration into something more enjoyable – the certainty of having an answer – and uses it to position herself as persistent and confident. This is an example of what I mean by working-on-yourself through mathematics. There is an interesting context to this mathematical friendship: Hayley comes from a lower GCSE set than Esther, and struggles throughout Year 12. Yet in Year 13, Hayley continues mathematics and Esther gives up. I suggest that we see here how Hayley can justify carrying on (to herself and others) despite some discouraging results and painful times. She uses the promise of eventual success as a means of feeling happy in her mathematics *and* in her self-work.

I chose this excerpt because it also links to the last of the common reasons: 'mathematics is hard'. At first sight this looks like a reason *not* to study mathematics. If maths is *too* hard, you are unlikely to enjoy it or do well. However it does feature significantly in students' reasoning. Hayley can work towards happiness by working on a mathematics problem, and the acknowledgement that mathematics is hard renders her own self-management even more impressive. Continuing with mathematics helps her demonstrate something special about herself. This notion of *proving yourself* with mathematics has been analysed by

Heather Mendick (2006). In 'proving themselves' with mathematics, students align themselves with a powerful authority and reconcile two contemporary discourses of adolescence: knowing who you 'really' are and ensuring that you will make progress.

Closing thoughts

In the discussion above I have highlighted approaches to choice that are relevant to thinking how mathematics courses differ and how students understand mathematics. The approach that is dominant in policy-making has been to consider mathematics and identity as separable, so that any patterns in who chooses mathematics are side-effects, treatable as mis-functions of our educational system. Or we can think about reasons for choosing mathematics (or not) as being closely connected with constructing identities of entrepreneurial progress, ability, enjoyment, challenge and masculinity. This is not deterministic; on the contrary, contemporary understandings of selfhood and adolescence place a high premium on managing oneself. Nor is it equitable since we cannot all take up different identities freely. But from this perspective we have another way of understanding and researching different mathematics courses: as contexts in which mathematics, success and difficulty are differently positioned in relation to adolescence and self-work.

Further reading

Matthews, A. and Pepper, D. (2007) *Evaluation of participation in GCE mathematics.* London: QCA. This Qualifications and Curriculum Authority (QCA) report reviews national survey data on who studies mathematics A-level and their different routes. It has been influential in critiquing mathematics as the perceived home of a 'clever core' of students.

Mendick, H. (2006) *Masculinities in mathematics.* Maidenhead: Open University Press. A readable introduction to post-structural perspectives on identity and how they play out in/through mathematics. The main focus is on gender, but the approach is equally influential in thinking about mathematics and social class.

Wake, G., Williams, J. and Drake, P. (2011) *Special Issue: Research in Mathematics Education*, 13, 2. This collection of Transmaths project papers analyses how students negotiate their identities as they move into 'advanced' mathematics. It illustrates how quantitative and qualitative analytic methods can be mutually supportive.

http://www.nuffieldfoundation.org/fsmqs. The website of the free-standing mathematics qualifications that support UoM. There are interesting Level 3 activities for teaching calculus, decision mathematics and dynamics.

http://www.furthermaths.org.uk. The website of the Further Mathematics Support Programme showing the teaching resources and events it offers. The student area page titled 'Why study mathematics?' exemplifies the FMSP discourse that choosing is both rational and expressive.

References

ACME (2010) *Post-16 in 2016.* London: Advisory Committee on Mathematics Education.

AQA (2008a) *Teacher support materials 2008 maths GCE.* Available from http://store.aqa.org.uk/qual/gceasa/exemplar/AQA-MFP1-W-TSM-EX-JUN08.pdf (accessed 7 January 2013).

AQA (2008b) *Teacher support materials FSMQ.* Available from http://store.aqa.org.uk/qual/gceasa/exemplar/AQA-UOM42-W-TSM-EX-JUN07.pdf (accessed 7 January 2013).

Ball, S., Maguire, M. and Macrae, S. (2000) *Choice, pathways and transitions post-sixteen.* London: RoutledgeFalmer.

Brown, M., Brown, P. and Bibby, T. (2008) '"I would rather die": attitudes of 16-year-olds towards their future participation in mathematics', *Research in Mathematics Education*, 10, 1, 2–18.

Coe, R., Searle, J., Barmby P., Jones K. and Higgins S. (2008) *Relative difficulty of examinations in different subjects*. CEM Centre, Durham University.

Educators for Reform (2009) *The misuse of mathematics*. London: Reform.

Hughes, S., Pollitt, A. and Ahmed, A. (1998) 'The development of a tool for gauging the demands of GCSE and A level exam questions', in K. V. Belfast (ed), (2012) *Mathematics in A-level assessments*. London: Nuffield.

Lesko, N. (2001) *Act your age! A cultural construction of adolescence*. New York: RoutledgeFalmer.

London Mathematical Society (2010) 'Comments on A-Level Mathematics and the A* Grade'. Available from http://www.lms.ac.uk/sites/default/files/Mathematics/Policy_repors/2010%20maths_admissions_letter.pdf (accessed 7 January 2013).

Matthews, A. and Pepper, D. (2007) *Evaluation of participation in GCE mathematics: final report*. Qualifications and Curriculum Authority.

Mendick, H. (2006) *Masculinities in mathematics*. Buckingham: Open University Press.

Morgan, C., Tang, S. and Sfard, A. (2011) 'Grammatical structure and mathematical activity', *Proceedings of the British Society for Research into Learning Mathematics (BSRLM)*, 31, 3, 113–118.

Murray, S. (2011) 'Declining participation in post-compulsory secondary school mathematics: students' views of and solutions to the problem', *Research in Mathematics Education*, 13, 3, 269–286.

Noyes, A. (2009) 'Exploring social patterns of participation in university-entrance level mathematics in England', *Research in Mathematics Education*, 11, 2, 167–183.

Reiss, M., Hoyles, C., Mujtaba, T., Riazi-Farzad, B., Rodd, M., Simon, S. and Stylianidou, F. (2011) 'Understanding participation rates in post-16 mathematics and physics: conceptualising and operationalising the UPMAP Project', *International Journal of Science and Mathematics Education*, 9, 2, 273–302.

Rose, N. (1999) *Powers of freedom: reframing political thought*. Cambridge: Cambridge University Press.

Smith, C. (2010) 'Choosing more mathematics: happiness through work?', *Research in Mathematics Education*, 12, 2, 99–115.

Solomon, Y. (2007) 'Experiencing mathematics classes: ability grouping, gender and the selective development of participative identities', *International Journal of Educational Research*, 46, 1–2, 8–19.

Wake, G., Williams, J. and Drake, P. (eds) (2011) 'Special issue: deepening engagement in mathematics in pre-university education', *Research in Mathematics Education*, 13, 2.

Index